Artistic Traditions of Inner Eurasian Cultures

Artistic Traditions of Inner Eurasian Cultures

Prehistoric, Ancient, and Medieval Golden Ages

Ardi Kia

LEXINGTON BOOKS
Lanham • Boulder • New York • London

Published by Lexington Books
An imprint of The Rowman & Littlefield Publishing Group, Inc.
4501 Forbes Boulevard, Suite 200, Lanham, Maryland 20706
www.rowman.com

86-90 Paul Street, London, EC2A 4NE

Copyright © 2022 The Rowman & Littlefield Publishing Group, Inc.

All rights reserved. No part of this book may be reproduced in any form or by any electronic or mechanical means, including information storage and retrieval systems, without written permission from the publisher, except by a reviewer who may quote passages in a review.

British Library Cataloguing in Publication Information Available

Library of Congress Cataloging-in-Publication Data

Names: Kia, Ardi, 1949- author.
Title: Artistic traditions of inner Eurasian cultures : prehistoric, ancient and medieval golden ages / Ardi Kia.
Description: Lanham : Lexington Books, 2022. | Includes bibliographical references and index. | Summary: "This book examines the cultural heritage of Inner Eurasia (Central Asia) through the arts, from prehistoric times to the ancient and medieval golden ages. The manuscript features extensive analysis of multiple Inner Eurasian cultural groups, their artistic traditions, and the development thereof throughout the region's history"— Provided by publisher.
Identifiers: LCCN 2022032157 (print) | LCCN 2022032158 (ebook) | ISBN 9781666918588 (cloth) | ISBN 9781666918601 (paper) | ISBN 9781666918595 (ebook)
Subjects: LCSH: Asia, Central—Civilization. | Art, Central Asian.
Classification: LCC DS328.2 .K43348 2022 (print) | LCC DS328.2 (ebook) | DDC 306.4/70958—dc23/eng/20220708
LC record available at https://lccn.loc.gov/2022032157
LC ebook record available at https://lccn.loc.gov/2022032158

In memory of my Dad
To Kay, Cameron, G.G., Mehrdad, Mike, Diana, John, Rebecca, and David
&
To my extended family, all the wonderful people of Central Asia, who have been so kind and helpful to us during our trips, and made us feel at home

This book is also dedicated to the memory of Don Bedunah, Arthur Pope, Phyllis Ackerman, Richard Frye, Roman Ghirshman, and Robert Greene

Contents

Acknowledgments	ix
List of Figures	xi
Introduction	1
Chapter One: Paleolithic and Mesolithic Artifacts of Inner Eurasia: Petroglyphs, Paintings, Drawings, and Etchings	5
Chapter Two: Inner Eurasian Pottery Art	17
Chapter Three: Prehistoric and Early Ancient Inner Eurasian Art of Figurines, Statues, and Sculptures	35
Chapter Four: Eurasian Cimmerian and Sarmatian Metal Arts	41
Chapter Five: Northern Cultures of Eurasia: Scythian/Saka Arts	49
Chapter Six: Early Migrations and Art Schools	67
Chapter Seven: Iron Age-Median Empire and its Art	79
Chapter Eight: Iron Age-Achaemenid Empire Arts	83
Chapter Nine: Satrapy of Khwarazmia: Cultures and Arts	91
Chapter Ten: Satrapy of Parthia & Parthian Empire Arts	105
Chapter Eleven: Inner Eurasian Art Schools of the East	115
Chapter Twelve: Sassanid Empire Arts	129
Chapter Thirteen: Satrapy of Sogdia and its Art Schools	139
Chapter Fourteen: Artistic Traditions of Middle Ages: Ceramics, Metal Works, Jewelry, Wood Working, Suzani, and Rug Making	153

Conclusion	161
Appendix I	163
Appendix II	165
Appendix III	167
Appendix IV	169
Appendix V	173
Appendix VI	175
Glossary	177
Maps	181
Bibliography	186
Index	203
About the Author	217

Acknowledgments

The author wishes to express his gratitude and thanks to the Central and Southwest Asian Studies Center at the University of Montana. This particular monograph is written exclusively for educational purposes. I would like to thank my students who have been my major source of inspirations. Also, I would like to thank Kasey Beduhn, Alexandra Rallo, Joyce Helena Brusin, Bryndee Ryan, and Ryan Dradzynski for helping me with their professional editing and revising this manuscript. Also, I would like to thank my colleagues and professors at the University of Montana for their comments, support and friendship, including: Irene Appelbaum, Susanne Bessac, Zhen Cao, Paul Dietrich, Kelly Dixon, Rick Graetz, Susie Graetz, Robert Greene, Nathan Lindsey, Doug MacDonald, Michael Mayer, Ona Renner-Fahey, Jeff Renz, Randy Skelton, and Clint Walker.

List of Figures

Map 1. Map of Scythia

Map 2. Map of Achaemenid Empire

Map 3. Map of Sassanian Empire

Map 4. Map of Silk Road

Map 5. Map of Timurid Empire

Map 6. Map of Russian Central Asia in 1895

Map 7. Map of Contemporary Inner Eurasia (Central Asia)

Introduction

This manuscript invites the reader on a journey through time, to explore the cultural heritage of Central Asia through the arts, from prehistoric times to medieval golden ages. Richly diversified, yet united by innumerable links, this heritage counted far more than the invasions, conflicts, and traditional alliances. The impact of powerful historical and cultural forces at work in large parts of Eurasia left their repercussions on iconography and styles of arts.

Central Asia has not received the attention it merits from the general public. The archeology of Central Asia is monumental; it has been conducted in the exploration of *kala* (town) sites and large cemeteries, many of which are concealed in the soil of Central Asia as *tepe* (mounds). The tepe, or kala, is the most characteristic monument of human settlement throughout Central Asia.

In many parts of Central Asia, groups of *kurgans* (burial mounds) commonly occur, often forming cemeteries of considerable size. These sites contain numerous examples of Central Asian artistic works. To appreciate the various artistic developments that occurred either simultaneously in different areas of Central Asia, or those that succeeded each other in a particular region, it is necessary to distinguish the precise characteristics of each local culture. The layout of towns, the plan of citadels, the disposition of sanctuaries, as well as the architectural techniques, carvings, or painted decoration of buildings, are among the evidence demonstrating social, economic, and cultural evolution in this region.

Scholars have achieved some spectacular success in Afrasiab, Nisa, Toprak-Kala, Varakhsha, and many other archeological sites. The results obtained in this area are of exceptional importance for the study and analysis of the history of cultures, arts, and civilization. Central Asia offers particularly favorable opportunities for studying the phenomena of cultural acculturation, contamination, and syncretism. The discovery in so many different areas of the remains of monumental art makes it necessary to reconsider or elaborate certain over-simplified theories about the spread of the great classical civilizations and the formation of hybrid styles.

Over most of Central Asia an "animal style art" was practiced by the various groups of people who were often related, yet distinct. The style flourished over so wide an area and so long a period of time that it is often called "the art of the steppe peoples." In the region and the period in which they lived, artists were influenced, to varying degrees, by trends prevailing in the great centers of civilization in their immediate neighborhoods. They were, in their turn, able to leave a mark on the major schools of art evolving in urban centers. This is especially true of the Scythian/Saka/Altaian communities, and even of their successors, the Sarmatians. Each of these groups produced individual variations on similar themes, but the creative genius and technical skill of the Scythians were generally of a far higher order than those of other communities.

Through transcontinental passages such as the Silk Road, Central Asia provided links among the major civilizations of China, India, Persia, and the Mediterranean, which in turn influenced the characteristics of the region and beyond. In late antiquity, the urban culture of Central Asia was predominantly Iranian, while the steppes were ruled by Scythians/Sakas and Huns, and from the eleventh century C.E. on, also by Turks. Central Asia was the site of an active and vibrant civilization for centuries prior to the Mongolian massacres of 1220, 1273, 1276, 1279, and 1316, and the Timurid massacres of 1379 and 1388.

Various religions and cults including Shamanism, Mithraism, Zurvanism, Buddhism, Zoroastrianism, Judaism, Manichaeism, Nestorian, and Melkite Christianity were practiced. In the eighth century C.E., an Arab army conquered some of the western parts of Central Asia and introduced Islam. The arts and cultures of Central Asia reflect these rich and varied traditions. The legendary poet, Rudaki, led the revival of Persian literature in the city of Bukhara during the golden age of culture and art of the Samanid dynasty (814–999). The next golden age arrived during the reign of the Timurids (1370–1507), when the city of Samarkand was filled with great architecture, art, and literature.

The Uzbek Shaibanids occupied large portions of Central Asia in the sixteenth century. By the end of the seventeenth century, three small Uzbek khanates were ruling parts of Central Asia through the eighteenth and nineteenth centuries till the year 1920, from the cities of Khiva, Bukhara, and Kokand. Russian czarist forces colonized the region in the nineteenth century, and after years of civil war (1917–1924), Soviet rule was established. Based on no historical or cultural foundations, Stalin fabricated five new Soviet states (1924–1936), replacing Khwarazmia, Soghdia, Baktra (Bakhtaran), and others, names of the Central Asian states since 500 B.C.E. Although, De-Stalinization, post-1953 dismantled some of the Gulag labor camps, the names Stalin made up are still with us. Since 1991, they are the independent republics of Uzbekistan, Kazakhstan, Tajikistan, Kyrgyzstan, and Turkmenistan.

In 1760, the eastern part of Central Asia was occupied by twenty-five thousand Chinese colonizing forces of the Qing Empire (1644–1911). Despite the resistance of the ancient Turks, Uyghurs, and other ethnicities to this invasion, Chinese occupation continued throughout the Republic of China era (1911–1949). In 1949, the region was, once again, invaded, this time by Mao's Red Army, and devastated during the Cultural Revolution (1966–1976).

The traditional world history written by Europeans in the eighteenth century meant the story of Greece. With great changes and tremendous advances in scholarship and scientific research in the fields of archeology, history, and arts over the last two centuries, particularly in studying the development of civilizations of Egypt and Mesopotamia, the boundaries of world history have been extended into India, China, Persia, and the Americas. Scientific research produced astounding results and surprises from these, the oldest civilizations of the world. Only in the twentieth century did European scholars recognize the importance of the historical development of all civilizations, and the view that none should be excluded from the portrait of the cultural evolution of humanity. Thanks are due to American and international scholars of the post-World War II era, who have expanded the perception of enthusiastic knowledge seekers beyond the former linear and traditional concepts.

There is, however, one vast and important area still frequently ignored by European scholarship, and that is Central Asia (Inner Eurasia). The archeological and historical studies of the twentieth and twenty-first centuries have brought to light the ancient inhabitants of Central Asia, and the highly sophisticated cultures, arts, and civilizations they built. Central Asia is a vast region rich in history, natural resources, and geopolitical importance. The birthplace of many of the world's religions and empires, it was the home to remarkable centers of learning, and devastating conflicts.

This book is a macro-historical analysis of some of the sophisticated, diverse, and pluralistic accomplishments of the Central Asian cultures and arts in prehistoric, ancient, and medieval golden ages.

The first chapter of this book starts with an analysis of *Paleolithic* (Old Stone Age) and *Mesolithic* (Middle Stone Age) artifacts (items made or given shape by humans) of Inner Eurasia. The second chapter of this book includes a historical analysis of pottery cultures of Inner Eurasia. Chapter three of the book elaborates the prehistoric and early ancient Eurasian art of figurines, statues, and sculptures. Chapter four includes an analysis of Eurasian Cimmerian and Sarmatian metal arts. Northern cultures of Eurasia including early ancient Scythian and Saka arts are analyzed and discussed in the fifth chapter of this book. Chapter six examines the ancient mass migration of the people of Inner Eurasia and the establishment of new art schools by them. Chapter seven includes an analysis of arts created in the Median Empire (728–553 B.C.E.). The book continues its analysis of the ancient arts of Achaemenid Empire (553–330 B.C.E.) in chapter eight. Princely patronage of the palace played a central role commissioning and supporting artistic creativities and architectural projects within this era and throughout most of the history of the region. *Satrapy* (state) of Khwarazmia's arts is discussed in the ninth chapter of this book. Chapter ten conducts an analysis of the arts of Parthian Empire (247 B.C.E. –224 C.E.). The arts of the schools of the eastern parts of Inner Eurasia are discussed in chapter eleven of this book. The arts of the Sassanid Empire (224–651) are analyzed and discussed in chapter twelve. Chapter thirteen of this book presents analysis of the Satrapy of Soghdia and its arts. Finally, artistic traditions of Middle Ages are analyzed and discussed in chapter fourteen.

Throughout the book, the arts of Inner Eurasia since prehistoric time comprise a wide variety of forms: petroglyphs, paintings, drawings, etching, pottery, figurines, statues, sculptures, sculptural reliefs, glazed brick compositions, mosaic art, metal art (copper, bronze, iron), jewelry (gold, silver, precious stones), crowns, book art, mural painting, calligraphical writing, manuscript illumination, silk making, fabric design, wood working, *suzani* (embroidery), rug making, and architectural projects. It is to this rich and varied array of human creativity we shall now turn.

Chapter One

Paleolithic and Mesolithic Artifacts of Inner Eurasia

Petroglyphs, Paintings, Drawings, and Etchings

This study includes research conducted by prominent scholars in the fields of archaeology, paleoanthropology, history and art history, numismatics, epigraphy, and comparative religious studies of prehistoric and early ancient sites of Inner Eurasia (Central Asia). Many of the petroglyphs, paintings, drawings, and etchings described are identified as sacred images, possibly associated with shamanic cults and Mithraism of prehistoric and ancient eras. Together, their association with burial sites, altars, sun-heads, and other artifacts provide substantial testimony to the lives and beliefs of pastoral peoples of the Eurasia since the Bronze Age. The oldest rock art of Eurasia dates from the ninth millennium B.C.E. and includes any markings made by humans on natural rock surfaces such as carved petroglyphs, etchings, or pictographs, paintings, and drawings.

XINJIANG: PREHISTORIC PAINTINGS AND PETROGLYPHS

At least three sites in the Altai Mountains area of Xinjiang have numerous polychrome rock paintings. In the area between the Haba River in the west and Altay City in the east, such rock paintings can be seen at ten locations. Three sites with substantial paintings are Arktas in Altay City, Tangbaletas in Fuyun County, and Dugat in Haba River County. Wang Bin Hua[1] identifies the rock paintings of the Altai Mountains in Xinjiang area dating to the late Paleolithic Age. This estimate derives from cultural features reflected in the paintings which depict social life belonging only to that specific prehistoric period.

One magnificent example of the life of these Paleolithic people consists of encircled hunting scenes, as shown in Dugat paintings, that rely on group collaboration. All the hunters are on foot, and the large animals are being killed by spears, not arrows. In the Altai Mountain area, there are more than eighty sites of rock carvings, with from a dozen to more than one hundred pictures at each site. Hunting activities are a very common subject. Many of the sites are surrounded by hand prints and mystic geometric symbols. Animals—horses, oxen, goats, and birds—frequently are composed in the rock art of this area.

Paleolithic art of the Xinjiang region also can be found in several burial sites at Tuo Gan Bai, dating between 4,000 and 4,400 years B.C.E. (on the basis of radiocarbon analysis). Several of the rock slabs lining the chambers bear both paintings and petroglyphs. The Kangjiashimenzi petroglyph site is more amenable to analysis. The site is located within the Tian Shan Mountain range, over four hours west of Xinjiang's capitol of Urumchi. The Kangjiashimenzi site consists of a relatively shallow rock shelter fifty meters wide at the base of a cliff 300 meters wide and 180 meters high.[2]

Much of the shelter's wall, as well as some blocks on the floor, are covered with hundreds of petroglyphs. The figurative elements of the site have been carefully polished and a number of them are painted in red, white, or yellow pigments. The petroglyphs of the main panel date between 2,000 and 4,000 years B.C.E. and include naturalistic animals in profile view, together with hand stencils.

INNER MONGOLIA: NEOLITHIC PETROGLYPHS

The ridge of Baimiaozishan, 130 kilometers north-east of Chifeng in the eastern part of the region, is 300 meters long and bears over 100 petroglyphs, many with face/mask motifs. This indicates extensive Neolithic occupation, evident in the region. At the site of Xiao Fengshan, north of the village Xia Paozi, located north of Chifeng, there is a series of granite hills. Close to a quarry, at the foot of the hillside slope, lies a block of several meters' length with rock art, which includes three face/mask motifs on the sloping surface. In addition, very faded, and only faintly detectable grooved designs are on the panel.[3]

A much richer petroglyph site, with thousands of motifs, is Daheishan, an hour north-west of Wengniute Banner. The petroglyphs at this location are generally shallow, implying the use of pointed metal tools, and include straight lines, patterns of circles, and faces/masks. In another area, twenty-five kilometers north-east of Hohhot, valley floors are surrounded mostly by schist mountains that are geologically dominated by significant deposits of rounded granite blocks. There are also a few scattered petroglyphs made by metal tools in this area. Thus, rock art of Inner Mongolia, at Xia Paozi and Baimiaozishan, is Neolithic, corresponding with extensive evidence from the Chifeng region.

KAZAKHSTAN: IRTYSH VALLEY AND ILLI VALLEY EXPEDITIONS

Stone Age excavations and research in Kazakhstan was conducted mostly by Chernikov and Okladnikov in the upper Irtysh valley, to the east and northeast of Kazakhstan.[4] Paleolithic as well as the Neolithic tools found by the archeologists exceeded 15,000 artifacts. In the Illi valley, to the southeast of Kazakhstan, Akishev found large quantities of tools belonging to the Neolithic period (between the fourth and third millennium B.C.E.).[5] Since 1957, expeditions near the Karatau Mountains to the southwest of Kazakhstan, led by Alpysbayev, have yielded rich results.[6] Kazakhstan's Sary-su region, the Moinkum desert, Kzyl-Dzhar, and Karaganda regions are areas where archeological excavation is being conducted under the supervision of Kh. Alpysbaev today.

KAZAKHSTAN: TAMGALY PETROGLYPHS AND PAINTINGS

A significant site for petroglyphs of Tamgaly is in the Zhetysu district, in the south-eastern part of modern Kazakhstan. The site has over 5,000 petroglyphs from four different eras. The earliest series belong to[7] the Middle Bronze Age, with the greatest cultural and aesthetics value, including anthropomorphic, zoomorphic, and syncretic images such as sun deities ("sun heads"), also, archers, chariots, bulls, boars, wolves, deer, and other fauna. In the Late Bronze Age, images have less variety, however, scenes from pastoral life appear with images of horses, bulls, and wild animals added in this period. In the Early Iron Age, many hieroglyphs were created with a variety of styles, quality, and different subject matter. Hunting scenes depicting the chase of deer or wild goats are still common. Finally, in the Middle Ages and Modern era more than 300 images of hunting scenes, warriors, horses, and horse equipment are portrayed.

Tamagaly became an UNESCO World Heritage Site in 2004. In the Karatau region of southern Kazakhstan, over 2,000 stone slabs with over 6,000 different scenes were found. The oldest ones represent chariots for hunting or warfare. A large number of the sites in Kazakhstan, and many surrounding regions, are identified with the Andronovo Culture (2,000–900 B.C.E.) which dominated western Eurasia in this era. The earliest fully developed horse chariots are evident in chariot burials of the Andronovo culture sites of Sintasha, dating from 2,000 years B.C.E. in the modern republic of Kazakhstan. The images of chariots appear in many rock art sites of this period in various parts of Eurasia. Other rock art sites of later eras are identified with the Scythian/Saka culture (900–300 B.C.E.) as the dominating culture from north of the Black Sea to the Altai Mountains.

KYRGYZSTAN: ROCK ART

In Kyrgyzstan, Okladnikov discovered Paleolithic sites in the Naryn district on the On-Archa River.[8] Other Paleolithic sites in the Alay valley and on the Kyzyl-Su River were excavated by Ranov.[9] (Kyrgyzstan rock art continues in this chapter, under Mesolithic Art of Inner Eurasia.)

TAJIKISTAN: PETROGLYPHS AND PAINTINGS

The systematic exploration and excavation of Stone Age sites in Tajikistan was begun by two scholars, Okladnikov and Ranov in 1953.[10] Okladnikov and Ranov explored the Kayrak-Kumy region, which has been the richest area for Paleolithic finds. A large quantity of interesting and significant material was found.

There are over fifty different petroglyphs sites within Pamir Mountains, the highest concentration of rock art sites in Tajikistan. Pamir petroglyphs portray wild goats, ibexes, yaks, deer, and hunting scenes, as well as cult rituals. The oldest petroglyphs of Pamir date back to the Bronze Ages.

There are more than 6,000 petroglyphs, on granite stone rock between Langar village and the Ratm fortress. The sites include animals and hunting scenes, some hunting mountain goats and deer with bow and arrow. Langar petroglyph images are commonly dated between 10,000– 8,000 B.C.E. There are also images of musical instruments, near the Ratm fortress, five kilometers from Langar, the last village of Vakhan valley, 3,300 meters elevation.

In 2007, along the Yaghnob River that joins the Fan River, before they both flow into the Zarafshan River, petroglyphs were discovered at the entrance of a gorge that included an ibex, two hunters, and a dog between them. A pack of ibexes, or goats, are running to escape the hunters.[11]

Other petroglyph sites in Tajikistan include the Dashte Eymatk petroglyphs near the village of Urmetan, on the banks of the Zarafshan River. There are also petroglyphs of Vagishton along the banks of the Vagishton Sai in the Panjikent District, and Soy Sabag petroglyphs in the Sogdia province of Tajikistan.

UZBEKISTAN: PETROGLYPHS AND PAINTINGS

In Uzbekistan, the oldest sites along the shores of the Akch-Darya belonged to fishermen and hunters living in dwellings of 100–120 residents, and were discovered by Tolstov.[12] The various material found on the site included implements of stone (flint) and bone, and fragments of round-bottomed pottery vessels with stamped and incised decoration.[13]

In 1938, to the south of Uzbekistan, Okladnikov discovered a cave (Tashik Tash) north of the town of Baysun.[14] A mass of Paleolithic tools and other objects, a skeleton with a well-preserved skull, surrounded by six pairs of mountain goat horns, was discovered.[15] This was the second occasion throughout the regions of the former Soviet Union that human remains dating back thirty to forty thousand years were found. Several Paleolithic cave sites, containing stone tools, were discovered on the upper Chirchik by Ranov and Okladnikov.[16] D. N. Lev discovered a large limestone cave at Aman Kutan, twenty-eight miles south of Samarkand, near the Takhta Karacha Pass. Paintings from the same period were found at Zaraut Say in Baba Tag Mountains, sixty miles from Termez. There are also two hundred paintings in red ochre representing animals and hunters dressed in skins shooting wild oxen with bows and arrows.[17]

UZBEKISTAN: SARMISHSAY ROCK ART

In the Navai region of Uzbekistan, in the Karatu range, near Zarafshan valley, there are over 10,000 ancient rock carvings. This area was a Neolithic area of Keltaminar culture, settled by hunters and fishermen. A portion of petroglyphs of this area belong to the Bronze Age (6,000–4,000 B.C.E.). Scythian tribes lived in this area from the ninth to the second centuries B.C.E. Many scholars have compared the Tamgaly site in Kazakhstan and Saymali Tash in Kyrgyzstan with the Sarmishsay site in Uzbekistan, since the other two sites also have contemporary examples of dominant segments of Scythian/Saka style paintings and petroglyphs. Scythians/Saka peoples developed a rich cultural style, characterized by luxurious tombs and metalwork. This cultural style continued during the Iron Age, from 800 B.C.E. at the peak of their dominance over the great Euraisean Steppe. Scythian/Saka empire's territory stretched from the Carpathian Mountains in the west all the way to central China in the east.

The Sarmishsay motifs are dominated by wild goats and sheep, snow leopards, hunting scenes, and dancers. There are burial mounds and sacred places near these rock art sites, and scattered petroglyphs near Tashkent, Fergana Valley, and Tien Shan Mountains in Uzbekistan. Besides Sarmishsay, the sites of Karakiyasay and Beldersay also have petroglyphs and paintings.[18]

TURKMENISTAN: PALEOLITHIC ARTIFACTS

The earliest excavation of Turkmenistan was conducted by Raphael Pumpelly, an American archeologist, who pioneered further exploration and research within the region.[19] From 1904–1906, Pumpelly concentrated his research in the Anau region, twelve kilometers to the south-east of the present Turkmenistan capitol of Eshqabad. The Anau culture was said to be one of the oldest agrarian cultures in the world, while southern Central Asia was declared the oldest center for cultivation of varieties of wheat.[20]

In 1938, a Paleolithic cave in Turkmenistan was discovered and excavated by Okladnikov, on the eastern shore of the Caspian Sea, in the region of Krasnovodsk. Dam Dam Chesme cave to the southeast of Krasnovodsk, was radio-carbon dated at 6,030 years old (+ or—240 years). A. A. Marushchenko discovered many ancient sites in southern Central Asia (today Turkmenistan) including Dzheytun associated with the earliest farmers in Central Asia.[21]

MESOLITHIC ART OF INNER EURASIA

Rock Art - Petroglyphs, Drawings, Paintings, & Etchings

Intermediate to Paleolithic and Neolithic is the Mesolithic period, or the Middle Stone Age. In Inner Eurasia (Central Asia), this period marks the origins of agriculture and stock-rearing. The Mesolithic begins 10,000 B.C.E. and is identified as a transition between a food-gathering and food-producing agrarian economy. The earliest segment of rock art creativity, including etchings, drawings, and paintings, were identified with the Mesolithic period, although rock art continues off and on in various parts of Central Asia later in the history of the region.[22]

Mesolithic Rock Art of the South and Southwest

The majority of Inner Eurasian groups developed a distinctly blade type industry, micro-lithic techniques, and tools of geometric shapes, resembling closely the Mediterranean culture complex in the Mesolithic period.[23] At present, the following groups of sites belong to this tradition in Western Central Asia including:

1. The Caspian Sea Group
2. The Western Tajikistan Group
3. The Fergana Valley Group
4. The Eastern Pamirs Group

The best known are the sites of the Caspian Sea group, represented by the caves of Djebel, Dam Dam Chashma I, Dam Dam Chashma II, in the Balkhan Mountains, and the Kailiu grotto on the Krasnovodsk peninsula.[24] The northerly spread of sites of this type in the Late Mesolithic site is seen in Hodja Su I on the eastern coast of Kara Bogaz. Among the earliest artifacts found on the Caspian shore are the flint implements from the Dam Dam Chashma I cave. These include piercers, pointed scrapers, backed blades, and lunates. The number of geometric tools here is large, and all are of a regular symmetrical form. By contrast, many trapezoid tools have concave edges. This is also true of the flint tools excavated in layers three and two, which contain pottery with incised and stamped decoration. The main activities of the Mesolithic people of the Caspian region were hunting and fishing. The osteological material shows that the principal game were onager and gazelle, with goats and sheep of secondary importance. Other game included water fowl, fox, and wild cat.

TAJIKISTAN: ROCK ART

A series of sites of Mesolithic origin was excavated in western Tajikistan. These sites were located along the tributaries of Amu Darya, or near sources of fresh spring water. At one of the earliest sites of this group, Kui Bulien, a number of artifacts including geometric-shaped implements have been found. The open sites and caves of the Fergana valley in the Obi Shir and Tah Kumir caves include Mesolithic artifacts similar, but smaller in size, than those recovered from caves near Caspian Sea and in Western Tajikistan.

Mesolithic culture of the eastern Pamirs evident in implements recovered in about twenty different sites, include two large open sites at Karatumshuk and Oshkhona. Both represent traces of seasonal camp sites of hunters who were attracted by the abundance of game in the alpine meadows. Bones of birds, mountain sheep, and goats found here reveal the hunting activities of the inhabitants. Examination of artifacts show thick blade scrapers, choppers, backed blades, and arrowheads, which radio carbon analysis date to 7580 B.C.E. (+ or—130 years). Hence, the artifacts of the Pamir area are almost as old as material found near the Caspian Sea.

A surprising discovery from this period was that of a painting in the Shakhta cave in the Eastern Pamirs, depicting a hunting scene with the outlines of boars and a large animal, possibly a yak, being showered with flying arrows. The hunters are portrayed in bell shaped skirts. The men in this painting are assisted by dogs accompanying them. The Mesolithic period in Western Central Asia also saw evidence of the perfection of micro-lithic techniques, and the initial stages of stock breeding.[25]

KAZAKHSTAN: ROCK PAINTINGS, DRAWINGS, ENGRAVINGS, AND CARVINGS

Throughout Inner Eurasia (Central Asia), numerous paintings, drawings, engravings, and carvings have been found. In Kazakhstan, elaborated rock art has been identified in the south and east. An engraving of animals recorded in Aktobe, south of Kazakhstan, was analyzed and elaborated by Senigova, dated in the sixth and fifth centuries B.C.E., and the first to second centuries C.E. In 1966, Marikovskiy found rock art, mostly of animals, in the Chulak Mountains.[26] Some of the paintings and etchings showed profile views of dogs, two-headed goats, and even an elephant. In the Tamgaly mountain pass, southwest of the Chu-Ili range, Maksimova discovered over one thousand engravings identified as belonging to the Saka period, seventh to fifth centuries B.C.E. In the Chirchik valley, south of Kazakhstan, especially in the Bostandy district, Alpysbayev identified many sites with representation of various animals, dating from the Saka period of the first millennium B.C.E. Chernikov, in the hills adjacent to the Irtysh River, discovered engraving of animals, believed to be from the sixth to the first century B.C.E.[27]

KYRGYZSTAN: ROCK ART

The early history rock art of contemporary Kyrgyzstan is of paramount importance. Zadnerprovskiy discovered and analyzed drawings at the Airymach-Tau site, eight kilometers from the city of Osh, in Kyrgyzstan.[28] A large number of profile-view silhouette drawings of horses from this area were identified, and dated from the first millennium B.C.E. Bernshtam discovered horse images engraved in the Aravan area. Ancient Chinese sources also refer to the heavenly horses of the Ferghana valley.

KYRGYZSTAN: SAIMALY-TASH - OVER 100,000 DRAWINGS, PAINTINGS, AND ENGRAVINGS

The site of Saimaly Tash in Jalal Abad province, Kyrgyzstan, bears over 100,000 petroglyphs and black and white paintings. UNESCO declared Saimaly Tash a World Heritage Site in 2001. (Saimaly-Tash site includes Saimaluu-Tash 1 and Saimaluu-Tash 2, petroglyph sites.)

Some of the rock art from the site was created in the Neolithic period between 3000–2000 B.C.E. Many other pieces of rock art from the Saimalu Tash were created during the Iron Age, 800 B.C.E. to the present. The most repeated subjects are animals: including horses, ibexes, wolves, and scenes hunting deer. The site has been identified as a sacred place, with spiritual and healing powers, even by some of the modern generations of Kyrgyz.[29]

In 1903, in the midst of the Ferghana range, at 3,200 meters elevation, the Saimaly-Tash site was discovered in Jalal-Abad province. A number of scholars, including Zima, Bernshtam, and Pomazkina, visited, explored, and analyzed the site, which includes well over 100,000 drawings, paintings, and engravings of many generations. Saimaly-Tash images include wild animals, hunting scenes, domesticated animals, and human beings. Bernshtam identifies some of the images as being from the Bronze Age, from the second to the first millennium B.C.E., and others from the third to the eight centuries C.E.

Situated high in the Ferghana mountain range, Saimaly-Tash is a grandiose natural sanctuary containing one of the largest collections of rock pictures in Central Asia and the world. Images identified date from the third to the early second millennia B.C.E., known as the Eneolithic and Bronze Ages. Saimaly-Tash is a rich source of knowledge about everyday life, history, culture, and mentality of prehistoric and ancient hunters, cattle breeders, and early peasants of Central Asia. The images on the rocks reflect the development of their spiritual and religious beliefs and worship of mountains, nature, and totems as reflected in solar-cosmic images.[30]

The study of this Bronze Age culture in the Farghana valley (an area shared across the independent states of Uzbekistan, Kyrgyzstan, and Tajikistan today) was initiated by B. A. Latynin in the 1930s. The sites discovered in this part of the valley are named Chust Culture (named after the village of Chust in the area). E. Voronets and I. V. Sprishevsky excavated Bronze Age sites of Chust; Y. A. Zadneprovsky investigated the extension of Chust Culture in the settlement of Dalverzin, which included a defensive wall. The houses were constructed on the ground level, and farming was the main occupation of inhabitants of Chust; although, stock rearing also played a considerable role in the local economy.

The excavations revealed the bones of sheep, horses, cattle, goats, pigs, asses, and dogs. Tools and implements made of bronze, stone, and bone were discovered. Many objects associated with weaving were found as well. The pottery of Chust is of great interest, showing a remarkable variety of forms. In addition to ordinary domestic ware, the find included some magnificent thin-walled table ware, covered with a red slip and after glazing, decorated typically with a pattern in black, in the form of cross-hatched triangles, as well as scrolls and volutes.[31]

KYRGYZSTAN: CHOLPON ATA PAINTINGS AND PETROGLYPHS

The site of Cholpon Ata, over 40 hectares on the north shore of Lake Issyk Kul, has more than 2,000 petroglyphs and paintings, some of them 4,000 years old. Motives are highly diverse, including humans, animals, and hunting scenes, especially wild goats, deer, dogs, and boars. There are more than 100 solar symbols in the Chopan Ata and Salmluu Tash sites.[32]

PAMIR, TAJIKISTAN: ENGRAVINGS

In Tajikistan, Ranov in the Pamir area, in the Shakhty caves, discovered rock engravings of the Paleolithic era, among which is a human figure with a bird's head. Rock engravings were discovered and analyzed by various scholars, including Litvinskiy, Mandelshtam, and Ranov along the Zarafshan River in Tajikistan and Uzbekistan.[33]

The excavations conducted by some of the early scholars in the field suggested that during the Bronze Age the earliest cultures expanded to surrounding regions, influencing the cultures beyond Inner Eurasia (Central Asia). Rock arts of the region are among the most significant and widespread Inner Eurasian arts from the late Paleolithic era to the early twentieth century. The primary engraving tool during this time was a pointed stone, and later, a metal tool harder than rock, used as a chisel. Inner Eurasian rock art comprises a unique cultural and historical monument to Eurasian art since prehistoric times.

The significance of the early excavations and research conducted by some of the prominent archeologists and historians was analyzed and discussed in this chapter. The next chapter acquaints readers with Central Eurasian pottery since prehistoric times.[34]

NOTES

1. Wang Binghua, *Paleolithic colored paintings in Altay Mountain caves*, Archaeology and Cultural Relics, 2002:03, pp. 48–55.

2. Tacon, P. S. C., Tang, H., and Aubert, M. *Naturalistic animals and hand stencils in the rock art of Xinjiang Uyghur Autonomous Region*, Rock Art Research 33(1): 2016, pp. 19–31.

Also, see: Bednarik, R. G. *Dating Rock Art in Xinjiang*, AURA Newsletter 32(1): 2015, pp. 6–8.

3. Fairservice, W. A. Jr. *Archeology of Southern Gobi of Mongolia*, Durham, 1993.

Also, see: Molodin V. I., Geneste Zh., Zotkina L. V., Cheremisin D. V., and Cretin C. *The "Kalgutinsky" Style in the Rock Art of Central Asia*. Archaeology, Ethnology & Anthropology of Eurasia. 2019; 47(3): 12–26.

4. Okladnikov, A. M. *On Stone Age,* Ch. 1, 2, 3 in Sredniaya Aziya, Academy of Sciences of Kazakhstan, 1966.

5. Akishev, K. A., *General Survey: Stone and Bronze Ages*, Izviestiya Academy of Sciences, Kazakhstan SSR, 1958, 3.

6. Alpysbayev, Kh. A., *Palaeolithic in South Kazakhstan*, Sovietskaya Arkheologiya, 1959, 7.

7. Baipakov, K. M., Maryashev, A. N., and Potapov, S. A. *Petroglify Tamgaly*, Almaty, 2006.

Also, see: Rozwadowski, A. *Symbols Through Time, Interpreting the Rock Art of Central Asia*, Poznan, 2004. Cf. Anthony, D. W. *The Horse, The Wheel and Language: How Bronze Age Riders from Eurasia Steppes Shaped the Modern World*. Princeton University Press, 2007.

8. Okladnikov, A. M., *On Stone Age*, Ch. 1, 2, 3 in Sredniaya Aziya, Academy of Sciences of Kazakhstan, 1966.

9. Ranov, V. A., *Toward a New Outline of the Soviet Central Asian Paleolithic*. Can, Vol. 20, No. 2, 1979, 249–70.

10. Okladnikov, A. M. *On Stone Age*, Ch. 1, 2, 3 in Sredniaya Aziya, Academy of Sciences of Kazakhstan, 1966.

Also, see: Ranov, V. A., *Toward a New Outline of the Soviet Central Asian Paleolithic*. Can, Vol. 20, No. 2, 1979.

11. Passarelli, M. *Petroglyphs Along the Yaghnob River*, U. of Bolobna, Yaghnob Valley Mission, 2007.

12. Tolstov, S. P. *Ancient Khorezm*, Essay in Historical Archeological Research, MSU, Moscow, 1948, 114.

13. Okladnikov, A. M. *On Stone Age*, Ch. 1, 2, 3 in Sredniaya Aziya, Academy of Sciences of Kazakhstan, 1966.

14. Okladnikov, A. M. *Djebel cave, an early prehistoric site on the Caspian shores of Turkmenia,* TYu—TAKE, VII, 1956.

15. Ranov, V. A., *Toward a New Outline of the Soviet Central Asian Paleolithic*. Can, Vol. 20, No. 2, 1979, 249–70.

16. Ibid, 249–70.

17. Korobkova, G. F. *The Mesolithic and Neolithic Cultures of Central Asia, problems in the archeology of Western Central Asia*, Leningrad, 1968.

18. Ibbotson, S. *Getting off the Silk Road: Uzbekistan's Hidden Archeological Sites*, Bradt Guides Ltd., 2020.

19. Pumpelly, R. *Explorations in Turkestan*, Carnegie institution, No. 73, Washington D. C., 1908.

20. Ibid, 10.

21. Markov, G. E. *Dam dam chashma cave no. 2 on the Eastern Shores of the Caspian* SA, 1956, 2.

22. Alpysbayev, Kh. A. *Bostandy Rock Engravings*, Trudy Instituta Arkheologii i Etnograffii, 1956, 1.

23. Okladnikov, A. M. *Djebel cave, an early prehistoric site on the Caspian shores of Turkmenia,* TYu—TAKE, VII, 1956.

24. Markov, G. E. *Dam dam chashma cave no. 2 on the Eastern Shores of the Caspian SA,* 1956, 2.

25. Ranov, v. A. *Stone Age engravings in the Shakhta cave*, SE, no. 6, 1961.

26. Bernshtam, A. N., *Scythian Art: Rock Engravings*, Materials of and Research into the Archeology of the USSR, 1952a, 26.

27. Korobkova, G. F. *The Mesolithic and Neolithic Cultures of Central Asia, problems in the archeology of Western Central Asia*, Leningrad, 1968.

28. Bernshtam, A. N., *Saimaly-Tash: Fergana Rock Engravings*, Sovietskaya Etnografiya, 1952.

29. Dyaduchenko, L. B. *Mystic Saimaluu-Tash*, Bishkek, 2008.

30. Kyrgyz National Commission for UNESCO, *Saimaly-Tash,* Bishkek, November 2015.

31. Dyaduchenko, L. B. *Mystic Saimaluu-Tash*, Bishkek, 2008.

32. Bernshtam, A. N., *Saimaly-Tash: Fergana Rock Engravings*, Sovietskaya Etnografiya, 1952.

33. Hermann, L. *Les Petroglyphes de Tcholpon-Ata*, Paris, 2010.

34. Litvinskiy, B. A., *Tadzhik Archeology*, Sovietskaya Arkheologiya, 1967a, 3. Also, see: Ranov, V. A. *Stone Age engravings in the Shakhta cave*, SE, No. 6, 1961. Also, see: Bernshtam, A. N., *Po Sledam Drevnikh Kultur: Tyan-Shan and Pamirs Engravings*, 1954.

Chapter Two

Inner Eurasian Pottery Art

DEVELOPMENT AND DIVERSIFICATION

The Copper Age (Chalcolithic period) refers to a period during which some weapons and tools were made of copper. This period is still largely Neolithic in character. The economic use of water within this period introduced village culture in the fourth millennium B.C.E. In these first villages and settlements, the production of painted pottery appears in Inner Eurasia (Central Asia). By the last quarter of the third millennium, still in the Neolithic period, a new economy develops with production, and domestication of animals and plants. While in northern Eurasia stock breeding was developing very early, in southern Eurasia it was developing in association with the cultivation of plants,[1] and farmers leading a more settled way of life, in one-roomed houses, built with cylindrical clay bricks. The Djietun culture, of Margiana, best illustrates this new process of production.

THE CHALCOLITHIC CULTURES OF SOUTHERN CENTRAL ASIA

The Chalcolithic cultures of southern Central Asia are linked with early agriculture. The excavations conducted under the direction of R. Pumpelly[2] at the Anau mounds supplied archeological information about Chalcolithic material in southern Inner Eurasia (Central Asia). The pottery of Anau I-A exhibits sand mixture, with well-levigated clay and skilled firing. The thin-walled, gracefully shaped vessels, mainly drinking bowls, have painted geometric decorations featuring large figures filled with cross hatching and concave bases. The ancient agricultural settlement of Govich-depe, west of Anau, included pottery typical of Anau I-A.

HAND MADE PAINTED POTTERY OF DJIETUN CULTURE

One Central Asian Copper Age site is the excavation site of Djietun, twenty miles northwest of Ashkhabad, the capital of Turkmenistan today. The site includes thirty-five houses, built of round blocks of sundried clay (the forerunners of bricks), which were excavated by B. A. Kuftin and V. A. Masson. The houses are small in size, each consisting of a single room with an area of 220 square feet. The pottery from Djietun, hand made without use of the wheel, already shows a form of decoration in the shape of parallel lines painted in ochre, identified by Ghrishman as the geometric style. Late Djietun levels at Chagilli Depe,[3] according to carbon-14 dating are 5050 years B.C.E. (+ or—110 years). Totally, there are twenty settlements from this period, which can be divided into three groups:

1. The Western Zone—consists of the territory between Kizil Arvat and Anau. This zone includes the settlements of Beurme, Karantki Tokai, Tilkin Depe, Dashli, Ovadan, Ekin Depe, and Anau. Each village in this group generally occupies an area between two and three acres, rising two to three meters above surrounding land. The inhabitants of these villages pursued a mixed farming economy. Houses were built of rectangular sunbaked bricks. Pottery was decorated with painted ribbon patterns; fuzzy lines are characteristic of pottery from this territory. Unfortunately, these villages have been studied very perfunctorily, based only on materials collected from the surface.
2. The Central Zone—occupies the area between Anau and Dushak, and includes large settlements at Kara Depe and Namazga Depe[4] as well as many smaller villages, such as Yassi Depe and Sermancha Depe.
3. The Eastern Zone—includes settlements situated along the lower course of the Chaacha Sai and Meana Sai. The houses of this region were generally built of standard rectangular sunbaked bricks tempered with chopped straw. The walls were covered with clay plaster, sometimes painted black. Stone sockets suggest that the doors were once made of wooden boards. Alongside the living rooms and storerooms, rooms believed to have been shrines have been excavated.

Almost a third of the pottery from this region is decorated with painted designs of which the most typical feature horizontal rows of triangles in black and dark brown. There are also patterns of zigzags, checker boards, wavy lines, and more rarely, outlined portrayals of horses, goats, and plants. The few human figurines found in the region represent specific human anatomy.

POLYCHROMATIC AND MONOCHROMATIC PAINTED POTTERY CULTURES

Middle Chalcolithic cultures[5] are characterized by polychrome decoration of pottery. In the western and central areas of southern Central Asia, monochrome painted decoration of earlier stages of pottery was replaced by bright polychrome friezes, comprised of small geometric figures on a light, predominately cream or yellow, ground. Occasionally, drawings of goats, and even people, were portrayed in an exaggerated and stylized manner. This culture was found in layers ranging in depth between two and six meters in the settlements of Tilkin Depe, in the northern mound of Anau, Kara Depe,[6] Elen Depe, and Namazga Depe. Polychrome decoration is found on 62 percent of all pottery, whereas monochrome painted pottery comprises 10 percent of the materials. The undercoated pottery includes red slipped hemispherical bowls, often highly burnished, while polished grey ware is much less. Thirty-five burials were excavated in level Two of Kara Depe. In many of the burials, necklaces and bracelets were discovered. Twenty-one burials were discovered in level Three of the Kara Depe site. A child's burial revealed 420 gypsum beads, as well as one of carnelian, two of azurite, and six of gypsum, wrapped in silver foil, on the wrist. The child had bracelets made of carnelian and azurite, and even gold beads, the oldest example of gold funerary discovered in western Central Asia.

Thus, in the fifth and fourth millennia B.C.E., southern Central Asia was a prosperous region of agricultural villages and farms, with developed architecture, sophisticated pottery, and superb figurines. This is in comparison with other parts of Central Asia, where, at this time, archaic Neolithic culture still predominated. It would seem that hunting, fishing, food gathering, and stock breeding were the chief activities of the local groups, features which continue in the north of Central Asia.

Pottery cultures of Central Asia are signifiers of the sophistication of some of these cultures in earlier stages. The cultures of Chust, Anau, Zaman Baba, and some of the excavation sites in Khorezm[7] are a few examples of the impressive accomplishments through the medium of pottery. Pottery from these cultures began to reflect similarities of style. These similarities by the end of the Bronze Age indicate assimilation among the different cultures of Central Asia. This assimilation intensifies in the Iron Age. In the Dam Dam Cheshma 2 cave, and in the Late Mesolithic of Debe, this process precedes and then develops through the Neolithic era, evidenced in handmade pottery.

NEOLITHIC POTTERY CULTURES

In the Neolithic period, a qualitatively new economy develops (known as the Neolithic revolution). This transition began with domestication of animals and plants, and developed further in association with the cultivation of plants, as farmers led a more settled way of life. This process is best illustrated by Djeitun[8] culture, which featured houses built of cylindrical clay bricks and flat-bottomed pots decorated with painted patterns. There are three periods within the Djeitun culture spanning 1000 years:

1. First period of Djeitun site has a lower layer, Chopan-depe, and also Togolok-depe.
2. Middle period represented in the upper layers of Chopan-depe,[9] Togolok-depe, Bami, Novaya Nisa, Pessedjik-depe, and the lower layers of Mondjukli-depe and Chagilli-depe.
3. Late period of Djeitun culture is best illustrated by the material from the upper layer of Chagilli-depe. Djeitun culture corresponds to one thousand years, with the Late Djeitun levels at Chailli-depe dated by the carbon-14 method to 5050 B.C.E.

The settled way of life and exploitation of plant foods by the Djeitun people was accompanied by the appearance of pottery, primarily rouletted ware, made by hand, and given a carefully polished surface. In the early period, about 12 percent of the pottery was decorated with red painted patterns on a yellow background. Most of the vessels decorated were cylinder-conical bowls. The painted patterns were simple, consisting mainly of parallel rows of wavy lines and vertical bracket-like lines and triangular patterns.

In the middle period of the Djeitun culture, pottery forms become more varied. Painted pottery excavated at Chopan-depe is only 3 percent of that found, with the percentage increasing in corresponding layers of Togolok-depe. Here, the wavy lines and bracket-like patterns give way to finely reticulated designs and dotted patterns. The pottery decoration becomes extremely and unusually small in the third period. Designs often were painted on the interior or inner surface of pots. In this period, decoration is in the form of horizontal lines, vertical zigzags, and tree-like patterns.

The Djeitun culture is an established and settled population, with clay brick architecture and improved standard of living, expressing the social transformation of the Neolithic revolution and an economic system based on agriculture and stock breeding: two major contributing factors to a food-production economy. The shape of vessels in this period resembled evolution from the pottery of preceding periods. The basic painted patterns derived inspiration from both Djeitun and Anau I-A pottery, while in general, features of the pottery were common to all these zones of southern Central Asia.

POLYCHROMATIC DECORATION OF POTTERY

The middle Chalcolithic period is characterized by polychrome decoration of pottery. At Namazga-depe it is represented in the assemblage of Namazga II.[10] The uniformity of southern Central Asian culture began to dissolve. Hence, in the western and central areas, monochrome painted decoration of the pottery of Anau I-Namazga I period was replaced by bright polychrome friezes, comprised of small geometric figures on a light, predominantly cream or yellow ground. This segment of cultural activities and polychromatic pottery were discovered in the settlements of Tilkin-depe, the northern mound of Anau, Kara-depe, Elen-Depe, and Namazga-depe. Polychrome decoration in pottery was found on 62 percent of all pottery, whereas the monochromatic painted pottery comprised only about 10 percent. The undecorated pottery includes red-slipped hemispherical bowls, often highly burnished, while the number of polished grey ware was much fewer. The coarse ware consists mainly of large vessels and round bowls. Thus, in the fifth and fourth millennia B.C.E., southern Inner Eurasia (Central Asia) had a prosperous agrarian economy, with developed architecture, colorful pottery, and superb figurines.

PROFESSIONALIZATION IN POTTERY

The transition of early settlements into settled villages was accompanied by the production of the finest painted pottery. Starting in the fourth millennium B.C.E., Central Asia began a period of five thousand years of pottery production, one of the longest and most fruitful ceramic traditions in the world, next to Chinese and pre-Columbian achievements. Some of the most compelling pottery were found at Susa in southwest Iran, where animal forms and abstract shapes were entwined. Some prehistoric sites were partially excavated, following the end of the Second World War. The oldest piece of pottery in this region dates to the eighth millennium B.C.E. At ten thousand years old, it was discovered between 1965 and 1974 by Philip Smith from the University of Montreal, at Tepe Ganje Dara[11] in Khuzestan province, present-day south-western Iran.

POTTER'S WHEEL AND GREY OR SOLID-COLORED POTTERY

The early phase of prehistoric pottery cultures included a polychromatic stage, wherein color was used as a decorative device. This phase was replaced, gradually, by the widespread availability of the potter's wheel. Multi-colored pottery gave way to grey, or solid-colored pottery. The early polychromatic stage emphasized aesthetic aspects of color, whereas the use of the potter's wheel emphasized greater delicacy and refined shape. Prehistoric pottery pieces were made in a variety of sizes for daily use; some have been found in graves and kurgans, where they held items necessary for the afterlife. The majority of these pottery pieces were vases, cups, beakers, teapots, flasks, and pitchers.

The most colorful material of this period is very fine painted pottery. As already noted, it began at Dzheytun, and later, decoration became more elaborate, both in pattern and coloring. The monochrome pottery shows a variety of geometric patterns, but frequently, figures of wild animals are found. The polychrome pottery is represented by vessels decorated with geometric designs, which are remarkable both for tonal range and accomplished craftsmanship. Kilns were developed for temperatures of 1200 Celsius.

Y. G. Gulyamov discovered, in the lower Zerafshan valley[12] (the western part of the Kyzylkum plains), Bronze Age Zaman Baba culture, which included houses, tombs, and a variety of objects indicating inhabitants engaged in farming and stock rearing. Their pottery is of great interest, with decorations stamped and occasionally painted.

ADVANCED FIRING TECHNIQUES AND TWO-LEVEL KILNS

In this period, the invention of the potter's wheel and important advances in firing technique in the two-level kiln are clear evidence of the beginning of professionalization of pottery production. A simplification and standardization of pottery production stages follows. Within this period, sculptural pottery figurines of animals are some of the most remarkable and expressive phenomena. The same process of professionalization occurred in metalworking, weaving, and other forms of production. Neolithic sites have been identified in the Chu valley, to the north of Kyrgyzstan.

POTTERY—EARLY BRONZE AGE (2500–2000 B.C.E.)

The Bronze Age refers to a new, more advanced stage of development observed at this time, both in material culture and in the economy as compared with the Chalcolithic Age that preceded it. In the middle of the third millennium B.C. there arose two kinds of settlement in southern Central Asia.

Emergence of Professional Potters

Two kinds of settlement arose in the southern part of Central Asia, from the middle of the third century B.C.E. The larger settlement was proto-urban and the other was a much smaller village settlement. Earlier pottery kilns of the Chalcolithic age were replaced by firing furnaces. Also, during this period, another important device, the potter's wheel came into use, and eventually replaced hand modelling entirely. A caste of professional potters emerged from among these farming and stock breeding communities.

In the early Bronze Age, the two pottery styles of the preceding period were replaced by a unified painted pottery style. The painted pottery of this period is chiefly monochrome, decorated with small patterns forming friezes. These were mostly geometric patterns. On exceptional occasions, bird motifs and goat figures were included.

As a result of this new development, changes in economy connected with the development of pottery manufacturing occurred. The massive appearance of firing furnaces and potter's wheel, both introduced to southern Central Asia midway during the third millennium B.C.E., are the two significant markers of this era. The caste of professional potters and discovery of sophisticated tools in manufacturing by stone artifacts, particularly stone vessels, are evidence of specialization in this craft. The discovery of copper smelting furnaces, appearance of the first stone and ceramic seals, and finally, the monumental structures preserved, all indicate complex transformation occurred among local tribes during the second half of the third millennium B.C.E. Three categories of pottery are distinguished in this period.

Painted Pottery, Unpainted Pottery, and Grey Pottery

The painted pottery of this period is chiefly monochrome, decorated with small patterns forming friezes. The patterns are mostly geometric, and zoomorphic motifs practically have disappeared. Although, occasionally bird motifs, goat figures, or tree motifs in a realistic style are represented. The grey ware was more common in the western districts of southern Central Asia. The techniques of pottery production were improved drastically by a new type of kiln, which became a feature of early Bronze Age, found in the excavation at Namazga Depe and Khapuz Depe. The new kilns are much larger, with complicated design. The use of potter's wheel and these kilns leave no doubt as to the existence of professional potters. Furthermore, pottery vessels in graves increase in number. One peculiar item discovered often with sophisticated pottery pieces are oil lamps carved of a stone similar to marble. Most of these lamps have cylindrical shapes.

The grey ware was more common in the western provinces of Central Asia, replacing the painted ware of the earliest periods, in Tepe Hissar, in southern Central Asia. Pottery objects, from the tombs of Marlik (1200–1000 B.C.E.), in simple though highly effective forms, such as vessels in the shape of human figures, and pottery bulls, called Amlash bulls, and other animals such as stag and a ram, have been found.

The most complete stratified sequence of habitation levels as a context for the local development of pottery from the late Chalcolithic Age to the early Bronze Age are the excavations in Khapuz-depe.[13] Decoration of painted pottery at Khapuz-depe is geometric, with new motifs emerging in the shape of stepped and un-stepped pyramids. The shape of vessels includes goblets with straight vertical sides, as well as hemispherical bowls, cups, and conical cups. These new features of pottery result from the use of the potter's wheel, which facilitated the manufacture of more fanciful forms.

In the Namazga IV culture layer, hand-shaped vessels occur alongside those bearing the unmistakable stamp of the potter's wheel. This enables us to date the introduction of the potter's wheel into southern Central Asia to the middle, rather the end, of the third millennium B.C.E. Similar development in pottery appear to be manufactured in other large settlements of the early Bronze Age in southwestern Central Asia. Altin-depe[14] pottery corresponds to that of Khapuz-depe, with black and brown painted designs on red or cream-colored ground. Nearly all the painted pottery from Altin-depe was wheel-turned. The clay is good quality, and the firing excellent. The decoration follows the general pattern of that at Khapuz-depe, but with finer workmanship, perhaps because Altin-depe was a more centrally located settlement.

The pottery from the settlement of Ulug-depe[15] dates to the Namazga IV period and is of great interest. Both the shape of vessels and decoration resemble pottery at Altin-depe, except that light colors are found alongside pottery with a red background.

Thus, there seem to be two ceramic traditions with origins in the older techniques of the eastern and central zones of southern central Asia. The pottery in Namazga-depe and Anau is distinguished by high standard workmanship and rather fanciful forms.

New Types of Kilns

Great progress in the technique of pottery production was achieved by a new type of kiln, which became a feature of the early Bronze Age, as we see attested in excavations at Namazga-depe[16] and Khapuz-depe.[17] Earlier primitive kilns were replaced by much larger kilns of a more complicated design: new kilns had two tiers, the firing chamber was built over the brick-lined furnace, and vertical partition or a thick pillar was built into the center of the furnace, to support the firing chamber above it, while the horizontal partition dividing the two chambers was perforated in many places to convey the heat. The furnace was loaded with firewood through a special, wide opening, so that the heated air was drawn into the chamber. The operation of the two-tiered kilns, where considerations of temperature adjustment and timing were of great importance, obviously required great technological skill. Both use of the potter's wheel and kilns of complicated design leave no doubt as to the existence of professional potters at the time.

Pottery reached the peak of its development in the middle Bronze Age. In the Namazgah V period, almost all was made on a fast potter's wheel, fired in two-tiered kilns at a temperature of 1400 degree Celsius. Improved techniques led to considerable modifications in appearance. Smooth, curved lines of handmade ware were replaced by intricate, deeply indented forms. At the same time, carelessly painted patterns, typical of Namazgah IV, were replaced almost entirely by wheel-defined decorative designs. Production by skilled professional artists, strictly standardized is evident in the sharp increase in variety in the Namazgah V period, with thirty basic types of pottery.

Prehistoric Pottery Centers of Eurasia

The rich tradition of production in the region is marked by particularly fine pottery at Sarazm, near Samarkand; at Hesar, Nurek, Regar, and Vakhsh in Tajikestan; at Bagram, Said Qala, Fullol, and Tella Tepe, in Afghanistan; in Iran at Persepolis, near Shiraz; at Tepe Sialk, near Kashan; at Tepe Hissar, near Damghan; at Tepe Gian, northeast of Susa; at Yarim Tepe, near Gurgan; at Marlik (1200–1000 B.C.E.), near Amlash in Gilan Province; at Hasanlu (1250–1050 B.C.E.), south of Lake Urumia, in Azarbaijan; at Shahre Sukhte, in Baluchestan; at Turang Tepe, in Mazandaran Province; at Namazgah and Altyn Tepe, in Turkmanistan; and at Sapalli Tepe and Kuchuk Tepe in Uzbekistan.

Art of Pottery and Origins of Trade

Social specialization in Central Asian communities coincided with a significant development of trade. Accumulated surplus production stimulated increased exchanges with surrounding communities near and far. A system of internal exchanges enabled the inhabitants of the residents of Altin Depe[18] to receive pottery and other professional products from other professional centers. Specific communities had specialized in the production of certain commodities; and these exchanges played an important role supplying agricultural villages with products of specialized crafts. For example, at Altin Depe, a grey ware vessel was discovered and identified as a product of the Hissar community, since there was no grey ware identified with Altin Depe pottery production units.

There is reason to believe that trade routes extended from southern Central Asia proto-urban communities far to the north and into the region of the steppe people.[19] The Zaman Baba culture, discovered in the lower reaches of the Zarafshan River, is dated to late third or early second millennium B.C.E. and is remarkable in this respect. Handmade pottery and other evidence, including the forms of beads, bronze pins, the presence of pottery kilns, and flat baked clay figurines reveals Zaman Baba as an early culture of the Steppe Bronze Age. At the settlement of Zaman Baba, grain impressions of wheat and barley were found, as well as bones of domesticated animals such as sheep, goats, cows, and asses. The bones of wild animals account for only 15 percent of the total, which demonstrates stock breeding and cultivation were established in Zaman Baba.[20]

Population Growth and the Great Migrations

According to C. Beckwith,[21] three distinct stages of migrations emerge from Eurasia: the first of Tokharians and Anatolians during the third millennium B.C.E.; the second includes Indic, Greek, Italic, Germanic, Armenians, and some of the Indo-Iranians people in the seventeenth century B.C.E.; and the third wave of Celtic, Baltic, Slavic, Iranian, and Albanian peoples in the late second millennium B.C.E.

The second millennium B.C.E. was a period of great migrations and changes in population, possibly resulting from rapid increases in population in the Eurasian steppes following the adoption of stockbreeding and agriculture, which replaced the archaic economy. The archeological material at our disposal leaves no doubt as to the spread of a population with Andronovo and Timber Grave cultural characteristics. There were two main movements of these steppe people into western Central Asia. The sources of the first were the Timber Grave culture of the Volga area, and the western Kazakhstan variant of Andronovo culture. There was a close association between the Timber Grave culture and some of the sites of western Andronovo culture, which has a large number of Timber Grave culture elements and their physical type. The second movement stems from the Andronovo traditions of central and eastern Kazakhstan, which extend into Kyrgyzstan, the Fergana Valley, and the shores of Zarafshan River.[22]

The first mention of gods with Indo-Iranian names occurs in Mesopotamian written records of the fourteenth century B.C.E., and the oldest parts of the Rig Veda, apparently of the same dates. Toponymic studies clearly show that from the ninth to the seventeenth centuries B.C.E., Iranian tribes appeared in large numbers in eastern Media and later moved west. It is quite logical to assume that western Central Asia was also affected by this process, especially if, as is mentioned in the Avesta and other sources, an Iranian-speaking population predominated here in the first half of the first millennium B.C.E. Some authorities believe that the sites of the Timber Grave culture, as well as the west Kazakhstan variant of the Andrononvo culture, are associated undoubtedly with an Iranian-speaking population, who laid the foundations of the Iranian-speaking Saka culture. Comparisons suggest that the great migrations in the second millennium B C.E. were connected with the spread of the Indo-Iranian tribes, and smaller tribal groups accompanying them. Worth noting are certain parallels between burial rites of these steppe Bronze Age cultures, and the burial rites described in the Rig Veda.[23]

Some scholars have discovered archeological sites to suggest before the mass migration of many Eurasian tribes to Europe, India, and the Iranian plateau, earlier migrations of smaller groups in the region occurred.

SIALK POTTERY CULTURES: PLAIN POTTERY, GEOMETRIC POTTERY, ANIMAL STYLE POTTERY, HUMAN FIGURE POTTERY, AND ORGANIC POTTERY STYLES

Sialk potters at this stage and of this era used symbolic motifs, for example, birds for funerary vessels.[24] There are, however, different and purely decorative elements elaborating many pottery pieces, including checker patterns, sun-wheels, circles containing crosses, rayed rosettes. Some of the pottery pieces elaborate fabulous wild or domesticated animals, including bulls, horses, and ibexes, some of which are winged. Human figures are found in three vases. Based on extensive archeological excavations in Sialk identifying nine to eleven layers of early pottery cultures and civilizations, R. Ghrishman[25] arrives at interesting conclusions (appendix I of this manuscript).

Ziwiyeh Pottery

In Ziwiyeh, a village where some of the Scythians migrating from the north settled in 700 B.C.E., a royal treasury was discovered with a collection of fascinating artifacts. Some of the pottery in Ziwiyeh tombs was of particular interest; pottery pieces forms and ornamentation revealed a branch of Scythian art.[26] A pitcher with a long beak-spout and a vase with a vertical cylinder-spout indicated a continuation of the traditions of Sialk, Khurvin, Hasanlu, and Luristan. Ziwiyeh pottery includes pots and pitchers with lugs in the form of a recumbent feline, a characteristically Scythian motif, which also figures on far more valuable gold objects. With its fine, well-baked clay, its burnished red slip and its decorative designs, it is the only pottery discovered so far that adheres to the technique of the Ziwiyeh potters, whose products were inspired by metal works.[27] There are a number of fascinating painted and glazed earthenware vases from Ziwiye (eighth to seventh centuries B.C.E.), at the Metropolitan Museum of Art.

Intricate Glazed Brick Walls of Susa

All ornamentation in the Achaemenid king Dariush's Apadana palace of Susa (sixth to fifth centuries. B.C.E.) consisted of glazed bricks. The walls of the palace were adorned with glazed bricks, to which Dariush added the profile view of a representation of his guardsmen, known as the Immortals, with whom he served in Egypt, and who helped him to regain his throne. These are materialized in the glazed brick wall pieces.

The third capital of the Achaemenid Empire was Susa, built by Darius I.[28] The palace of Darius I (522–486 B.C.E.) is built at Susa around a central court, measuring 116 by 118 feet. Susa was a powerful fort and flourishing administrative city, with a large civilian population, in the heart of the satrapy of Khuzestan. Many of the art objects discovered from the Achaemenid excavation sites have synthesized motifs of animals, either in naturalistic or stylized animal forms.

The first systematic excavation of Susa took place in 1884, led by the French archeologist J. de Morgan. There was no conservation, nor preservation. On the contrary, the Apadana Palace of Dariush at Susa, was reduced severely to rubble. Its animal style columns displaying bulls, horses, and lions, and the walls of the site of the capitol, with some of the earliest glazed bricks and figural images of humans and animals, were dismantled and stored in a newly built fortress. Although they were excavating and working to preserve the site of ancient Susa, the excavators used the ancient bricks with cuneiform writings from the ancient site to construct a new building, now known as Susa Castle.

The Apadana palace of Dariush was built on a platform of 820 by 490 feet in 521 B.C.E. and was the center of a complex. Many scholars, including many archeologists, have condemned the vandalism of this site. One remarks that eight hundred eighteen-wheel trucks moved from Susa to the Louvre Museum in Paris. Although this may be exaggeration, the inventory of "Susa at the Lourve" lists the collection of artifacts taken from Susa, leaving only rubble behind.

Amphoras, Craters, and Bowls of Parthian and Sassanid Dynasties

Examination of pottery pieces from the Parthian era at the ancient capital of Nisa, presently under excavation by Turkmen and Italian scholars and researchers from Turin University, continues.[29] Ongoing excavation and research in the southern part of Central Asia reveals pottery from the time of the Sassanids.[30] These pottery pieces can be divided into three major groups: bowls, amphoras, and craters, in a variety of sizes, and then further divided into forty sub-categories, or sub-groups. The majority of pottery pieces are elaborated with geometric patterns, such as parallel lines, checker board patterns, zig zags, or chevrons on the upper parts, around the shoulder of the bowl, amphora, or crater.

Pottery Schools of Eurasia: Bokhara, Khiva, Afrasiab (Samarkand), Kashgar, Chach (Tashkand), Herat, Khotan, Urganj, Turfan, Merv, and Nishapur

In the late ancient and early medieval times, especially between 105 B.C.E. and 721 C.E. and between 815 and 999 C.E., and again in the later fourteenth and early fifteenth centuries, there were many cultural and economic centers in Central Asia. Some of these cities enjoyed prosperity, being located on either the northern or southern extensions of the Silk Road, the primary trade and commerce freeway of communication and interactions. In fact, many of these cities became centers of artistic creation and production of various cultural products. Also, these cities became destinations for many enthusiast talents seeking training, education, and a chance to join active artistic communities, especially potters. They included the cities of Bokhara, Khiva, Afrasiab (Samarkand), Kashgar, Chach (Tashkand), Herat, Khotan, Urganj, Turfan, Merv, and Nishapur. These cities were among the most active in pottery production. Potters occupied large quarters in each city. From the ninth century to the beginning of the thirteenth centuries, pottery was divided into two major categories of glazed and unglazed ware. Stamped ware became widespread in the twelfth century, offering a wealth of inscriptions and organic and geometric decorative patterns, or abstractions.

Pottery of southern Inner Eurasia (Central Asia) did not neglect the human figure. There are examples of human figures against backgrounds abounding in animals, flowers, and inscriptions. The pottery pieces were elaborated with decorative motifs of birds, including doves, pheasants, and ducks; animals such as mountain goats, horses, cheetahs, and lions; mythical creatures such as phoenixes; plants, pomegranates, and flowers; and even scenes from royal receptions. The geometric patterns included squares, triangles, and varieties of lines. Inscriptions occupied the rim of the plates, while the remaining surface was undecorated usually. One glazing technique with particular appeal was a lead glaze that resulted in a particular gloss to the ware.

One fine example this decorative technique is the tenth-century alabaster panel from Afrasiab (Samarkand), which shows traces of a rich and ancient tradition. It is composed of trefoils, sinuous leafed stems, circles filled with small squares, six-pointed stars, and so on. The degree of sophistication attained in the applied arts is demonstrated by the Afrasiab, glazed ceramics of the ninth and tenth centuries C.E., the peak of Central Asian artistic achievement in ceramic technique and decoration. A white or red engobe covering was initially applied to this type of ware as a ground; it was then painted white, red, black, or other colors, and a transparent glaze was applied on top, giving the ware a luminous sheen. The surfaces of dishes, bowls, and other vessels were ornamented with various geometric designs and plant motifs, as well as inscriptions conveying greetings. Animals and birds were sometimes depicted as well.

Samanid Golden Age of Culture and Arts

Thus, in the ninth and tenth centuries C.E., intellectual life in Transoxiana and Khurasan attained a high level. It was inevitable that the local Samanid dynasty, seeking support among its literate classes, should cultivate and promote the local cultural traditions, literacy, and literature. Poetry in Persian spread rapidly, and is best exemplified in the work of A. A. Rudaki, the father of Tajik-Persian poetry, as well as A. Q. Firdawsi, the greatest poet of the Shahnama (Book of Kings). Poetry was the highest, but not the only, manifestation of this culture; equally interesting was the development of scholarship in various branches of inquiry: mathematics, astronomy, chemistry, medicine, history, and philology, with such outstanding exponents as Ibn Sına (Avicenna), A. R. Biruni, and many others.[31]

The main towns—Bukhara, Samarkand, Balkh, Merv, Nishapur, Khujand, Bunjikat, Hulbuk, Termez, Kashgar, Khotan, and others—became the major cultural centers of this era. Scholars, poets, artists, and other men of culture from many countries gathered in the Samanid capital of Bukhara, creating a fertile place for burgeoning creative thought; Bukhara became an outstanding cultural center of the known world. In Bukhara, a rich library a known as the Storehouse of Wisdom was assembled, containing books on various branches of learning, including the most esoteric; the rarest and best works of scholarship were to be found in the Bukhara book bazaar.

This era was followed by one when the Seljuk Turks occupied Central Asia, between 1040 and 1141 C.E. Central Asia was ruled by Seljuk sultans Arsalan (1156–1172) and Takish (1172–1200) and the Sufi dynasty Qongrat independently by the mid thirteenth century. Sufi Lord Yusuf and Sufi Lord Sulayman were famous local rulers of this period. By the early thirteenth century, Gurganj had become the capitol of the powerful Khwarazm Shahian Empire. The economic situation greatly improved, as towns were revived and irrigated farms were reclaimed. Crafts, especially pottery, also recovered. This particular era is identified in the archaeological record by new forms of richly decorated and elaborated jars. Glazed ceramics were decorated in diverse colors of red, ochre, yellow, or cinnamon, on white or yellow background. Silk Road trade was once again revived on all of its routes. In 1220 and again in 1273, 1276, 1279, and 1316, Central Asia was devastated by the Mongol army, which destroyed the dams built on the Amu Darya, flooding low lands of Central Asia.

After the Mongol invasion of the thirteenth century, and the massacre of many urban inhabitants in the region, particularly artisans and craftsmen, we witness a sharp decline in the quality of ceramic products in the archaeological record. However, ceramic production regains some of its former quality when Timur decided to rebuild Samarkand as his capitol, and brought artisans from all parts of his empire, especially from the city of Shiraz, since Shiraz had not been affected by the Mongol invasion. The architects and tile makers brought by Timur to Central Asia from Shiraz left a profound impact on architectural styles of the fourteenth and fifteenth centuries, especially a particularly obsessive fashion with which some buildings' interiors and exteriors were covered with exquisite polychromatic ceramic tiles. Thirty Majestic schools, palaces, caravansaries, vaulted markets, and mausoleums were built all with ceramic tile work.

Timurid Exquisite Ceramic Tiles as Interior and Exterior Wall Covers

During his reconstruction of Samarkand, Timur carried out other superb construction works. He built a citadel in 1370, and within its walls, included a residence and guardhouse, as well as administrative and military buildings. He then set about redesigning the city and planning other new buildings.

Bibi Khanum complex, named after the queen of his empire, was the largest Timurid architectural project. It was never completed by Timur, nor by his successors. Only in 1975 did Soviet authorities decide to finish the building. Several years after the end of the Soviet Union in 1991, the Uzbek government declared the completion of the building.

The Bibi Khanum complex stood surrounded by a high wall. Its rectangular plan measured 110 by 170 meters. In a typical Persian fashion, it contained a courtyard of 65 by 75 meters with four ivans, one in the center of each façade. At the four corners of the great enclosing wall, four polygonal minarets, in pairs, flanked a monumental pishtaq and framed the principal ivan that led to the room containing the mihrab, or great central hall.[32] A dome forty meters high covered with blue-green ceramic tiles stands next to two shorter domes. The tallest dome included thirty-six thick ribs enlivened by blue, white, and orange ceramic tiles.

Other architectural structures built in Samarkand in the latter fifteenth century C.E. include Ak Saray (White House), built in the 1470s. Sixteen relatively small architectural monuments covered with ceramic tiles were built at the Shah Zinda, where a number of Timur's relatives were buried.[33] The next golden age of Central Asian culture and arts would begin after Shah Ismail Safavi founded the Safavid Empire in Iran in the sixteenth and seventeenth centuries, While the drastic changes discussed resulted in changes to ceramic tile color and their decorative motives, by the fifteenth century, these tiles remained among the outstanding achievements of ceramic art in the world. Under the khanate rule in Khiva, Bokhara, and Kokand, styles and techniques of the Timurid era continued in Central Asia until the Russian Bolshevik revolution of 1917.

NOTES

1. Kuftin B. A. *Field Report on the work of Yu TAKE Team No. XIV on the Study of the Culture of the Settled Agricultural Population of the Copper and Bronze Age*, 1952. Masson, V. M. *Kara Depe near Artyk*, TYuTAKE, t, X, 1960.

2. Pumpelly, R. *Expolartion in Turkestan, Expedition of 1904: Prehistoric Civilizations of Anau*, V. I-II, Washington, 1908.

3. Litvinsky, B. A. *Namazga -Tepe: 1949 – 1950 Excavations*, SE, No. 4, 1952. Also, see: Khlopin, I. N. *The Tower of Namazga Depe*, Arkheologicheskiye otkrytiya goda, Moscow, 1966. Also, see: Khlopin, I. N. *Excavations at Namazga Depe*, Arkheologicheskiye otkrytiya goda, Moscow, 1968.

4. Masson, V. M. *Kara Depe near Artyk*, TYuTAKE, t, X, 1960.

5. Itina, M. A. *Excavations of a Cemetery of Tazabaiab Culture at Kokcha*, Materaly Khorezmskoi Eksepeditsii, V. 5, Moscow, 1961. Also, see: Itina, M. A. *The Farmers of Ancient Khorezm*, Moscow, 1968. Also, see: Vorobeva, M. G. *Reports of*

Khorezm Archeological and Ethnographical Expedition, IV, 1959. Also, see: Nerazik, E. E., *Village Settlements of Khorezm*, Moscow, 1966.

6. Korobkova,G. F. *The determination of the Function of Stone and Bone Implimentsas the Djeitun Site on the basis of Working Traces*, TYuTAKE, t. X. Ashkhabad, 1961.

7. Korobkova,G. F. *The Production tools from the Settlements o Chopan-depe, Togolok-depeand Pessedjik-depe,* Karakumskiye drevnosti, I, Ashkhabad,1968.

8. Litvinsky, B. A. *Namazga -Tepe: 1949 – 1950 Excavations*, SE, No. 4, 1952. Also, see: Khlopin, I. N. *The Tower of Namazga Depe*, Arkheologicheskiye otkrytiya goda, Moscow, 1966. Also, see: Khlopin, I. N. *Excavations at Namazga Depe*, Arkheologicheskiye otkrytiya goda, Moscow, 1968.

9. Smith, P. E. L. Ganj Dareh Tepe, Paleorient, V. 2 No. 1, pp. 207–209, 1974.

10. Guliamov, YA. Islamov, G. Askarov, A. *Prehistoric Culture and the Rise of Irrigation Agriculture in the Lower Reaches of Zarafshan,* Tashkent, 1966.

11. Sarianidi, V. I. *Khapuz Depe, A Bronze Age Site*, KSIA, V. 98, 1964. Also, see: Sarianidi, V. I. *Excavations at Khapuz Depe and Altin Depe*, Arkheologicheskiye otkrytiya goda, Moscow, 1967.

12. Ganialin, A. F. *The 1959 – 1961 Excavations at Altin-depe*, SA, No. 4, 1967.

13. Sarianidi, V. I. *Further Investigations at Ulug-depe, Arkheologicheskiye otkrytiya* 1966 goda, Moscow, 1969.

14. Litvinsky, B. A. *Namazga -Tepe: 1949 – 1950 Excavations*, SE, No. 4, 1952. Also, see: Khlopin, I. N. *The Tower of Namazga Depe*, Arkheologicheskiye otkrytiya goda, Moscow, 1966. Also, see: Khlopin, I. N. *Excavations at Namazga Depe*, Arkheologicheskiye otkrytiya goda, Moscow, 1968.

15. Sarianidi, V. I. *Khapuz Depe, A Bronze Age Site*, KSIA, V. 98, 1964. Also, see: Sarianidi, V. I. *Excavations at Khapuz Depe and Altin Depe*, Arkheologicheskiye otkrytiya goda, Moscow, 1967.

16. Ganialin, A. F. *Altin Depe*, The 1953 excavations, TIIAE AN TSSR, t. 5 Also, see: Masson, V. M. *The Fourth Season of Excavation at Altin Depe*, Arkheologicheskiye otkrytiya goda, Moscow, 1969.

17. Kuzmina, E. E., The Cemetary of Zaman-baba, SE, No. 2, 1958.

18. Sarianidi, V. I. Pottery Manufacture in the settlements of Ancient Margiana, TYu-TAKE, t. VIII, Ashkhabad, 1958. The following examples illustrate the rich tradition of pottery within the region in the early historical era. Particularly fine prehistoric pottery was produced at Sarazm, near Samarkand; at Hesar, Nurek, Regar, and Vakhsh, in Tajikestan; at Bagram, Said Qala, Fullol, and Tella Tepe, in Afghanistan; in Iran: at Persepolis, near Shiraz; at Tepe Sialk, near Kashan; at Tepe Hissar, near Damghan; at Tepe Gian, northeast of Susa; at Yarim Tepe, near Gurgan; at Marlik (1200 B.C. –1000 B.C.), near Amlash in Gilan Province; at Hasanlu (1250 B.C. –1050 B.C.), south of lake Urumia, in Azarbaijan; at Shahre Sukhte, in Baluchestan; at Turang Tepe, in Mazandaran Province; at Namazgah and Altyn Tepe, in Turkmanistan; and at Sapalli Tepe and Kuchuk Tepe in Uzbekistan.

19. Beckwith, C. I. *Empires of the Silk Road,* Princeton University Press, 2009.

20. Grousset, R. *The Empire of the Steppe*, Rutgers University Press, 1991.

21. Ghirshman, R. *L'Iran et la migration des Indo-Iraniens*, Leiden, 1977.

22. Ghirshman, R. *Fouilles de Sialk pres de Kashan*, 1933, 1934, 1937, V. 1, P. Geuthner, 1938.

23. Ghirshman, R. *Fouilles de Sialk*, V. 2, P. Geuthner, 1938.

24. Rice, T. T. *Ancient Arts of Central Asia*, Thames and Hudson, 1965.

25. Dyson, R. H. *Glimpses of History at Ziwiye*, Expedition 4, 1963.

26. Muscarella, O. W, Caubet, A., and Tallon, F*., Susa in Achaemenid Period*, in The Royal City of Susa, The Metropolitan Museum of Art, Harry N. Abrams, New York, 1993, 215–52. Also, see: A. Caubet, *Achaemenid Brick Decoration,* in P. O. Harper, J. Aruz, and F. Tallon, eds., The Royal City of Susa: Ancient Near Eastern Treasures in the Louvre, New York, 1992, 223–25.

Also, see: O. W. Muscarella, "Achaemenid Art and Architecture at Susa," in P. O. Harper, J. Aruz, and F. Tallon, eds., The Royal City of Susa, New York, 1992, 216–22. Also, see: A. Caubet, "Achaemenid Brick Decoration," in P. O. Harper, J. Aruz, and F. Tallon, eds., The Royal City of Susa: Ancient Near Eastern Treasures in the Louvre, New York, 1992, pp. 223–25.

27. Cellerino, A. *La ceramica, In Nisa Partica, Ricerche nel compleso monumentale, Arsacide*, Monogra, 2008. Also, see: Bruno, J. *Ceramics of Parthian Homeland: New data about the ceramic production of the early Arsacd period,* from the Italian excavation in Old Nisa, 2008.

28. Priestman, S. *Sassanian Ceramics from the Gogan Wall and other Sites on the Gorgan Plain*, 2013.

29. Frye, R. *The Samanids*, The Cambridge History of Iran, V. 4, Cambridge University Press, 1975.

30. Chuvin P. and Degeorge, G. *Samarkant, Bokhara and Khiva*, Flummarion, Paris, 1999, pp. 89–162.

31. Starr, S. F. *Lost Enlightenment*, Princeton University Press, 2015. Starr's Lost Enlightenment suggests that the golden age of Central Asia in Bokhara in ninth and tenth centuries continues after interruptions in Samarkand in the fourteenth and fifteenth centuries. Also, see:

Lenz T. W. and Glenn, D. L. *Timur and Princely Vision*, Persian Art and Culture in the Fifteenth Century, Washington, D. C., 1989, pp. 17–66. Also, see: Hookham, H. *Tamburlaine the Conqueror*, London, 1962, pp. 37–58.

Chapter Three

Prehistoric and Early Ancient Inner Eurasian Art of Figurines, Statues, and Sculptures

The cultural zone of the early Metal Age comprises almost all of the Central Eurasian region. The great mining and metallurgical production include the Altai region and northern and southern Central Asia. Mobile pastoralist cultures, armed with metal weapons, emerge on the steppe, where their influence would be felt by the neighboring peoples of Eurasia and beyond for millennia.[1] Although, nearly all northern cultures of Central Asian economies were based on hunting, fishing, and gathering in the Neolithic period, between the eight and sixth millennia B.C.E., the southern Central Asian cultures were committed to a productive economy, based on agriculture and animal husbandry. Copper tools appear first in Central Asia during the fifth millennium B.C.E.

EARLIEST METAL ART OF CENTRAL ASIA: NAMAZGA AND DJEITUN CULTURES

The earliest metalworks in Central Asia appear in levels belonging to Namazga I culture, and increase in number during the Namaga II and III periods, when a range of distinctive artifacts appear, with average length of 5–10 cm. Scholars have traced the Djeitun culture to the sixth millennium B.C.E. Numerous artifacts were found on sites of Djeitun culture.[2] There are a variety of pendants and beads; some of the pendants are figurines of animals made of bone, seashells, and semi-precious stones, including turquoise. Many figurines of unbaked clay have holes made with sharp sticks. Djeitun culture was replaced by the Copper Age culture of Anau, now referred to as Namazgah I–III type (beginning in the earliest levels of Namazgah I and

Dashlydzhi depe). In the early Chalcolithic period for southern Central Asia, there are few human figurines. All together twenty settlements from this period can be divided into three groups:[3]

1. The Western Zone—occupies the territory between Kizil Arvat and Anau. This zone includes the Settlements of Beurme, Karantki Tokai, Tilkin Depe, Dashli, Ovadan, Ekin Depe, and Anau. Each village in this group generally occupies an area of 2–3 acres and rises 2–3 meters above the surrounding area. Residents of these villages pursued a mixed farming economy. Houses of this zone were built of rectangular sun-baked bricks. Pottery decorated with painted ribbon patterns and fuzzy lines are one of the characteristics of the sites of the western group. Unfortunately, the villages of the western zone have been studied very perfunctorily, using only material collected on the surface. Very few have been investigated by trial excavations. Mural frescoes, however, were discovered on the northern mound at Anau in 1953.[4] Furthermore, the frescoes at the settlement of Yassi Depe also were discovered by Kuftin.
2. The Central Zone—occupies the area between Anau and Dushak, and includes large settlements such as Kara Depe[5] and Namazga Depe and many smaller villages, such as Yassi Depe and Sermancha Depe.
3. The Eastern Zone—includes settlements situated in the lower course of the Chaacha Sai and Meana Sai. The houses of this region were generally built of standard rectangular sunbaked bricks tempered with chopped straw. The walls were covered with clay plaster, sometimes painted black.

FIGURINE ART STYLE

It is interesting to note that almost all the figurines are portrayed in a standing position, including one female figurine from Kara-depe. By the end of the second millennium B.C.E. figurines in the seated position were more common. The number of zoomorphic figurines, mostly sheep and cattle, are greater. Many are made of unfired clay. The anthropomorphic figurines of Geoksyur have distinctive features. Here, just as at Kara-depe, figurines were portrayed in a standing position, but they are more schematized. One of the figurines of Dashlidji-depe[6] has survived intact. It was modeled without arms, and its facial contours are completely dominated by a large nose.

Dashlidji-depe[7] conceptual figurine style is in sharp contrast to the realistically portrayed female figurines from Kara-depe. Thirty-five burials were excavated in Kara 2 level, where one of the most ancient figurines of a man was found. He is shown bearded, and in a seated position. Kara 3 level contained twenty-one burials. In Geoksyur, in a Neolithic, early Chalcolithic agricultural village with one-roomed houses,[8] the remains of ancient ditches were excavated around the outer side of a defensive wall. A collection of more than one hundred female figurines was discovered in this village.

Yalangach-depe Female Deity

Next door, at Yalangach-depe from the same period, a complete figurine, 28 cm high was found, giving a good idea of the iconography of the female deity. It shows a woman in a sitting position, her head slightly tilted back, and her facial features were schematized, with round holes for eyes and black-painted eyebrows. Two broad, painted bands around her neck may represent ornaments. Below these, in front, three rows of dotted lines form a kind of necklace. The figurine has no arms. The thighs are painted with circles dotted on the inside, possibly in imitation of the sun. The artist may be conveying an image of a fertility deity, or mother goddess. Most of the female figurines from this area resemble the one described above.

One difference among female deities is the size of the figurine. There are also differences as far as the details of the painting of the figurines; for example, goats painted around the hips, instead of the sun. Some of the figurines have their arms folded on their stomach, with their hands cupped under the breasts. This iconographic image of a sitting female goddess, with certain variations, survived until the end of the second millennium B.C.E. over the entire territory of southern Central Asia.[9]

During the late Chalcolithic period, the early agricultural communities of southern Central Asia show great cultural advances: Irrigation systems improved, decorations on painted pottery grew more refined, and figurines of high quality were produced, while contacts grew with settlements of neighboring countries.

Male Statuettes

Male statuettes are sharply distinct from the general typology of female figurines. Only three figurines of this kind were discovered in the foothills of the Kopet Dag Mountains, all from the upper layer of Kopet Dag. One of them, shown in a standing position, is known as the priest. The second, whose skillfully fashioned head has been preserved, possibly represents the same type of religious figure. Another figurine has broad features, an aquiline nose, and a long neck.

Zoomorphic Figurines

Zoomorphic figurines vary, relative to those of human figurines. Most of the animal representations are modeled in clay. Occasionally, they bear painted patterns, which may represent harnesses. It is crucial to mention that within this segment of time (3000–2500 B.C.E.). The site of Geoksyur I[10] alone yielded three hundred figurines, compared to only thirty figurines from Kara-depe.

South-Eastern Central Asia Female Figurines

The female figurines of south-eastern Central Asia may be divided into two types:

1. The first type was more common in early Geoksyurian times, late fourth to early third millennia B.C.E. These were relatively large female figurines (25–30 cm. tall), made of clay heavily tempered with finely chopped chaff and straw, and their upper part covered with pink or red slip. All of them were modeled in sitting position and are noted for their realistic portrayal. Their faces have large noses, and their long neck merges with sloping shoulders. Their narrow waist merges with broad hips from which their legs project forward. Many figurines have painted eyebrows, painted necklaces, and other ornamentations. There is one figurine of a mother with a baby painted on her stomach.
2. The second group of statues (later in this period) include highly stylized figurines (some 7–10 cm. tall) made of close-textured clay. These are all shown in a sitting position as well, their bird-like heads attached to long necks. They have neither arms nor breasts. In some instances, the head was given a complicated hairstyle.

BABAS AND/OR BALBALS SCULPTURE ART OF INNER EURASIA

A symbolic stone entity ranging from flat, engraved outlines of human faces to more elaborate reliefs is widely dispersed throughout the regions of Kyrgyzstan, Kazakhstan, Southern Siberia, Caucasus, the Altai, the Tuva, and Mongolia. However, they have not been found in Tajikistan, Uzbekistan, or Turkmenistan. Grach[11] believed that Babas, or Balbals were sculptures of the enemies of the region: eastern Huns, or Hephtalites, who occupied the region for over one hundred years and were defeated by an alliance between the Sassanid Persian Emperor Khosrow (Anushervan) and Western Turk

Khaghan Sinjibu in 567 C.E. Kyzlasov, in his analysis, identified Babas or Balbals as the memorial representations of ancestors, or those deceased.[12]

INDIVIDUALIZED STYLES AND VARIOUS TYPES OF EURASIAN FIGURINES

Figurines of this period were executed in a highly individualized style. For example, one statuette found in Altin Depe shows a pregnant woman, symbolizing motherhood.[13] Figurines of Southern Central Asia held significant meaning and as a result of a preliminary survey, they have been classified in six different types:

1. The first type, a triangle with cilia, occurs only with figurines of Altin Depe, where they were very common, distributed all over the settlement. In 1968, a small clay vessel bearing two similar symbols was discovered at Taichanak Depe.[14]
2. The second type, a crucifixion star, was more widespread, and occurs on figurines from Altin Depe, Ullug Depe, and Taichanak Depe.
3. The third type, in the form of marks which sometimes resemble the letter K, occurs on figurines from three sites of Altin Depe, Khapuz Depe, and Taichanak Depe.
4. The fourth type represents a stylized branch of a plant, and has been found at Khapuz Depe and Altin depe.
5. The zigzag type.
6. The row of vertical lines type is confined to Altin Depe. The constant repetition of these symbols is proof that motifs were not random. Most likely, these marks were symbolic of gods, deities of water, or female spirits.

NOTES

1. Chernykh, E. N. *Ancient Metallurgy: The Early Metal Age*, Cambridge University Press, 1992.

2. Hiebert, F. T. *A Central Asian Village at the Dawn of Civilizations at Anau*, Turkmenistan, University of Pennsylvania., 2003.

3. Masson, V. M. *The south Turkmenistan Center of Early Agriculturalists*, TYuTAKE, t. X, Ashkhabad, 1960.

4. Kuftin, B. A. *Research into the Anau Culture by the South Turkmenistan Archeological Expedition in 1952*, IAN TSSR, I, 1954.

5. Masson, V. M. *Kara Depe near Artyk*, TYuTAKE, t, X, Ashkhabad, 1960.

6. Khlopin, I. N. *Dashlidji Depe and the Chalcolithic Farmers of Southern Turkmenistan*, TYuTAKE, t. X. Ashkhabad, 1960.

7. Khlopin, I. N. *The Geoksyur Group of Settlements in the Chalcolithic Period*, Moscow- Leningrad, 1964.

8. Chernykh, E. N. *Ancient Metallurgy: The Early Metal Age*, Cambridge University Press, 1992.

9. Khlopin, I. N. *The Geoksyur Group of Settlements in the Chalcolithic Period*, Moscow- Leningrad, 1964.

10. Grach, A. D. *On Early Burials with Cremation: Balbals of Tuva*, Archeological Discoveries, 1968, 1.

11. Kylasov, L. R. *The Meaning of Babas* Sovietskaya Arkheologiya, 1964, 2.

12. Ganialin, A. F. *Altin Depe, The 1953 Excavations*, TIIAE AN TSSR, t. 5.

13. Shchetenko, A. Y. A. *Taichanak Depe*, Karaumskiye drevnosti, V. 2, Ashkhabad, 1969.

14. Masson V. M. Sarianidi, V. I. *The Symbols on the Central Asian Bronze Age Figurines*, VDI, No. I, 1969.

Chapter Four

Eurasian Cimmerian and Sarmatian Metal Arts

CIMMERIAN ART

Some scholars believe that from 1200 B.C.E. the Cimmerians, a people of Iranian origin from Eurasia, crossed the Caucasus and settled in western Iran and Asia Minor; and in the eighth century B.C.E., their descendants began to inhabit the Eurasian steppe, including the north area of the Black Sea.[1]

Cimmerians either migrated from Hungary and Romania, or inhabited those countries as well. The most important Cimmerians of numerous finds of this period in the Dnieper and Kuban region include the Borodino treasure (1300–1100 B.C.E.), the Shetkovo treasure with its bronze sickles (1400–1100 B.C.E.), the bronze foundry of Nikolayev (1100 B.C.E.), and the bronze sickles of Abramovka (1200 B.C.E.). All these discoveries were made between the lower Danube and the lower Dnieper. At Kuban, there are gold plaques and silver oxen of Saromishastovskaya (1300 B.C.E.). On the Trek River, there are kurgans of Piatigorsk (1200 B.C.E.) and the beginning of Koban (the age of pure bronze, 1200–1000 B.C.E.). This Cimmerian art in the south of Eurasia is also related to Talysh culture, where bronze art flourished about 1200 B.C.E.[2] As early as 1300–1200 B.C.E. we see the spread of Cimmerian civilization using bronze, from the Volga to the Urals. From 1150–950 B.C.E. the Cimmerian civilization continued to develop north of the Black Sea.

The last phase of Cimmerian cultural complex occurs between 900 and 750 B.C.E. This is the period of the Mikhailovka treasure in Galicia, with its famous golden crown. It is also the period of the Podgortsa treasure, south of Kiev, and of the bronze socketed axes of Koblevo, east of Odessa. The Cimmerian bronze culture extended to Romania and then into present-day

Hungary. According to Hungarian Professor J. Harmatta[3] "the rise of the Scythian kingdom represented an event of intra-ethnic character, because both Cimmerians and Scythians were Iranian peoples." M. A. Dandamaev and V. G. Lukonin indicate that "ethnically and linguistically, the Scythians and Cimmerians were kindred groups since both people spoke Old Iranian dialects." The first record of the Cimmerians, however, appears in Assyrian annals in the year 714 B.C.E. Assyrians recorded the migration of Cimmerians because the Assyrian king Sargon II, was killed in battle against them.[4]

LURISTAN—A METALLURGY MEGA CENTER BRONZE ART (EIGHTH CENTURY B.C.E. TO SEVENTH CENTURY B.C.E.)

In the first decades of the eight century B.C.E., Cimmerians were acting as allies of Urartu, and Cimmerian mercenaries were serving in the Assyrian army, while others were co-operating in the Median revolt. Cimmerians split up into two groups; one moved westward toward Asia Minor, and the other traveled into a region that is today the province of Luristan. They established themselves in Luristan, with its isolated valleys, as herders and horse breeders. Thousands of objects have been found in the tombs and shrines of Luristan; great quantities of ornaments, horse gear, and weapons were unearthed from excavation sites.[5]

SURKH DUM: A TREASURY OF METAL ART

The great majority of known examples of these artifacts emerged from plundering and international market distribution. The British Museum acquired some Luristan bronzes in 1854, followed by other purchases in 1885, 1900, 1914, and 1920. Between 1927 and 1930, museums in New York, Boston, Philadelphia, Chicago, Brussels, and Hamburg acquired numerous pieces of Luristan bronzes. Erich Schmidt excavated the site of Surkh Dum in eastern Luristan in 1938.[6] Surkh Dum is recognized by many international archeologists to be the most important site in Luristan. Over one hundred objects of bronze, ivory, bone, faience, and terracotta, as well as two hundred cylinder and stamp seals, were recovered. The Metropolitan Museum of Art in New York acquired forty objects excavated at Surkh Dum.[7]

The art of Luristan reached its zenith in the second half of the eighth and into the seventh century B.C.E. A large portion of the diverse objects found in Luristan funerary sites center on the glorification of the powers presiding over life and death of every individual. There is no hint of any Shamanic cult in these bronzes. They represent the most ancient images of the Iranian religion, as it existed before Zoroaster, in the period when Yashts, the oldest part of Avesta, the sacred book of Iranians was taking form. The Yashts section of Avesta is composed of twenty-one chapters, each dedicated to a different deity or supernatural force (see apendix III).

In the Cincinnati Art Museum, a silverplate from Luristan depicts Zurvan, the deity of infinite time, who gave birth to Ahuramazda and Ahriman, Good and Evil, or, Prince of Light and Prince of Darkness. This ancient Iranian belief was incorporated into official Zoroasterianism under the Sassanian Empire (241–651 C.E.) when they declared Zoroasterianism as their state religion. Ahuramazda is a supreme god, the creator of the world, named "the Wise, the Lord" in the reformed religion introduced by Zoroaster, in opposition to his twin brother, Ahriman, lord of evil. In his funerary images, he is shown in the gesture of a prayer, with both arms raised and the palms of the hands turned forward, expressed more or less elevated forms of religious emotions. Art in this case was put to the service of religious imagery and symbolism, the rich diversity of age-old mythology condensed and epitomized by the artist in a single work of art.[8]

The animal style art of Luristan bronze pieces includes hybrid creatures composed of the foreparts of two animals. It is quite possible that these objects made in the workshops of the Luristan smiths were the origin of the famous Achaemenid column capitals composed of two animals, which after being used in Iran for edifices, made their east way to India and westward to the Aegean. In which case, the theory that the column capital, as we find it in the palaces of Susa and Persepolis, originated from proto-Elamite seals, calls for reconsideration. The animal effigies were also used for decorating objects of daily use, such as seals, tools, chariots, and furniture. The plasticity of animal style art of Luristan has a certain power, in fact simplified geometric or organic structure of the some of the work reminds us of the artwork of modern, or postmodern animal sculptures.

Many of the horse strappings and weapons found in the cemeteries and shrines of Luristan have never been used. Most of this group of artifacts were merely symbolic objects, which the dead took with them to the other world for personal use. Another peculiar characteristic of the animal style art of Luristan bronzes was the practice of attaching wings to creatures, creating a surreal and imaginary world. The same style was followed in some Achaemenid art pieces.

A great number of axes were discovered in the tombs of Luristan. They are symbolic objects intended for the use of the dead in the next world. There are three varieties of fibula found in Luristan. The first kind is the more common, from late eighth or early seventh century onward. The second kind has no spring, and its pin is fastened to the arc by a small ring, turning on a stud.

The third fibula from Luristan has a certain significance, because it is formed in the shape of animals, a specialty of the Cimmerians.

Potters of Luristan imitated bronze-workers and took from the bronze vessels their new elements. Potters of Luristan elaborated their vases with painted decorations. No other civilization has yielded such a wealth of metal objects, with so great a diversity of forms, and so wide range of subjects and techniques, as those of the metal works of Luristan. They represent an extraordinary growth of Iranian metal industry in the eight and seventh centuries B.C.E.

According to Herodotus (440 B.C.E.), Cimmerians were expelled from their homeland by Scythians. Between 750 and 700 B.C.E., according to the Greek historians and Assyrian sources, Cimmerians were dispossessed of steppes of southern Central Asia by the Scythians, who came from the north of Central Asia. These were the people called Ashkuz by Assyrians, Scyths by Greeks, and to whom Persians gave the name of Saka.

SARMATIAN GOLD, SILVER, AND BRONZE ART

In the second half of the third century B.C. E., the Sarmatians of the same lineage as the Scythians, belonging, like them, to the northern nomadic Iranian group, and until then, established north of the Aral Sea, crossed the Volga River, driving the Scythians to Crimea. The Scythians were mounted archers, wearing a cap and roomy garments, and had developed an animal style art, stylizing naturalistic forms.[9]

Sarmatians were essentially lancers, with conical caps, and coats. Sarmatian's animal style art displayed a far more exclusive taste than that of the Scythians for stylizing floral motifs.[10] The transition from Scythian to Sarmatian art occurred at the beginning of the third century B.C., as may be concluded from the great discoveries made at Alexadropol near Ekaterinoslav. Sarmatian art became established in southern Eurasia during the third and second centuries, as shown by jewelry of Buerova Mogila, Akhtanizovka, Anapa, Stavvropol, Ksinskoye, and Kurdzhips in the Kuban. It is also revealed by the Sarmatian layer at Elizavetovskaya near Azov, and may be seen in the celebrated silver and enamel belt in Maikop. A griffin devouring a horse, the Maikop belt is said to be an example of Sarmatian art dating from the second century B.C.E. This group, and in particular the plaque of the Maikop belt, are associated with the gold and silver plaques of Eurasia, part of the treasure of Peter the Great, which are ornamented with fights between griffins and horses, tigers and horses, griffins and yaks, and eagles and tigers, and treated in a highly stylized manner.[11]

The same style continues in the Sarmatian plaques of the succeeding period, and is found at Taganrog and Fedulovo near the mouth of the Don, at Siverskaya near the mouth of the Kuban (second to first century B.C.E.), and as of the first century of this era, at Novocherkask, near Azov; at Ust-Labinskaya; at the Zubov farm; and at Armavir in the Kuban. The Altai group comprised, besides Pazyryk, the kurgans of Shibe, Karakol, and Oirotin, dating mainly from the first century B.C.E., having Sarmatian affinities. Objects of Shibe group display an animal style art with stylization not far removed from realism.

ORDOS ARTS

Ordos refers to a Bronze and early Iron Age culture from the sixth to second century B.C.E., occupying a large portion of what is Inner Mongolia today. The Ordos culture is known for significant discoveries of Scythian/Saka art representing its easternmost extension.[12] The Ordos plateau was an ideal grazing land covered by grass, bushes, and trees with numerous rivers and streams running through the area. Overgrazing and climate change turned the area into a desert. The Ordos culture, from 500 B.C.E. to 100 C.E., has horse gear, small plaques, tent poles, and blade weapons, including bronze artifacts using animal style decorations related to Scythian art.[13] The Ordos culture is also identified as the easternmost of Iranian peoples of the Eurasian Steppe, which gradually included Chinese elements and motifs in their art. J. Harmatta, the Hungarian scholar writes: "From the first millennium, we have abundant historical, archaeological and linguistic sources for the location of the territory inhabited by the Iranian peoples. In this period the territory of the northern Iranians, they being equestrian nomads, extended over the whole zone of the steppes and the wooded steppes and even the semi-deserts from the Great Hungarian Plain to the Ordos in northern China."[14]

XIANG'NU

According to Chinese historian Ssu-ma Ch'ien, in the latter half of the third century B.C.E., Xing'nu twenty-four tribes were united as a strong nation.[15] They wore a loose robe to the calf, split at the sides and gathered in by a girdle, whose ends hung down in front. Because of the cold, sleeves were gathered tightly at the wrists. A short fur cape covered their shoulders, with the head protected by a fur cap. Their shoes were leather, and they wore wide trousers strapped at the ankle. The sheath of the bow hung from the belt in front of the left thigh. The Xiang'nu livelihood was regulated by their flocks of sheep, herds of horses, cattle, and camels. They migrated with their livestock in search of water and pasture. They dressed in skins, slept on furs, and camped in felt tents. Xiang'nu art is often known as Ordos art, named after the Mongol Ordos tribe, which, since the sixteenth century C.E., has occupied what is today Inner Mongolia.[16]

As far as Xiang'nu art is concerned, many scholars see a double current in the aesthetics of Eurasia. On the one hand, by the third century B.C.E., there is a naturalism rooted in Scythian/Saka animal style art, which is replaced by the decorative art of Sarmatians, geometrical and floral, and equally stylized exclusively for decorative purposes. It is a combination of these two tendencies—naturalistic and decorative art—that is transmitted, through the great metallurgical centers of Eurasia: namely, Pazyryk, Minussinsk, and Katanda to the Xiang'nu tribes of Mongolia, eastern Siberia, and northern China. Hence, the art of the eastern part of Eurasia merges as a branch of the stylized animal art of the steppes, influencing Chinese art and also that of the eastern nomads. Also, as a result of mass migrations to the south, southwest, and west, we find the influences of this art in those regions as well.[17] The next chapter of this book includes an analysis of combined Scythian/Saka Art.

NOTES

1. Tallgren, A. M. *La Pontide prescythique apress l'introduction des metaux*, ESA II, 1926.

2. Kristensen, A. K. G. *Who were the Cimmerians, and where did they come from?: Sargon II, and the Cimmerians, and Rusa I*. Copenhagen Denmark: The Royal Danish Academy of Science and Letters, 1988.

3. Harmatta, J: *Scythians*, UNESCO Collection of History of Humanity: Volume III: From the Seventh Century BC to the Seventh Century AD, Routledge, 1996, p. 181.

4. Hancar. F. *Luristan, Archéologie, Art et histoire*, Persée - Portail des revues scientifiques en SHS, Vol. 16, 1935, p. 311–12. Also, see: Kohl, P. L.; Dadson, D. J., eds. The Culture and Social Institutions of Ancient Iran, by Dandamaev, M. A. and Vladimir G. Lukonin. Cambridge University 1989, Press, p. 51.

5. Overlaet, B. *Luristan Metalwork in the Iron Age*, Persia's Ancient Splendour: Mining, Handicraft and Archaeology, Deutsches Bergbau-Museum: Bochum, 2004.

6. Schmidt, E. Maurits, N., and Curvers, H. H. Expedition to Luristan, The Oriental Institute of the University of Chicago, 1989.

7. Muscarella, O. W. *Surkh Dum at The Metropolitan Museum of Art*, Journal of Field Archaeology, Vol. 8, No. 3, 1981, pp. 327–59.

8. Moorey, P. R. S. *Ancient Bronzes from Luristan.* British Museum: London, 1974.

9. Sinor, Denis, ed. *The Cambridge History of Early Inner Asia*, Cambridge University Press, 1990.

10. Perevalov, S. M. The Sarmatian Lance and the Sarmatian Horse-Riding posture. *Anthropology & Archeology of Eurasia* 40(4): 7–21, 2002.

11. Hinds, Kathryn, *Scythians and Sarmatians*, Marshall Cavendish, 2009. Also, see: Brzezinski, R.; Mielczarek, M. *The Sarmatians 600 BC—AD 450*, Bloomsbury USA; Osprey Publishing, 2002.

12. Harmatta, J. *The Emergence of the Indo-Iranians: The Indo-Iranian Languages.* In Dani, A. H. and Masson, V. M. (eds.). *History of Cicilizations of Central Asia: The Dawn of Civilization: Earliest Times to 700 BC*, UNESCO, pp. 346–70, 1992.

13. Lebedynsky, I. *Les Nomades, les peuples nomades de la steppe des origines aux invasions mongoles*, IXe siècle av. J.-C. - XIIIe siècle apr. J.-C. Paris: Errance, 2007.

14. Harmatta, J. *The Emergence of the Indo-Iranians: The Indo-Iranian Languages.* In Dani, A. H. and Masson, V. M. (eds.). *History of Civilizations of Central Asia: The Dawn of Civilization: Earliest Time to 700 BC*, UNESCO, pp. 346–70, 1992.

15. Maenchen-Helfen, O. J. *The Legend of the Origin of the Huns*, Byzantion, Vol. 17, pp. 244–51, 1944–1945.

16. Ma, L. *The Original Xiongnu, An Archaeological Exploration of the Xiongnu's History and Culture*. Hohhot: Inner Mongolia University Press, 2005.

17. Bunker, Emma C. *Nomadic Art of the Eastern Eurasian Steppes: the Eugene V. Thaw and other New York collections*, New York: The Metropolitan Museum of Art, 2002.

Chapter Five

Northern Cultures of Eurasia
Scythian/Saka Arts

There are three important cultural and territorial groups and sites within the northern zone of Central Asia during the Bronze Age:

1. The group of burials of Timber Grave[1] culture in the western Central Asia
2. The very large group, or perhaps several groups, belonging to Androvono[2] culture
3. The Caspian Sea[3] group

The people of these steppe cultures, their coexistence, and mutual assimilation comprise a very complex situation with different ethno-cultural contacts involved.

ANDRONOVO CULTURE: METALLURGY ART OF EURASIA (2300–900 B.C.E.)

The first prehistoric culture to extend all across the steppe from the Urals to western China was the Andronovo culture. Many scholars have identified Andronovo culture as one of the most powerful cultures of Central Asia. Andronovo culture burials found in the Tarim basin, radiocarbon datable to 2000 to 400 B.C.E., contained well-preserved corpses with distinctly Caucasian features, implying that Indo-Europeans inhabited that region, now part of Xinjiang province occupied by China. These early Iranians appear to be the ancestors of the Tokharians who inhabited the region; in fact, a new discovery at the Baigetuobie cemetery features human genetics of an Andronovo community residing to the east of the Tianshan mountains.[4]

The Andronovo culture was of special importance in the history of Eurasia, with its most southerly monuments found in the foothills of the Altai. The most northerly monuments of Andronovo culture are in the Ob River region in the zones between the forest and the steppe. One of the most important centers of the Andronovo culture was the Minusinsk basin, which extended from the west of the Altai to the Yenisei and included present Kazakhstan and the steppes of the southern Urals.[5] The culture developed advancements in cattle breeding and agriculture in which horned cattle and sheep played an important role, producing meat and wool for clothing and felt. The wool was processed and used for knitted caps, the remains of which have been found in graves. Horses were also bred, and grain was ground with grinders made of stone slabs.

Andronovo Metallurgy

Metal was obtained in the Altai and Kalbin ranges in northern Kazakhstan from shallow open shafts. The primary source of raw metal was oxidized ore from surface deposits. The ore was beaten with stone hammers then smelted in furnaces. The metalworkers used clay pouring molds, composite stone molds, and often a combination of the two in which objects were simultaneously molded. The Andronovo agriculturalists and cattle breeders lived a more or less sedentary life in permanent settlements near their plowlands or cattle corrals. The regular sedentary life necessitated many clay vessels including flat-bottomed jar-like pots with straight sides and vessels with convex sides. Such vessels were ornamented by comb-like stamps with zigzags, triangles, and rhombs. In Kazakhstan, a culture known as Andronovo reached Minusinsk, and around 1000 B.C.E. was prolonged by that of Karasuk. This was the first Siberian Bronze Age, with its socketed axes.[6]

Art of Gold, Pottery, & Bronze Tools

According to G. Frumkin,[7] the Bronze Age of Kazakhstan corresponds roughly to the second millennium B. C. E. Some archeologists, including A. Kh. Margulan in 1960, M. N. Komarova[8] in 1962, and V. P. Aleksieyev in 1967, have shown in their analyses of Andronovo culture that it extended from north of the Black Sea, along the shores of Ural River, to the heart of the Altai mountains, to the shores of the Aral Sea and Khwarazm. Andronovo culture was common in major parts of Kazakhstan and the Siberian Minusinsk region.

Dwelling sites from the Andronovo period in central Kazakhstan were usually comprised of huts for ten to fifty inhabitants. The burial places consisted of groups of tombs surrounded by megalithic granite slabs, sometimes several hundreds of them. In 1946 archeologists A. Kh. Margulan,[9] M. K. Kadyrbayev,[10] and A. M. Orazbayev[11] conducted the first excavation on the Central Kazakhstan Andronovo culture of the Bronze Age. In 1959 and 1966, M. K. Kadyrbayev continued his expedition around Karaganda in central Kazakhstan. He explored many kurgans of the Tasmola burial site of the seventh to third century B.C. near the Shiderty River. Numerous ornaments in bronze, gold, bone, and iron were discovered. The significance of Kadyrbayev's discovery was the fact that it was the earliest evidence of the Scythian/Saka Animal Style in Central Kazakhstan. To the east of Kazakhstan in Chiliktin Valley, south of Lake Zaysan, S. S. Chernikov[11] in 1956 and 1960 and A. G. Maximova[12] in 1959 discovered several hundred gold objects in kurgan number five, known as the Golden Kurgan, from the seventh and sixth centuries B.C.E.

In the districts of Borovoye, Kokchetav, Petropavlovsk, and Akmolinsk, north of Kazakhstan, archeologists K. A. Akishev[13] in 1959 and A. M. Orazbayev in 1958 investigated many Andronovo tombs. The tombs contained a great deal of pottery, some bronze tools, and a few bronze and gold ornaments.[14] To the west of Kazakhstan, north of the Caspian Sea in the region of Novaya Kazanka or Dzhangaly, two expeditions were underway by the late 1940s. The leading figures of the expeditions, I. V. Sinitzyn[15] and T. N. Senigova[16] in 1956 and E. E., Kuzmina[17] in 1961, identified and analyzed four-thousand-year-old Bronze Age tombs consisting of Neolithic flints, bronze objects, and iron weapons, as well as a great deal of pottery. To the south and southeast of Kazakhstan, A. N. Bernshtam[18] explored the shores of the Talas, Ili, and Chu Rivers in 1950. He then explored the area between Syr Darya river and the Karatau range. L. I. Rempel[19] explored the banks of Talas River in 1957. Rempel discovered several Zoroasterian ossuaries in terracotta within this area. In 1956, 1959, and 1967 on the shore of the Ili River, Akishev[20] found Bronze Age ornaments and jewels with early indication of animal-style art in twenty large-size kurgans of the Scythian/Saka period. In the Bes Shatyr area in 1962, Akishev discovered several thousand tombs including some belonging to Scythian/Saka emperors.

According to M. A. Itina's[21] (1960) analysis, Andronovo Bronze culture spread across the steppes of Kazakhstan in the second half of the second millennium B.C. E. A. N. Bernshtam[22] in 1949 and 1950, M. N. Komarova[23] in 1962, and S. S. Chernikov[24] in 1960 identified and explored the Bronze Age Andronovo culture of the second and first millennium B.C.E. in the Chu, Talas, and Fergana Valleys and the Tian Shan and Alay Mountains in Kyrgyzstan. In the Chu Valley in 1949 and 1950, Bernshtam[25] discovered and explored a variety of kurgans with elements indicating a fire cult, Shamanism, and some Zoroasterianism. Also in 1949, Bernshtam discovered figures of animals in an early Scythian style in Semirechiye near lake Issykul in Kyrgyzstan. The objects belonged to the fifth to third century B.C.E.: bronze utensils, tables, lamps, and a bronze yak figure.

Andronovo Culture and Indo-Iranians

Anthony and Vinogradov's[26] 1995 analysis indicated that the Andronovo culture is strongly associated with the Indo-Iranians and is often credited with the invention of the spoke-wheeled chariot around 2000 B.C. E. Sintashta, a site on the upper Ural River, is famed for its grave offerings, particularly chariot burials. Sintashta is often pointed to as the premier proto-Indo-Iranian site. Abetekov and Yusupov's[27] 1996 work indicates that many Greek writers referred to all the nomads of Eurasia, including those of Central Asia, as Scythians. Persians designated all nomadic tribes of the Eurasian steppes, including the Scythians, as Sakas. These broad classifications were based on the similarity of the culture and way of life of all the nomads who spoke Iranian languages. Abetekov and Yusupov, through their 1996 analysis, interpret the similarity of Scythian cultures as a single original culture, agreeing with Herodotus that Scythians originally came from Asia. Terenozhkin's 1976 analysis of recent discoveries refers to the Arzhan site (an older archeological site in the Tuva region from the ninth and eighth centuries B.C. E.), as the place from which the spread of Scythian/Saka culture across the Eurasian steppes first took shape.

A second group of scholars including K. A. Akishev[28] and Kushaev who conducted excavation and research in Semirechye in 1963; B. A. Litvinsky who conducted research in the Pamir Area in 1972; and Vishnevskaya who conducted excavation on the shore of Syr Darya in 1973, have a slightly different interpretation of the region's early cultures. They agree with the strong cultural similarities, resemblances, and ethnic ties between these people; however, they also believe that politically the region was a distinct decentralized entity of various indigenous kingdoms, with each entity having its unique and peculiar historical development. In fact, Scythia was only once unified as an empire under the leadership of King Ateas (429–339 B.C.E). Within this segment of time, certain tombs examined were found to contain considerable quantities of grave goods, a practice unknown in earlier stages. This also reflects changes in social structure in which the beginning of social differentiation is noticed. Andronovo people lived in the vast steppe with large deep rivers, predominately stock breeders. Their Indo-Iranian language has numerous terms for horse breeding. Their gods are constantly asked to grant rich livestock, especially horses. They knew metallurgy and metal processing.

Turning from material culture, we will address the reasons for the early migration of various Indo-Iranian tribes from the northeast regions of Central Asia to southern Russia and Iran. These early tribes were seeking grazing lands for their animals and cattle. Horses, sheep, goats, and yaks were central to their livelihood. Other factors, including a population explosion, control of grazing and water rights, early invasions from the north-east, and a gradual change of temperature also contributed to the mass migration of early Central Asian tribes.

SCYTHIAN/SAKA ANIMAL ART STYLE

Central Asia, consisting of vast expanses of steppe land with fine seasonal pasture, was destined by nature for the development of cattle breeding. Between the seventh and third centuries B. C. E. the region was inhabited by a large number of Indo-European tribes called Sakas by the Persians and Scythians by the Greeks. Scythians were Indo-European tribes of Iranian stock who lived partly on the steppe and the wooded steppe zone of Central Asia and partly in its oasis zone.

In the fifth millennium B.C.E., the ancestors of these Iranian tribes separated from the Proto-Balts and the Proto-Slavs. Their first mass migration occurred during the second millennium B.C. E. and related to the rise of animal husbandry, in particular horse breeding. Following their invention of two- and four-wheeled horse drawn vehicles, their migration reached the Caucasus, the shores of the Don and Danube Rivers, India, Central Asia, the Iranian plateau, Mesopotamia, the Altai Mountains, and even China and Korea.[29]

Early or ancient cultures of Inner Eurasia (Central Asia) are divided into different sub-cultures of Timber Grave, Pit Grave, Scythian/Saka, and Hunnic. The transformation of Timber grave and pit grave to family-size mounds or kurgans were characteristics of Bronze Age people, especially Scythian/Saka/Siberian cultures of the eighth to third century B.C.E. Scythian/Saka kurgans have been discovered and explored in the Altay Mountains, the Caucasus, Ukraine, Poland, Romania, Bulgaria, Siberian Russia, and many parts of Central Asia. Hunnic culture dates from the third century B.C.E. to the six century C.E., and some of the later constructed kurgans are identified as belonging to this era.

The ancient inhabitants, the Scythian or Saka, were dependent on animal husbandry as the principal source of livelihood. It also determined their mobile way of life. Raising horses, sheep, and cattle, they moved from one pasture to another. The mobility of their pastoralist lifestyle made great migrations possible. Thus, massive waves of nomadic Scythians rolled beyond the boundaries of the Eurasian steppes.

A major wave of Scythian/Saka migration began in the late eighth century B.C.E. with the invasion of the kingdoms of southwest Asia and Asia Minor. According to an inscription written by the Assyrian king Esarhaddon (681–668 B.C.E.), the Scythian tribes appeared in southwest Asia around 670

B.C.E. where they contributed heavily to the military divisions of some of the southern kingdoms.[30]

Historiography of the Scythians: Herodotus and Strabo

Scythians/Sakas were among the earliest people to master the art of riding, and wherever they went they astonished their neighbors by the civilization they created. According to the Greek historian Herodotus, the Scythians/Sakas spoke Iranian languages and migrated from the Altai Mountains at the eastern extreme of the Eurasian steppe. Also, according to Herodotus, Scythians conquered numerous towns and settlements around the Black Sea area in ancient times. Within the vast Eurasian steppe land, from the Altai Mountains across the Eurasian steppe into the southern Russian and Crimean territories and shores of the Black Sea, the royal Scythians left elaborate graves filled with richly worked "Animal Style" articles of gold and other precious metals.

The historian Strabo, who described the nomadic tribes from Mongolia to Ukraine as Scythians, classified some of them as: Dayes, Massagetes, Saki, Assian, Passians, Toharss, Attasians, and Khoresmians.[31] The Naqsh-I Rustam inscription of Achaemenid Emperor Darius I (sixth century B.C.), lists three Saka tribal confederations:

1. the Saka Haumavarga, in Ferghana, who converted to a settled form of life;
2. the Saka Tigraxauda, in the region beyond Syr Darya and in Semirechye;
3. the Saka Tayaiy Paradraya.

Many archeologists agree that in addition to a common language, other cultural similarities unified the Scythians/Sakas as a people.[32]

ART TREASURY OF KURGANS

A characteristic feature of the landscape of the steppes from the Altai Mountains to Mongolia, southern Siberia, Ukraine, and the shores of the Black Sea, was the kurgan, an earth and stone mound erected over ancient graves.[33] The population of Central Asia was no longer only composed of hunters and fishermen. Inner Eurasia (Central Asia) was rich in deposits of copper, and it was the site of an industrial and agricultural revolution. The people had access to metal tools, instruments, and arms and were engaged in agriculture and stock breeding. It is within this segment of time that, according to many scholars, the collective Andronovo culture (covering various regional cultures of the Bronze Age over a long period of time) emerges.

Dwelling sites from the Andronovo period in Central Asia were usually comprised of huts for ten to fifty inhabitants. The burial places consisted of groups of tombs surrounded by megalithic granite slabs, sometimes several hundreds of them. Most of the kurgans served as graves for the Scythian/ Saka kings and queens. Many also included burial plots for family members of rulers, horses, dogs, and even cats.

Unfortunately, the majority of these kurgans were looted over time, but those that were spared contain a variety of artifacts including numerous gold and silver objects. At Tolstaya Mogila, the graves of a young queen and a child remained undisturbed. The queen's entire costume once gleamed with gold; large gold plates were fastened to her headdress, and all her clothing, including her footwear, was sewn with little gold plaques or platelets. The Queen's neck was jeweled with a massive gold piece weighing 478 grams and depicting seven little lions attacking a young deer. On her temples the queen wore large gold pendants depicting a goddess. Massive gold bracelets adorned her wrists, and her fingers were covered with rings.[34] The skeleton of the child was covered with gold plates that all but obscured his clothing.

Very rich mausoleum complexes of the royal leaders of Scythia were unearthed in the Tagisken and Uygarak cemeteries on the lower reaches of Syr Darya,[35] in the Chilik kurgan, and in the Issyk kurgan in Kazakhstan. At Pazyryk, in the Altai Mountains, Russian archeologists unearthed five thousand objects of wood, textiles, felt, leather, and fur preserved in ice.[36]

Kunstkammer Museum

Kunstkammer, the first real museum of anthropology and etymology in Russia, was founded in 1714 by Peter the Great. The following year, Alexis Demidov, owner of a metallurgical industry with many mines in Siberia, donated twenty gold objects found in kurgans to the museum. The next year, one of the regional governors, M. P. Gagarin of Tobolsk, sent the museum fifty-six more gold objects. During the first half of the eighteenth century, the Academy of Sciences of Russia sent scholars to southern Siberia for excavations and research around the Irtysh, Ob, and Yenisei Rivers.

The director of the first expedition was D. Messerschmidt, who in 1721 expressed his surprise in his diary that digging up gold and silver from ancient graves had become a trade in Siberia already. One of the most surprising areas of southern Siberia is the Minusinsk district, where thousands of ancient kurgans surrounded by vertical stones are a distinctive feature of the landscape. Meanwhile, by the first half of the eighteenth century, G. F. Miller, had conducted research in Siberia from 1733–1743. At that time, the Scythian/Saka culture was unknown to everyone; hence, the mysterious ancient gold and silver objects skillfully formed and shaped as domesticated or wild animals created naturally or conceptually, caused great shock and awe. Miller wrote a history of this vast area, mentioning the archeological finds.[37] The earlier gold and silver objects from the Siberian burials entered Kunstkammer Museum in the eighteenth and the first half of the nineteenth centuries. In 1859 they were moved to the Hermitage Museum.

Semirechye

A great deal of work has gone into analyzing the eastern kurgans of Kazakhstan including the Semirechye region. Semirechye, the land of seven rivers of Ili, Karatal, Bien, Aksu, Lepsy, Baskan, and Sarkand, lies in central region of the Eurasian steppe belt.[38] In the Semirechye region over ten thousand small burial mounds have been identified, but also hundreds of monumental kurgans are known. K. Akishev (d. 2003) is the expert archeologist who has conducted extensive excavation and research, writing over 200 scientific articles and books. Two of his major projects, bringing him international recognition, were the excavations of Scythian/Saka complex of Besshatyr and Issyk Kurgan.[39] Besshatyr Kurgan is the largest of the mounds in the Semirechye area, with a diameter of 350 feet and height of sixty feet. The kurgans date to the sixth to third centuries B.C.E. and reflect Scythian/Saka horse and/or sheep cultures of the steppe with an abundance of gold, tin, and copper objects buried in them. The wealth buried in the kurgans has made them a tempting target for looters ever since ancient times.[40]

The idea that Scythian animal-style objects follow, mimic, or blindly copy objects from another school of art is rejected by a number of scholars who have done extensive work on Central Asian archeological sites. Thousands of Scythian "Animal Style" art pieces have been found over a wide territory from west of Mongolia and the Altai Mountains through the Eurasian steppes into southern Russia, Crimea, and Ukraine. The Institute of History of the Ukrainian Academy of Sciences has excavated more than three hundred kurgans around the Black Sea from this period belonging to the Scythians.

HUN WARRIORS IN NORTHERN MONGOLIA

In 1924 and 1925, eight kurgans containing the remains of Hun warriors were excavated in northern Mongolia.[41] Wool fabrics, tapestries, embroideries, silk cloths, pottery, and jewelry pieces, along with leather and bronze pieces were discovered in these burial mounds. Scholars found elements of shamanistic practices, as well as strong evidence of the Huns' close ties to Mongolia, Soghdia, eastern Europe, and the Near East.

Many more burial mounds in the Tien-Shan territory have not yet been excavated. Three major kurgans in Hissar, Tajikestan have also not been excavated. Some of the larger burial mounds extend over ten meters high and one hundred meters in diameter. On the Black Sea steppes, the kurgans of Kul' Oba, Solokha, Pyat'brat'ev, Tolstaya Mogila, and Chertomlyk are some of the well-known burial mounds that have been excavated.[42]

SCYTHIAN/SAKA ART OF JEWELRY MAKING

Across the Eurasian steppe from the Altai Mountains to southern Russia and Ukraine, so-called "animal style" jewelry was prevalent and widespread. These pieces of jewelry depict wild and domesticated animals. The wide use of this powerful decorative style reflects the cultural unity of the Scythian/Saka world despite its widespread dispersal from the Altai Mountains to southern Russia and Ukraine.[43] One of the most fascinating discoveries of the twentieth century was a warrior's costume that was found in the 1960s in a Scythian/Saka kurgan near Issyk, about 40km east of Almaty. The warrior costume was made up of over 4,000 separate gold pieces, many of them in the form of animal motifs. The Scythian/Saka warrior's costume included a two-foot-high headdress with pointed arrows on top and snow leopards and two-headed winged mythical animals covering it.[44]

Animals and birds—standing, running, or in flight—with exaggerated or accentuated horns, paws, hooves, jaws, beaks, and ears were the favored subjects of the era. The gold and silver figures depicted animals including reindeer, horses, ibexes, and snow leopards on necklaces, bracelets, and earrings.[45] Jewelry making was the most popular art form between the eighth and third centuries B.C.E. Today, some of the most impressive pieces of Scythian art are at the Hermitage Museum in St. Petersburg, Russia.

Scythian/Saka art pieces were created in a variety of materials including leather, felt, bone, bronze, iron, and silver. The tombs of Pazyryk in the Altai Mountains yielded many well-preserved articles of clothing covered with embroidery dating from the eighth to third century B.C.E. No subsequent moment in the history of Eurasian nomads was as uniform as the ancient period, when a sense of cultural and artistic unity transcended local differences.[46]

According to Tallgren, Scythian art[47] from approximately 700 to 550 B.C.E. reflects that the center of Scythian culture remained in the southeast, in the Kuban region and Taman Peninsula. The Scythians were already dominant in the south of Ukraine as is proved by the finds at Martonocha and Melgunov.

It was between approximately 550 and 450, according to Tallgren, that the Scythian culture sprang vigorously into being in the Ukraine of today, to reach its peak from about 350 to 250 B.C.E., as may be seen from the great royal kurgans of lower Dnieper at Chertomlyk, Alexandropol, Solokha, Denev, and others. The most northerly area in the west to be reached by Scythian expansion ran along the border of the forest steppes south of Kiev in the Voronezh region. Scythian expansion moved eastward up the Volga to Saratov, where important discoveries have been made.[48] No other Eurasian people has been dealt with so often and in so much detail in European scholarship, but the testimony of the written sources must be completed by archeological data.

From the start we observe the rise of Scythian animal art. A naturalistic, decorative art that appears in its definitive form with the golden deer of the Kostromskaya tomb whose antlers are stylized in spirals. It also appears in Kuban in the sixth century B. C. E. Scythians' decorative natural aesthetics of the steppe bends, twists, and diverts for ornamental and stylized purposes. Scythian/Saka luxuries were reflected in the richness of their dress, personal adornment, ornamentation of equipment, harnesses, and so on. Objects of this sort—hooks and plaques for belts, harness plates, sword belt buckles, wagon panels, handles, and hilts, and of course carpets—provided Scythian/Saka artists with many opportunities to represent a dramatic art of horse scuffles or deer seized by snow leopards, bears, birds of prey, or griffins.

The varied elements and tendencies of steppe art are unevenly distributed over a huge area extending from Odessa in Ukraine to Manchuria and the shores of the Yellow River. The Scythian art of the steppe spreading toward the forest region of the upper Volga influenced the Ananino culture near Kazan (600–200 B.C.E.), which was a Finno-Ugrian civilization. A rich burial ground discovered there has yielded axes and some animal motifs in which animal bodies are curved up.

There are well-documented cases that convincingly show that identical mythical conceptions found in Near Eastern, Chinese, and Greek writing are not, as is often thought, borrowings, but independently generated from a common Eurasian substratum. It is most likely that the peculiar early art form that for many centuries flourished all across the continent—the so called "animal style art" is also based on such common conceptions.[49]

The first phase of painting in Central Asia is clearly of Scythian/Saka inspiration. During the 700 to 300 B. C. E. period, the whole of Central Asia formed a peripheral area within the Scythian/Saka-Tokharian sphere of influence. This classical background synthesized ideas and elements from Achaemenid, Hellenistic, and school of Gandhara (that flourished in northwest of India) and went on to shape the whole future evolution of Central Asian art.

The Scythians, or royal Scyths of southern Central Asia, created an animal-style art of superb quality. The earliest of their known works date from the seventh century B. C. E. and come from the Kuban district and southern Central Asia. Yet Scythian art is an important branch of prehistoric expression, an early ancient art. Scythian art essentially is decorative in character and primarily animalistic in content. It includes astral, geometric, organic, floral, and figural motifs. It is complex in its imagery and composition and achieves great technical subtlety and polish. The finest examples include gold plaques representing stags or other wild animals.

The excellence of these plaques and other outstanding works owes something of its quality to the skillful use of the play of light on the surface by inclining sections of the metal, often gold, in slightly different directions in order to recreate the ripple of the animal's muscles and body when in motion. The gold stag from Kostromskaya and the gold leopard from Kelermes show the art of the Royal Scyths at its best. The leopard's ears were originally inlaid with amber and its eyes with enamel, and both were from seventh to sixth century B.C.E.[50]

The Altai people shared the way of life and outlook of Scythians and practiced an art similar to theirs between the fifth and second centuries B. C. E. Many of the artifacts survived in the funerary sites of Scythians and other Altai cultures preserved in the ice or freezing air. The Altaian burial grounds of Pazyryk, Tuekt, Shibe, and Katanda, to name a few, excavated by Griaznov, Rudenko, and other scholars revealed numerous artistic objects. In addition to gold, silver, and bronze objects, there were a great many objects in wood, felt, wool, and silk.[51]

From the collection of Peter the Great at the Hermitage Museum, belt buckles number amongst the most interesting objects. The majority of them are cast in bronze, but a number of them are in gold. In both cases, the clasps were made separately and soldered to the plaques; the molded design was then finished by hand. At times, additional decorations were added in gold wire. Occasionally buckles were adorned with turquoises.

MINUSINSK: A METALLURGY CAPITAL

The metalworking center of Minusinsk, on the upper Yenisei, was from approximately the beginning of the fifth century B. C. E., the scene of a new activity. This period is characterized by a profusion of animal motifs, especially those of recumbent or standing deer, of deer looking backward, and of the curled-up animal, which, according to Tellgren, originated in southern Central Asia. It is between 500 and 300 B.C.E. that the first manufacture of Central Asian bronze instruments and tools occurs, and also that of the "cup cauldrons" which were to spread from Minusinsk both to the Ordaos of the Xiang'nu period and to Hungary of the great invasions.[52]

At Minusinsk during the most flourishing period of the Bronze Age (sixth to third centuries B. C. E.), this important metalworking center of Altai went on producing socketed axes. From the same period, the site yields animal bronze of a sober stylization. Was it at Minusinsk, the geographical center of this art, situated halfway between the Black Sea and the Gulf of Chihli, that the ancient smiths of the Altai hammered out the first animal design?

About 330–220 B.C.E. the Iron Age triumphed at Minusinsk where spiked axes (partly bronze and partly iron) were produced and where a group of large collective burial places occurred. Minusinsk has also provided ornamental bronze plaques dating to the second and first centuries B. C. E. Minusisnk plaques reveal bulls and horses with ears, hoofs, tails, muscles, and hair treated in the hollow trefoil manner. This technique is clearly related to the Sarmatian art of Central Asia, which many archeologists think was handed on by Minusinsk to the art of the East and West. Masks, dating from approximately the second and first centuries B. C. E. are found in the Minusinsk group at Trifonova, Bateni, Beya, Kali, and Znamenka. During the first two centuries of this era, animal patterns in transitional culture continued to flourish in the Minusinsk area. Shortly afterward, these centers of cultures with Scytho-Sarmatian affinities were found in the Altai.[53] Indeed, metallurgy was developed in the Minusinsk area at a very early date.

PAZYRYK: ANOTHER METALLURGY CAPITAL

Farther south on the north side of the great Altai, near the headwaters of the Ob and the Khatun Rivers, the Griaznov[54] mission of 1929 uncovered burial places dating from 100 B. C. E. and earlier containing the bodies of horses masked as reindeer. There were twenty-five kurgans identified in Pazyryk. While Griaznov excavated one of them, Rudenko[55] excavated many others within the area. People of the region had replaced the reindeer with the horse. Horses have masks, and their harnesses of leather, wood, and gold, are ornamented with stylized animal motifs: ibexes and stags at full gallop, a winged griffin fighting an ibex, snow leopards leaping upon a deer or an ibex, a bird of prey attacking a deer on the ground, and cocks confronting one another. All these themes are still fairly close to Scythian animal realism. The stylization produces a splendid decorative effect. For the first century C.E., the Altai culture is represented by the kurgan of Katanda where there are wood carvings of fights between bears and deer, the deer having antlers burgeoning into birds' heads. There are also bronze plaques and fragments of fabric adorned with stylized animal patterns, including fights of griffins and deer.

Before disappearing, the cultural centers of Minusinsk, Pazyryk, and Katanda had played a considerable part in handing down stylized animal art—the art of the steppes—to the Hunnic nations of Mongolia.

The Pazyryk people must have been in contact with both China and Persia, for fine textiles produced in those countries were found among their tomb furnishings. The Persian fabrics included two woven stuffs and the oldest knotted carpet known to us. One of these is in perfect condition and is displayed at the Hermitage Museum at St. Petersburg. It dates from the fifth century B.C.E. The Pazyryk tombs were particularly lavishly equipped with objects virtually covered in decorations similar to other Scythian tombs, indicating a sharing of the same culture. The Pazyryk burials, like other Scythian/Saka burials, are all horse burials.

Animal Art Style: Tattoo Art of Pazyryk

Exceptional examples of animal art were discovered on tattooed mummies in Central Asia, including kurgan 5 of Pazyryk. At least two of the Pazyryk mummy bodies of the fifth century B. C. E. were covered with animal-style tattoos. A beast was tattooed on the body of a man identified as a Scythian high-status individual. There are images of other animals, including a fish, and some organic dots and curvilinear lines that are elaborated on his body, too. Another mummified body from kurgan 2, perfectly preserved, elaborates tattoos on the back, arms, and one leg. Besides an unbroken sequence of highly fantastic animals in most unlikely postures, there were images of animals he had hunted or tended in his lifetime. Some scholars identify the tattoo figuration as indicating the high rank of the deceased.[56]

THE FIRST KNOTTED WOVEN CARPET IN THE WORLD & OTHER TEXTILE ART

More than 4,000 artifacts were discovered from Pazyryk's kurgans by Grazinov and Rudenko.[57] One of the most striking and impressive objects from the frozen tomb of a Scythian/Saka chieftain in Pazyryk is a wool carpet. It is the oldest woolen knotted-pile carpet in the world, dating back to the fifth century B. C. E. The carpet design is composed of 28 horseback riders and 24 deer. The carpet has a highly sophisticated design with a combination of abstract motifs, organic and geometric decorative symbolic shapes and forms. The famous pile carpet from kurgan 5 has often been called Achaemenid. The woven carpet is made with a row of horses and horsemen along the outer frieze. However, the spotted fallow deer, which appears on the inner frieze of the carpet, is an animal characteristic of Transcaucasia and Siberia.[58]

The central square of the carpet includes 24 smaller squares; each small square contains similar abstract designs of four-rayed stars. Furthermore, the central large square is surrounded by a procession of 24 deer in profile view. The outermost border of the carpet includes another procession, elaborating 28 horseback riders in profile view. The wool carpet is dominated by maroon, yellow/orange, black, and white colors.[59]

NOTES

1. Mandel'shtam, A. M. *Timber Graves in Southern Turkmenia*, KSIA, v. 108, Moscow, 1966. Also, see: Mandel'shtam, A. M. *New Timber Graves in Southern Turkmenia*, KSIA, v. 112, Moscow, 1967.

2. Askrov, A. *Sites of Andronovo Culture in the Lower Basin of the Zarafshan*, Istoriyamaterial'noi kul'tury Uzbekistana, v. 3, Tashkent, 1962.

3. Korobkova, G. F., Krizhevskaya, L., and Mandel'shtam, A. *The Neolithic of the East Coast of the Caspian Sea*, The History, Archeology and Ethnography of Central Asia, Moscow, 1968.

4. Zhu, J., Ma, J., Zhang, F. *The Baigetuobie cemetery: New discovery and human genetic features of Andronovo community's diffusion to the Eastern Tianshan Mountains (1800–1500 BC),* Sage Journals, 2020.

5. Mandel'shtam, A. M. *Timber Graves in Southern Turkmenia*, KSIA, v. 108, Moscow, 1966. Also, see: Mandel'shtam, A. M. *New Timber Graves in Southern Turkmenia*, KSIA, v. 112, Moscow, 1967.

6. Beckwith, Christopher I. *Empires of the Silk Road: A History of Central Eurasia from the Bronze Age to the Present*, Princeton University Press, 2009. Beckwith indicates that "Archeologists are now generally agreed that the Andronovo culture of Central Steppe region in the second millennium BC is to be equated with the Indo-Iranians" p. 49.

7. Fraumkin, G. *Archaeology in Soviet Central Asia*, E. J. Brill, 1970. A component of the Soviet excavation and research according to Frumkin can be summarized and interpreted as the following: The bronze age of Kazakhstan corresponds roughly to the second millennium B.C. Some of the archeologists, including A. Kh. Margulan in 1960, M. N. Komarova in 1962, and V. P. Aleksiyev in 1967, in their analysis of Andronovo Culture have shown that it extended from north of the Black Sea, the shores of Ural River, to the heart of Altai Mountains, to the shores of Aral Sea and Khorazm. Andronovo culture was common to major parts of Kazakhstan and the Siberian Minussinsk region.

8. Komarova, M. N. *Detailed Survey of Andronovo Civilization: Analysis of Pottery in the Hermitage*, 1962.

9. Margulan, A. Kh., Akishev, K. A. *Analysis of nomad Tribes: Origin of Scythian Art,* 1966.

10. Kadyrbayev, M. K. *Early Nomads: Central Asia Tasmola Kurgan Culture, Funeral rites, Early "Animal Style,"* 1966.

11. Orazbayev, A. M. *Survey on Bronze Age and early Nomads in North Kazakhstan*, 1958.

12. Maximova, A. G. *Bronze Age of East Kazakhstan: A comprehensive survey of Chernikov's writings,* 1959.

13. Akishev, K. A. *South Kazakhstan: Ili Basin, Gigantic Saka Kurgans*, Bes-Shatyr, 1959. Also, see: Akishev, K. A. *Andronovo Cultures of Central Kazakhstan*, 1966.

14. Orazbayev, A. M. *Survey on Bronze Age and early Nomads in North Kazakhstan*, 1958.

15. Sinitzyn, I. V., *West Kazakhstan: Neolithic, Bronze Age, Scythians and Sarmatians*, 1956.

16. Senigova, T. N. *Novaya Kazanka, West Kazakhstan, Bronze Age: Sarmatian Period*, 1956.

17. Kuz'mina, E. E., *Emba Region, West Kazakhstan: Neolithic and Bronze age Analysis*, 1961.

18. Bernshtam, A. N. *Reports of the Semirechye Archeological Expedition: The Chu Valley*, MIA, 14, Moscow and Leningrad, 1950.

19. Rempel, L. I. *Taraz, South Kazakhstan, Zoroastrian ossuaries*, Figurines, 1957.

20. Akishev, K. A. *Andronovo Cultures of Central Kazakhstan*, 1966.

21. Itina, M. A. *The Steppe Tribes of the Central Asian Inter-River Area in the Second Half of the 2nd and the Early 1st Millennium BC*, 25th International Congress of orientalists: Moscow, 1960.

22. Bernshtam, A. N. *Reports of the Semirechye Archeological Expedition: The Chu Valley*, MIA, 14, Moscow and Leningrad, 1950.

23. Komarova, M. N. *Detailed Survey of Andronovo Civilization: Analysis of Pottery in the Hermitage*, 1962.

24. Chernikov, S. S. *"Golden" kurgan in Chiliktin Valley: Origin of Scythian Art*, 1964.

25. Bernshtam, A. N. *Reports of the Semirechye Archeological Expedition: The Chu Valley*, MIA, 14, Moscow and Leningrad, 1950.

26. Anthony, D. Vinogradov, N. *Birth of the Chariot*, Archaeology, 48(2), 1995, pp. 36–41.

27. Abetekov, A. and Yusupov, H. *Ancient Iranian Nomads in Western Central Asia*, UNESCO, 1994.

28. Akishev, K. A. *Andronovo Cultures of Central Kazakhstan*,1966. Also, see: Akishev, K. A. *South Kazakhstan: Ili Basin, Gigantic Saka Kurgans*, Bes-Shatyr, 1959.

29. Abetekov, A. and Yusupov, H., *Ancient Iranian Nomads in Western Central Asia*, History of Civilization of Central Asia, Vol. II, UNESCO Publishing, 1994, 23–34.

30. Pavlinskaya, L. R., *The Scythians and Sakians*, Eight to Third Centuries B.C., Nomads of Eurasia, Academy of Sciences of the U.S.S.R. and Natural History Museum of Los Angeles County, 1990, 19–40.

31. Scythian and Saka warriors played active role in the military politics of the region. Also, see: Beckwith, C., *Empires of the Silk Road*, Priceton University Press, 2009.

32. Jones, H. L., The Geography of Strabo, The Loeb Classical Library, 8 V.

33. Pavlinskaya, L. R. *The Scythians and Sakians*, Eight to Third Centuries B.C., Nomads of Eurasia, Academy of Sciences of the U.S.S.R., Natural History Museum of Los Angeles County, University of Washington Press, 1991, 19–40. Also, see: Grousset, R., *The Empire of the Steppes - A History of Central Asia*, Rutgers University Press, 2002.

34. Frumkin, G., *Archeology in Soviet Central Asia*, Leiden/Koln, E. J. Brill, 1970. A component of the Soviet excavation and research according to Frumkin can be summarized and interpreted as the following: The Bronze Age of Kazakhstan corresponds roughly to the second millennium B.C. Some of the archeologists including A. Kh. Margulan in 1960, M. N. Komarova in 1962, and V. P. Aleksiyev in 1967, in their analysis of Andronovo culture have shown that it extended from north of the Black Sea, the shores of Ural River, to the heart of Altai Mountains, to the shores of Aral Sea and Khorazm. Andronovo culture was common to major parts of Kazakhstan, and the Siberian Minussinsk region. Semirechye: T. Gorka and J. W. E. Fassbinder 2011, *Classifying and documenting kurgans,* Siberia, 2011. (Analyzing eastern kurgans of Kazakhstan including Semirechye region. Semirechye, the land of seven rivers).

35. Ibid, pp. 23–38.

36. Rudenko, S. I., *Frozen Tombs of Siberia*, the Pazyryk Burials of Iron Age Horsemen, University of California Press, 1970. 37.

37. Bernshtam, A. N. *Reports of the Semirechye Archeological Expedition: The Chu Valley*, MIA, 14, Moscow and Leningrad, 1950. Also, see: Orazbayev, A. M. *Survey on Bronze Age and early Nomads in North Kazakhstan*,1958.

38. Akishev, K. *Art and mythology of Sakas*, Alma Ata, Science, 1984. Also, see: Akishev, K. *Andronovo Cultures of Central Kazakhstan*, 1966.

39. Akishev, K. *Ancient gold of Kazakhstan*, Alma-Ata, 1983.

40. Gryaznov, M. P., *On the Question of the Formation of the Scytho-Siberian-type Cultures in Connection with the opening of the Arzhan Kurgan,* Moscow institute of Archeology, 1978, 9–12.

41. For more information on Scythian Art see: Artamonov, M. I., *The Splendor of Scythian Art: Treasures from Scythian tombs*, F. A. Praeger Publishers, New York, 1969.

42. For more information on Scythians see: Artamonov, M. I., *The Splendor of Scythian Art: Treasures from Scythian tombs*, F. A. Praeger Publishers, New York, 1969.

43. Fergus M. and Jandosova J., *Kazakhstan—Coming of Age*, Stacey International, London, 2003, 103.

44. Rice, T. T., *Ancient Arts of Central Asia*, F. A. Praeger Publishers, New York, 1965. In two earlier Scythian kurgans, at Kelermes in the North Caucasus, and at the Melgunov kurgan in Ukraine, objects have been found very similar to the Ziwiye treasure of early sixth century discovered in Iran between the borders of Kurdistan and Azarbijan provinces. The idea that Scythian animal style objects follow, mimic, or blindly copy objects from another school of art is rejected by a number of scholars who have done extensive work on Central Asian archeological sites. Thousands of Scythian"animal style" art pieces have been found over a wide territory from west of

Mongolia and the Altai Mountains through the Eurasian steppes into southern Russia, Crimea, and Ukraine.

45. Pavlinskaya, L. R. *The Scythians and Sakians*, Eight to Third Centuries B.C., Nomads of Eurasia, Academy of Sciences U.S.S. R., Natural History Museum of Los Angeles County, 1989, 19–40. Also, see: Herodotus, *The History, The Fourth Book: Melpomene*, translated by G. Rawlinson, N.Y. Tudor Pub. Co., 1956, 204–11. According to Herodotus: In one account, after eighteen years of famine in Lydia (east of the Republic of Turkey today), the king deported half of the population to look for a better life elsewhere. Under the leadership of the crown prince of Lydia, Tyrrhenus, the emigrants were loaded onto the ships and sailed from Smyrna until they reached Umbria in Italy. This raises the question about the strong possibility that the deported people from Lydia were of Scythian origin. Italian geneticists are conducting DNA testing on the Etruscans found in the graves to trace their origins. Also, see: Bonfante, L., *Etruscan Life and Afterlife*, Wayne State University Press, 1986.

46. For more information on Siberian Shamanism see: Michael, H. N., *Studies in Siberian Shamanism*, Toronto: University of Toronto Press, 1963. According to some scholars, the revival of shamanism in Siberia and Central Asia followed the fall of the Soviet Union, particularly among: Altaians (Kyrgyz and Kazakhs); the Khakass (in the Russian Republic of Khakassiya, Republic of Tuva, and in Krasnoyarsk Kray northeast of Kazakhstan); Tuvinians (in the Russian Republic of Tuva north of Mongolia and northeast of Kazakhstan);.the Yakuts (in the Russian Republic of Sukha or Yakutia, east of Siberia); and the Buryats (in the Russian Republic of Buryatia, to the southeast of Lake Baikal). Altaian male and female shamans utilized ceremonial garments, which were constructed from sheepskin or deer skin according to specific dreams. The Altaian shaman drum was made from the hide of a deer, or horse, stretched over the rim of the drum. The drum handle was shaped like a human figure, representing the spirit of the master of the drum and the ancestral shaman. Before and after the rites, the tribal people would hang cloth ribbons on the crosspiece of the drum as offerings to the spirits. Altaians believed that the drum was a living creature—a horse on which the shaman in ecstasy made his voyages into the other world. When the Altaian shaman died, there were holes made into his drum, symbolizing the death of his drum. The drum of the shaman was hung in a tree close to the grave of the shaman. A number of festivals and ceremonial customs reflect the strong impact of belief in the spirit world and shamanism. Djer-suutayi refers to the festivities that include sacrifices to the divinities of earth and water. When a new building was erected, or a yurt was installed, a sacrificial animal was offered. The first spoon of the broth of the animal was dropped on the fire to make the fire deity, Umaiene, happy. The richness of Eurasian cultures is apparent from the diversity and pluralism of the religions and cults the area has inherited. The history of sacred sites goes back to ancient times. Burial mounds hold the remains and the personal belongings of the deceased.

47. Tallgren, A. M. *Dolmens of North Caucasia*, Antiquity Journal, 1933.

48. Tallgren, A. M. *Eyrasia Septentrionalis,* Antiqua III, Journal of East European and North Asiatic Archeology and Ethnography, ESA III, 1928.

49. Jettmar, K. *The Altai before the Turks*, Bulletin of the Museum of Far Eastern Antiquities, No. 23, pp. 135–223. Stockholm 1951.

50. Pavlinskaya, L. R., *The Scythians and Sakians*, Eight to Third Centuries B.C., Nomads of Eurasia, Academy of Sciences of the U.S.S.R. and Natural History Museum of Los Angeles County, 1990, 19–40.

51. Jettmar, K. *Art of the Steppe*, New York, 1967.

52. Gryaznov, M. P. *Drevnjaja bronza Minusinskich stepej.* I. Bronzovye kelty. Gosudarstvennyj Ermitaz. Trudy otdela istorii pervobytnoj kul'tury, t. I, str. 237–71. Leningrad 1941.

53. Tallgren, A. M. *Collection Tovostine des antiquites prehistoriques de Minoussinsk*. Helsing fors 1917.

54. Gryaznov, M. P. *Southern Sibiria.* Geneva: Archaeologia Mundi, 1969.

55. Rudenko, S. I., *Frozen Tombs of Siberia, the Pazyryk Burials of Iron Age Horsemen*, University of California Press, 1970.

56. Hiebert, F. T. *Pazyryk Chronology and Early Horse Nomads Reconsidered*, Bulletin of Asian Institute, New Series, Vol. 6, pp. 117–29, 1992.

57. Azarpay, G. *Some Classical and Near Eastern Motifs in the Art of Pazyryk.* Artibus Asiae XXII/4. 1959.

58. Rubinson, K. S. *A Study in the Transfer and Transformation of Artistic Motifs, The Textiles from Pazyryk,* Penn Museum, Vol. 32, Issue one, 1990.

59. Rudenko, S. I., *The Pazirik burial of Altai*. American Journal of Archaeology XXXVII, 1933. Also, see: Azarpay, G. *Some Classical and Near Eastern Motifs in the Art of Pazyryk*. Artibus Asiae XXII/4. 1959. Also, see: Gryaznov, M. P. *Southern Sibiria*. Geneva: Archaeologia Mundi, 1969. Also, see: Gryaznov, M. P., *On the Question of the Formation of the Scytho-Siberian-type Cultures in Connection with the opening of the Arzhan Kurgan,* Moscow institute of Archeology, 1978, 9–18.

Chapter Six

Early Migrations and Art Schools

According to C. Beckwith[1] there were three distinct stages of migrations from Eurasia. The first wave happens at the end of the third millennium B. C. E. and includes Tokharians and Anatolians. The second wave happens around seventeenth century B. C. E. and includes Indic, Greek, Italic, Germanic, Armenian, and some Indo-Iranian groups. The third wave happens in late second millennium B. C. E. and includes Celtic, Baltic, Slavic, Iranian, and Albanian people.

Scholars have undertaken analyses of a series of migrations from Inner Eurasia (Central Asia) in late prehistoric times and early ancient era. When and how extensions of the Scythian/Saka tribes—specifically the Medes and Persians—reached the Iranian plateau is still an open question.[2] Some scholars believe that the original homeland of the Iranians lay in Eurasia from which some of the tribes reached the Iranian plateau between the ninth and eighth centuries B.C.E. Other scholars hypothesize that the Iranian tribes occupied vast steppe areas of Eurasia in the early second millennium B.C.E. and that, subsequently, some of them left for Iran via the Caucasus while many others, who were also of Iranian stock, remained in the Eurasian steppe. Regardless of the exact date of their arrival and the location of their original homeland, these Iranians had already developed complex and sophisticated social institutions, cultural traditions, and economic practices. They engaged in both pastoral and agricultural modes of life and were thoroughly acquainted with metals, reared horses, and used chariots.[3]

Some of the scholars have discovered a number of archeological sites that suggest that before the mass migration of many Eurasian tribes to Europe, India, and the Iranian plateau, there were earlier migrations of smaller groups of people in the region.

SIALK: THE OLDEST SILVER PRODUCTION CENTER IN THE WORLD/POTTERY CAPITAL

"Solomon Spring," has been the major source of water since prehistoric time for Sialk, a suburb of the city of Kashan, in Isfahan province. The oldest settlements in Sialk date to 6000–5500 B.C.E.; however, Sialk ziggurat was built around 3000 B.C.E. Sialk's excavation was initiated by R. Ghrishman and his wife, Tania, in 1933 and continued for number of seasons.[4]

The excavation site was constructed as a massive polygonal terrace, covering 3,000 square yards and standing 65 feet above the plain. The northern mound is the oldest segment of the excavation site, Sialk I, and composed of two levels; it dates to seventh millennium B.C.E.

The second level, Sialk II, sees the first appearance of metallurgy. The jewelry, mostly in copper and occasionally in silver, was always very thin and simply decorated. Women wore braided hair ornaments and a special type of eardrop in metal or terracotta that seems to imitate a bunch of grapes; the pins almost always end in a gazelle's or lion's head. Men wore torques and leather helmets with silver plaques sewn on as decorations. Potters at this stage and of this era used, however, different and purely decorative elements to elaborate many pottery pieces, including checkerboard patterns, sun-wheels, circles containing crosses, and rayed rosettes.

Sialk III and Sialk IV include the southern mound and are divided into seven sub-periods. A significant amount of metallurgical remains, especially silver artifacts and the oldest silver products in the world, were found from Sialk III excavations. Radiocarbon fragments of the remains date back to 3660 B.C.E. –3520 B.C.E. As far as pottery production, the potter's wheel appears at this stage of time in Sialk, and some of the pottery pieces elaborate fabulous wild or domesticated animals, including bulls, horses, and ibexes, some of which are winged. Sialk IV begins in the second half of the fourth millennium. The remains of Sialk IV includes one of the oldest Ziggurats (if not the oldest) of the world, belonging to this era of around 3000 B.C.E.

Sialk V and Sialk VI are dated to the second millennium B.C.E. Sialk V pottery pieces include human figures. Human figures are found in three vases at this time. The artifacts of the two periods are mostly found in two cemeteries A and B. Objects in bronze, jewelry, iron items, ceramic pieces, and some weapons were found in the cemeteries. The ceramic pieces are in gray-black or red with some decorations.[5]

(See: Appendix I of this manuscript - The summarized Sialk archeological excavations, based on R. Ghirshman and G. Contenau analysis)

KHURVIN

In 1954, a team of archeologists conducted excavation on fourteen tombs of the early Iron Age (ninth and eighth centuries B.C.E.) at the village of Khurvin, sixty miles northwest of Tehran, in the Alborz Province. More than 577 artifacts including pottery and metal objects were discovered. Khurvin's tombs lacked weapons, indicating that the emphasis was on farming and herding in the area. Streams coming down from the Alborz range mountains provided water for irrigations. Khurvin pottery is monochrome, black or gray-black, and occasionally red. There is an absence of any painted decorations. Many of the pottery pieces have the shape of a bird-vase with a long beak-spout. Most of the pottery produced at Khurvin closely resembles that of Sialk. The potters of Khurvin also made square and triangular vessels, whose surfaces were decorated with incised lines, and in some cases adorned with the heads of rams and ibexes.[6]

Metal workers of Khurvin created figurines that tried to liberate the limbs from the mass of the trunk and torso. The bronze statue of a warrior has a pose of a worshipper, with stressed arms and hands. The face is bisected by a prominent nose, and the eye-sockets must have been inlaid. The warrior's helmet has a semicircular crest, and there are no ear guards. The warrior wears a large belt. Jewelry pieces of Khurvin covered with gold foil include crescent shape ear-rings with a ball attached to one of the tips. The bronze ornaments—torques, pins, bracelets, and pendants with animal motifs—are simply and carefully executed. Khurvin's miscellaneous objects include mirrors, testifying to a higher artistic standard. A number of mirrors with handles were produced; in particular, there is one consisting of a disk upheld by a figurine.

HASANLU

To the south-west of Lake Rezaieh, in the Gadar River Valley, there is an archeological site near the town of Solduz. There is a cemetery in the plain near the twenty-five-meter-high mound covering the site of the ancient town. Hasanlu was a major center of commerce and artistic production. Many gold, bronze, and pottery pieces were discovered in this excavation site.[7] The black and red pottery and the gold jewelry at Hasanlu give the impression of a sophisticated culture. J. Dyson from the University Museum of Philadelphia, who led the expedition in 1958, has thrown new light on this highly complex phase of Iranian art and civilization. A magnificent and surprising gold vase decorated with legendary scenes showing varied artistic expression was discovered there. The scenes seem to show a warrior fighting to save a man whose bust rises from a hiding place decorated with leaves. The scene also includes a ferocious animal killed by the hero, a woman with extended arms holding a cloak and standing on a ram, and an eagle in full flight carrying off a human being.

Scythian influences can also be discerned in the equine grave goods of Hasanlu tombs. A peculiar type of horse harness and bit from the Hasanlu tombs resembles the type of bit that has also been found in Scythian tombs at Kelermes in the Kuban, dating to the first quarter of the sixth century B.C.E. Hasanlu cemetery is one of the earliest tombs discovered so far in which evidence of the sacrifices of horses has been found.[8] The gold pieces of Hasanlu also included earrings, necklaces, and bowls. The discovery of a solid gold vase, found in what was apparently a palace at the top of a mound, suggests a magnificent cult object, decorated with religious and mythological scenes and dating from late second and early first millennium B.C.E. The pottery pieces include different sizes and shapes of vases.

There are ten distinct periods within the Hasanlu archeological site. Dates range from the Neolithic era to the sixth millennium B.C.E. to tenth and ninth centuries B.C.E. to the Iron Age period when a fire in a devastating battle of 800 B.C.E. destroyed the site. According to the scholars' analysis, the richest period of Hasanlu cultural activities was the tenth and ninth centuries B.C.E. From the golden age of Hasanlu there were thousands of ceramics, iron, bronze, stone, glass, ivory, and gold artifacts excavated.

The bronze pieces included some animal-style art including a winged horse, stag's head, and a lion. The nature of Hasanlu art, the shapes of the red and black pottery, and the gold jewels found make it clear that the culture linked up with other proto-Iranian civilizations. The pottery found on this site, mostly black and few red pieces, are exceptional. Hasanlu jewelry, despite being larger than the jewelry of Khurvin and Sialk sites, belongs to the same stylistic family (e.g., earrings in clusters; necklaces consisting of round gold beads; tubes adorned with soldered gold double spirals; and white stones, either cylindrical or cask shaped).

AMLASH

In the early 1960s, the peasants in Amlash, a mountain region in Gilan province, to the south-west of the Caspian Sea, accidently discovered several megalithic tombs from the eighth and ninth centuries B.C.E. Amlash's pottery has a distinctive touch not to be found elsewhere. Human figures and interpretation of animals made by Amlash potters have an immediate appeal. Gifted Amlash artists perform inventive power of a high order. Silver and gold objects including necklaces, cups, and beads in the form of birds were also discovered in the funerary sites of Amlash. Some of the metal pieces from Amlash include a great variety of small animal figures, among which the humped ox and the stag predominate.[9] Amlash is identified as one of the regions traversed by the Iranians in the course of their migration to Luristan province and the rest of the plateau.

MARLIK

In 1961, a team of archeologists under the direction of Dr. Negahban of the National Archeological Museum of Iran explored the intact royal necropolis of Marlik about twelve miles from Rudbar, in the Goharrud Valley, in Gilan province. Over fifty tombs were excavated, and over twenty thousand artifacts, including gold beakers, silver and bronze vessels, figurines and statuette of humans and animals, many tools, and pink pottery rhytons, which we might attribute to the Scythian/Saka or proto-Iranian peoples of the beginning of the first millennium B.C.E., were discovered.[10] Some scholars argue that the Royal cemetery of Marlik was utilized between fourteenth and tenth century B.C.E.; however, others believe it was used in early Iron Age, between eighth and seventh centuries B.C.E.

LURISTAN - MEGA CENTER OF METALLURGY & BRONZE ART (EIGHTH–SEVENTH CENTURIES B.C.E.)

In the first decades of the eighth century B.C.E., Cimmerians are acting as allies of Urartu. Cimmerian mercenaries are serving in the Assyrian army, and others are cooperating in the Median revolt. The Cimmerians split up into two groups: one moved westward toward Asia Minor, and the other into a region that is the present-day province of Luristan, in the Zagros Mountains. They established themselves in the region of Luristan with its narrow, isolated valley, as herders and horse breeders. There have been thousands of objects found in the tombs and shrines of Luristan. Great quantities of ornaments, horse gear, and weapons were recovered from their excavation sites. The great majority of known examples were derived from plundering and international market distribution.

The British Museum acquired some Luristan bronzes in 1854, followed by other purchases in 1885, 1900, 1914, and 1920. Between 1927 and 1930 museums in New York, Boston, Philadelphia, Chicago, Brussels, and Hamburg acquired numerous pieces of Luristan bronzes. E. Schmidt excavated the site of Surkh Dum in eastern Luristan in 1938. Surkh Dum is recognized by many international archeologists to be the most important site in Luristan. Hundreds of bronze, ivory, bone, faience, and terracotta objects, as well as two hundred cylinder and stamp seals were recovered. The Metropolitan Museum of Art acquired forty objects excavated at Surkh Dum.[11]

The art of Luristan reached its zenith in the second half of the eight and in the seventh century B.C.E. A large portion of the diverse objects found in Luristan funerary sites centers on the glorification of the powers presiding over life and death of every individual.[12] There is no hint of any Shamanic cult in these bronzes. They represent the most ancient images of the Iranian religion, as it existed before Zoroaster, as it existed in the period when Yashts, the oldest part of Avesta, the sacred book of Iranians, was taking form. The Yashts section of Avesta is composed of twenty-one chapters each dedicated to a different deity or supernatural force. (See appendix II of this manuscript.)

In the Cincinnati Art Museum, a silverplate from Luristan depicts Zurvan, the deity of infinite time, who gave birth to Ahuramazda and Ahriman, Good and Evil, Prince of Light and Prince of Darkness. This very ancient Iranian belief was incorporated into official Zoroastrianism under the Sassanian Empire (241–651 C.E.) when they declared Zoroastrianism their state religion. Ahuramazda is the supreme god, the creator of the world. He was named "the Wise, the Lord" in the reformed religion introduced by Zoroaster in his opposition to his twin brother Ahriman, the lord of evil. In funerary images, the gesture of a prayer with both arms raised and the palms of the hands turned forward expressed more or less elevated forms of religious emotions.[13] Art in this case was put to the service of religious imagery and symbolism, and the rich diversity of age-old mythology condensed and epitomized by the artist in a single work of art.

Some of the animal style art of Luristan bronze pieces include hybrid creatures composed of the foreparts of two animals. It is quite possible that these objects made in the workshops of the Luristan smiths lay at the origin of the famous Achaemenid capitals composed of two animal protomes, which after being used in Iran for edifices, made their way east to India and westward to the Aegean. In which case, the theory that the capital as we find it in the palaces of Susa and Persepolis originally derived from proto-Elamite seals calls for reconsideration. The animal effigies were also used for decorating objects of daily seals, tools, chariots, and furniture. The plasticity of animal-style art of Luristan has certain power; in fact, the simplified geometric or organic structure of the some of the work reminds us of the work of some modern or postmodern animal sculptures.

Many of the horse trappings and weapons found in the cemeteries and shrines of Luristan had never been used. Most of this group of artifacts were merely symbolic objects that the dead took to the other world for personal use. Another peculiar characteristic of the animal-style art of Luristan bronzes was the practice of attaching wings to creatures, creating a surreal and imaginary world. The same style was followed in some of the Achaemenid art pieces.[14]

A great number of axes were discovered in the tombs of Luristan. They are symbolic objects made for the use of the dead in the other world. There are three varieties of fibula found in Lurestan. The first kind is the more common from late eighth or early seventh century B. C. E. on. The second kind has no spring, and its pin is fastened to the arc by a small ring turning on a stud. The third fibula from Lurestan had a special significance since it is animal-shaped, which was a specialty of the Cimmerians.

Potters of Luristan imitated bronze workers and took from the bronze vessels their new elements. Potters of Lurestan elaborated their vases with painted decorations.

No other civilization, except perhaps that of Etruscans, has yielded such a wealth of metal objects, with so great a diversity of forms, so wide a range of subjects and techniques as those of the metal-works of Luristan. There was an extraordinary growth in the Iranian metal industry in the eighth and seventh centuries B.C.E.[15]

THE OXUS TREASURE (TAKHT-I-KOBAD)

In Bactra (Bakhtaran) on the right bank of Amu Darya, the Oxus Treasure (now in the British Museum, Room 52), containing 180 pieces of gold and silver, around 1,500 coins, and several dozen gold plaques engraved with figures, flowers, and other decorative elements, was discovered in 1877. Although some of the scholars identify the Oxus Treasury as an Achaemenid collection, R. Ghrishman's analysis identifies the Oxus Treasure as a Median collection (728–553 B.C.E.), and concludes that its study would surely throw new light on Iranian art of the pre-Achaemenian period. The Oxus treasure dates to the seventh or early sixth century B.C.E.[16] One of the most famous items of this treasury is a gold armlet with four parts of horned griffins at the open ends. Hollows in the bodies and cloisons of wings, necks, and horns originally held inlays that were lost in the fifth to fourth century B.C.E. The height of this piece is 12.3 cm.; width is 11.5 cm.[17]

ZIWIYEH

Ziwiyeh is a village twenty miles east of the town of Sakkis, (Scythians refer to themselves as Sakaii), one of the kingdoms that some of the Scythians migrated to from the north and settled in 700 B.C.E.[18] The structure of the archeological complex of Ziwiyeh is composed of three sections: a lower triangle area at one end, a second level higher up, and a smaller and higher third level. A royal treasury, which was buried below the walls of a citadel, was discovered that included a collection of fascinating artifacts. Some of the pottery discovered in Ziwiyeh tombs was of particular interest.[19] The pottery forms and ornamentations revealed the nature of a branch of Scythian art. A pitcher with a long beak-spout and a vase with a vertical cylinder-spout indicated a continuation of Iranian traditions of Sialk, Khurvin, Hasanlu, and Luristan.

Ziwiyeh pottery includes pots and pitchers with lugs in the form of a recumbent feline, a characteristically Scythian motif that also figures on the far more valuable gold objects. With its fine, well-baked clay, its burnished red slip, and its decorative designs, it is the only pottery so far discovered that keeps to the technique of the Iranian potters whose products were inspired by metal works.[20] The pottery of Ziwiyeh is predominately Late Buff ware, associated with the spread of Median power.

KALAR DASHT

A Neolithic archeological site was identified in the Alborz Mountains on Kalar Dasht plain in Mazandaran province. The site was a gigantic mound 10 meters high and covering an area of 6,000 hectares. A group of tombs was found in Kalar Dasht south of the Caspian Sea containing artifacts made of gold, bronze, and pottery pieces. The famous golden cup decorated with a lion's figure was unearthed during excavations for construction of Ejabat Palace on a mound named Ganj Tappeh (or Tepe Kalar) in Kalar Dasht in 1939. Other artifacts included animal rhytons and gold jewelry. Tepe Kalar was named after an ancient city called Paradise of Explorers. R. Ghrishman identified some of the art objects as Median arts of the ninth to seventh centuries B.C.E.[21]

TURANG TEPE

A prehistoric site called Turang Tepe, in the province of Gurgan, was first excavated in 1931 by F. Wulsin, curator at the University of Pennsylvania Museum in Philadelphia. Amazing painted pottery pieces and metal tools, terracotta and stone figurines, instruments, and jewelry pieces were discovered.[22] A French team led by J. Deshayes conducted excavations from 1960 to 1979. The French archeologists excavated 150 burials and several remains of houses. Artifacts including pottery, beads, and jewelry pieces were discovered.

Turang Tepe consists of a group of mounds rising to 15 meters off the ground and approximately 900 meters in diameter. Turang Tepe complex has 15 layers of cultures and civilizations, including three Neolithic and Chalcolithic layers, followed by three Bronze Age layers (3100–2100 B.C.E.). The Bronze Age layer includes an enormous mud-brick terrace constructed in the center of the complex. Three Iron Age layers of Turang Tepe follow (seventh to second centuries B.C.E.). From the first century B.C.E. to the thirteenth century C.E. there were six independent civilizations (the third layer consists of Sassanian civilization, from the third to fifth centuries C.E.).[23]

NOTES

1. Beckwith, C. I. *Empire of the Silk Road*, Princeton Press, 2009.
2. Mandelshtam, A. M. *The Nomads on the Route to India*, Materials and investigations of the Archeology of U.S.S.R., Moscow, 136, 1966, 61–65. Also, see: Potemkina, T. M., *On the Question of Bronze Age Steppe Tribal Migration to the South: Interaction between Nomadic Cultures and Ancient Civilization*, Science, Alma-Ata, 1987, 76–78. Also, see: Pyankova, L. T. *The Bronze Age Cemetery of Tigrovaya Balka*, Soviet Archeology, 3, 1974, 171–80. Also, see: Yablonsky, L. T., *The Saka of the Southern Aral Sea Area: The Archeology and Anthropology of the Ceremonies*, Moscow, 1966, pp. 6–12. Also, see: Klyosov, A. A., *The 3 R's in R1 Haplogroup*, Journal of Genetic Geneology, Vol. 5, No.2, pp. 217–56, 2009. According to Klyosov's genetic analysis the Andronovo culture embraced Kazakhstan, Central Asia, and South Ural and Western Siberia, and about 3600 ybp they migrated to India and Iran. Those who were left behind re-populated Eastern Europe (present-day Poland, Germany, Czech, Slovak, etc.) between 3200 and 2500 years bp. Also, see: Parlato, S., *The Saka and Xiongnu: A Comparative Reading of Literary Sources*. In B. Genito, The Archeology of the Steppes—Methods and Strategies, Naples, 1992, 9–12. Also, see: Rice, T. T., *Ancient Arts of Central Asia*, F. A. Praeger Publishers, New York, 1965.
3. Pavlinkaya, L. R., *The Scythians and Sakians*, Eight to Third Centuries B.C., Nomads of Eurasia, Academy of Sciences of U.S.S.R., Natural History Museum of Los Angeles County, 1989, 19–40. Also, see: Beckwith, C., *Empires of the Silk Road*, Princeton, 2009. Also, see: Parlato, S., *The Saka and Xiongnu: A Comparative Reading of Literary Sources*. In B. Genito, The Archeology of the Steppes—Methods and Strategies, Naples, 1992, 9–12. Also, see: Rice, T. T., *Ancient Arts of Central Asia*, F. A. Praeger Publishers, New York, 1965.
4. Biscione, R. *Ceramica di Amlash*, Museo Nazionale d'Arte Orientale, Schede 6, Rome, 1974.
5. Ghrishman, R. *Fouilles de Sialk pres de Kashan* 1933, 1934, 1937; I, II (Musee du Louvre, department des antiquites orientales; serie archeologique IV, V. Paris, 1938, 1939). Also, see: Ghirshman, R. *Sept Mille Ans d'art en Iran* (Exposition: Petit

Palais, Oct. 1961–Jan. 1962. Paris, 1961). Also, see: Ghirshman, R. *Fouilles de Sialk*, Vol. 2, Paul Geuthner, 1939. Ghirshman conducted series of the following excavation including: 1931–1972 (Head of archeological mission in Persia) Tepe giyan 1935 Sialk 1931–1938 Bishapur 1938 1941 (A.D. 241–A.D. 272), 1971 Begram 1943 Susa 1967 Masjid-I Soleiman 1976.

6. Berghe, L. V. *La Necropole de Khurvin,* Nederlands Historisch Archaeologisch Instituut in het Nabije te Istanbul, XVII, 1964.

7. Dyson, Robert H (1989). *"Constructing the Chronology and Historical Implications of Hasanlu IV"*; Iran, Vol. 27, pp. 18–19, 22.

8. Crawford, E. *Hasanlu,* Bulletin of the Metropolitan Museum of Art, Nov. 1961. The Republic of Azerbaijan (historically Arran and Shirvan) was fabricated by Stalin; Historically Azerbaijan was referred to the region south of Aras River.

9. R. Biscione, *Ceramica di Amlash*, Museo Nazionale d'Arte Orientale, Schede 6, Rome, 1974. Also, see: Parrot, A. *"Acquisitions et inédits du Musée du Louvre,* 13. Animaux et ceramiques d'Amlash," *Syria* 40, 1963, pp. 236–41. Also, see: Mongiatti, A. *A gold four horse mode chariot from the Oxus Treasure: A fine Illustration of Achaemenid goldwork*, The British Museum Technical Research Bulletin. British Museum, 2010, 4: 27–38. Also, see: Curtis, John, *The Oxus Treasure*, British Museum Objects in Focus series, 2012, British Museum Press.

10. Negahban, E. *Excavations of Marlik*. Tehran: Cultural heritage Organization Iran, (Research center). Vol. 1, 1st ed., 1999. Also, see: Negahban, E. *Royal Gold of Marlik Tepe*, Hhorizon Magazine, V, Nov. 1962. Also, see: Ghirshman, R. *The Arts of Ancient Iran*, New York, 1967, pp. 31–38.

11. Berghe, L.V. *Les Bronze du Luristan*, Archeologie, pp. 177–87, 1959.

12. Godard, A *Les Bronzes du Luristan,* Ars Asiatica XVII, 1931.

13. Dussaud, R. *The Bronzes of Luristan*, Survey, I, pp. 254 –77, 1956.

14. Overlaet, B. *Luristan Metalwork in the Iron Age*: *Persia's Ancient Splendour: Mining, Handicraft and Archaeology*, Deutsches Bergbau-Museum: Bochum, 2004.

15. Fleming, S. J., V. C. Pigott, C. P. Swann, and S. K. Nash. *Bronze in Luristan: Preliminary analytical evidence from copper/bronze artifacts excavated by the Belgian mission in Iran*. Iranica Antiqua: 2005.

16. Curtis, John, "The Oxus Treasure in the British Museum," *Ancient Civilizations from Scythia to Siberia*, Vol. 10, pp. 293–338, 20.

17. Yamauchi, E. M., Review of *The Treasure of the Oxus with Other Examples of Early Oriental Metal-Work, Journal of the American Oriental Society*, Vol. 90, No. 2, JSTOR, pp. 340–43, Apr. –Jun., 1970.

18. Ghrishman, R. *The Scythians and the Royal Tomb of Ziwiyeh*, in Art of Ancient Iran, New York, 1964, pp. 98–125.

19. Dyson, R. H. Jr., *"Glimpses of History at Ziwiye,"* Expedition 4, Spring, pp. 32–37, 1963. B.

20. Goldman, B. *The Animal Style at Ziwiyeh, IPEK* 24, pp. 54–68, 1977.

21. Ghirshman, R. *Sept Mille Ans d'art en Iran* (Exposition: Petit Palais, Oct. 1961–Jan. 1962. Paris, 1961).

22. Moreau, K. Tureng Depe, Expedition records, University of Pennsylvania, Penn Museum Archives, 2010. Also, see: Moreau, Kathy.

23. Olson, Kery G.; Thornton, Christopher P. *"Tureng Tepe, a Bronze Age Centre in Northeastern Iran Revisited."* Journal of the British Institute of Persian *Studies*. 59(1): 2021, 4–35. Also, see: Wulsin, F. R., *Excavation at Tureng Tepe, near Asterabad*. Supplement to the Bull. American Inst. Persian Art and Archaeology, New York, 1932.

Chapter Seven

Iron Age Median Empire and its Art

The Iranian world was divided between the nomadic Scythian/Saka northern zone and the southern Persian zone.[1]

EXPANSIVE MIGRATIONS FROM EURASIA

As a result of a series of explosive and expansive migrations from north and northeast toward the south and southwest, the establishment of a number of powerful and historically significant empires occurred between 728 B.C.E. and 651 C.E. including:

The Median Empire	728–553 B.C.E.
The Achaemenid Empire	553–330 B.C.E.
The Parthian Empire	247 B.C.E. –224 C.E.
The Kushan Empire	30–320 C.E.
The Sassanid Empire	224–651 C.E.

MEDES

Medes were people of Indo-Iranian origin. By the sixth century B.C.E. Median tribes established an empire that stretched from the beautiful regions of Shirvan and Eran to Central Asia.[2] They include:

1. Busae group
2. Paraetaceni group (Herodotus referred to them "Royal Scythians")
3. Strukhat
4. Arizanti (noble tribe, clan)

5. Budii (found also among the Black Sea Scythians as Budi-ni)
6. Magi (hereditary caste of priests of the Zurvanism/Zoroastrianism)

Medes and Scythians

The above named six Mede tribes are similar to tribal names of the Scythians, suggesting a definitive link between these two groups. Today's population of the western part of the Iranian plateau consider themselves to be descended of ancient Iranian warrior tribes of Scythian/Saka, Medes, Parthians, and many other Iranian sects. The language of Medes was most likely similar to the Avestan and Scythian/Saka languages. The Medes, appear in history first in 836 B.C.E. Earliest records show that Assyrian conqueror Shalmaneser II received tribute from the "Amadai" in connection with wars against the tribes of the Zagros. His successors undertook many expeditions against the Medes.[3]

The Medes were usually mentioned together with the Scythians. They were divided into many districts and towns, under petty local chieftains; from the names in the Assyrian inscriptions, it appears that some of them had already adopted the religion of Zoroaster and some others converted to Mithraism.

An Assyrian military report from 800 B.C.E. lists twenty-eight names of Mede chiefs. A second report from c. 700 B.C.E. lists twenty-six names. In spite of repeated rebellions by the early chieftains against the Assyrian yoke, the Medes paid tribute to Assyria through the first half of the seventh century. In the second half of the seventh century B.C.E., the Mede kings Phraortes and his son Cyaxares established the Mede Empire. Medes great powers were maintained until the rise of Cyrus.

Medes and Cyrus

Cyrus, king of Persia, rebelled against the Medean king Astyages and won a decisive victory in 550 B.C.E. Thus were the Medes subjected to their close kin, the Persians. In the new Persian Empire, Medes in honor and war stood next to the Persians. Many noble Medes were employed as officials, satraps (governors), and generals of the Persian Empire. Media proper, or Greater Media, as it is often called, was formed by Darius' as the eleventh satrapy of the Persian Empire.[4] Macedonians occupied Media in the summer of 330 B.C.E. In 328, Atropates, a former general of Darius, was appointed as the satrap of Media. During the reign of Demetrius I, the disintegration of the Seleucid Empire began, and shortly afterward, in about 150, Medes celebrated their liberation when the Parthian king Mithradates I entered Media.

History of Medes and their Arts

Excavations at Godin Depe, Depe Nushi, and Baba Jan

The origin and history of the Medes was quite obscure, as we possessed almost no contemporary information, and not a single monument or inscription from Media itself until the 1960s. In 1965, T. C. Young, Jr. started excavation of Godin Depe, 15 km east of Kangavar. Godin Depe is a Bronze Age fortified palace of a Median king.[5] Between the years 1966 and 1969, C. Goff conducted the excavation of Baba Jan, a Median site in East Azerbaijan. Baba Jan is 10 km from Nurabad. In 1967, D. Stronach started excavation of Depe Nushi Jan, 15 km west of Malayer in Hamadan Province.[6] There are four main buildings in the site: 1. The central temple; 2. The western temple; 3. The fort; and 4. The columned hall. The discoveries revealed the four different wares known as common ware: buff, cream, or light red in color with gold or silver mica temper, including jars in various sizes. Smaller vessels were in gray ware. They displayed smoothed and burnished surfaces. The cooking ware and crumbly ware are also recognized products. According to the Achaemenid inscription the capital of the Median Empire was Hegmatana (Ecbatana), today Hamedan. The cities of Malayar and Kangavar were major cities of the empire.[7]

The artifacts discovered at Depe Nushi Jan, Godin Depe, and Baba Jan show the existence of urban settlements in Media in the first half of the first millennium B.C.E. These settlements were centers for production of arts and crafts and also of an agricultural and cattle breeding economy.

NOTES

1. Godley, A. D. (ed.) *Herodotus'* Histories, with an English translation. Cambridge: Harvard University Press, 1920, 110.

2. Diakonoff, I. M. *Media*, The Cambridge History of Iran, 2, Cambridge University Press, 1985, pp. 36–148.

3. Radner, K., *An Assyrian view on the Medes*, in G. B. Lanfranchi et al. (eds.), Continuity of Empire: Assyria, Media, Persia (History of the Ancient Near East Monographs 5), Padova: Sargon, 2003, 37–64. Also, see: Dalley, S., *Foreign charioteer and cavalry in the armies of Tiglath-Pileser III and Sargon II*, Iraq 47 1985, 31–48. Also, see: Reade, J. E., *Iran in the Neo-Assyrian period*, in M. Liverani (ed.), Neo-Assyrian Geography (Quaderni di geografia storica 5), Rome: Università di Roma 'La Sapienza,' 1995, 31–42.

4. Young, T. C. *The Early History of the Medes and the Persians and the Achaemenid Empire*, in Cambridge Ancient History, 4, Cambridge University Press, pp. 1–52. Also, see: Godley, A. D. (ed.) *Herodotus'* Histories, with an English translation. Cambridge: Harvard University Press, 1920, 110.

5. Young, T. C. *Excavations of the Godin Project: First Progress Report*. Toronto Royal Ontario Museum 1969. Also, see: Young T. C. Jr and Louis D. Levine L., *Excavations at Godin Tepe*. Second Progress Report, Royal Ontario Museum Occasional Paper 26, 1974. Also, see: Young, T. C. *The Kangavar Survey, Periods VI to IV*, in A View From the Highlands: Archaeological Studies in Honour of Charles Burney. Edited by Antonio Sargona. 645–60. Herent, Belgium: Peeters, 2004. Also, see: Smith, P. and T. Cuyler Young T. C. *The Evolution of Early Agriculture and Culture in Greater Mesopotamia*. In Population Growth: Anthropological Implications, edited by B. Spooner. 1–59. Cambridge, MA: MIT Press, 1972. Also, see: Matthews, R. *Administrative Activity and Technology at Godin Tepe in the Later Fourth Millennium BC*. In Proceedings of the International Symposium on Iranian Archaeology: Western Region, (Kermanshah, 1–3 November 2006). Teheran: ICAR (Iranian Center for Archaeological Research).

6. Stronach, D. *Depe Nush-I Jan: A Mound in Media*, The Metropolitan Museum, New Series, 27, 3, 1973, 177–86.

7. Young, T. C. *The Kangavar Survey, Periods VI to IV*. In A View From the Highlands: Archaeological Studies in Honour of Charles Burney. Edited by Antonio Sargona. 645–60. Herent, Belgium: Peeters, 2004. Also, see: Diakonoff, Igor M. (1985). "*Media,*" In Ilya Gershevitch. Cambridge History of Iran, Vol 2. London: Cambridge University Press. pp. 36–148.

Chapter Eight

Iron Age
Achaemenid Empire Arts

Cyrus, king of Persia, rebelled against the Medean King Astyages and won a decisive victory in 550 B.C.E. Thus were the Medes subjected to their close kin, the Persians.[1] In the new Persian Empire, Medes in honor and war, stood next to the Persians. Many noble Medes were employed as officials, satraps, and generals of Persian Empire. Media proper, or Greater Media, as it is often called, was formed by Darius as the eleventh satrapy of the Persian Empire.[2]

ACHAEMENID EMPIRE AND THE FIRST CENTRAL ASIAN STATES

The Achaemenid Empire, established by the emperor Cyrus, extended from the shores of the Indus River and Hindokush Mountains in the east to the Balkans in the west. The empire's political philosophy was based on the oath or commitment that Cyrus made with his people and is written on a cylinder, found in the middle of nineteenth century in Babylon (Iraq today). On the cylinder Cyrus writes:

> I am Cyrus. King of Kings, King of Babylon, Sumer, Akkad, Son of Camboujiah, The great king, King of Anshan, Grandson of Cyrus, Descendant of Cheshpesh, The great king, I announce that I respect the customs and religions of the nations of my empire and never let any of my governors and subordinates look down or insult them until I am alive, I will never let anyone oppress any others, I will never let anyone take possession of properties of the others by force or without compensation, I declare that everyone is free to choose a religion, people are free to live in all regions, I denounce slavery and my governors have to prohibit exchanging men and women as slaves within their domains.

As far as the territory into which the Achaemenid Empire extends, the Inscription of Behistun found in the western Iran of today includes five elaborate written columns carved from solid rock that describe the extension of the empire. The detailed inscription begins with an introduction from the emperor Darius:

> "I am Darius, the great king, king of kings, the king of Persia, the king of countries, the son of Hystaspes, the grandson of Arsames, the Achaemenid." The sixth section of the first column then lists the countries under the rule of Darius: "Persia, Elam, Babylonia, Assyria, Arabia, Egypt, the countries by the sea, Lydia, Greece, Media, Armenia, Cappadocia, Parthia, Drangiana, Aria, Chorasmia, Bactra, Sogdia, Gandhara, Saka, Sattagydia, Arachosia and Maka: twenty-three lands in all."[3]

With this declaration, the Central Asian states, of Parthia, Chorasmia, Bactra, and Sogdia or Soghdiana clearly were established by the Achaemenids as distinct provinces with their own governors.

ACHAEMENID EMPIRE CAPITAL CITIES AND MEGALITHIC ARCHITECTURE

The history of architecture of this region goes back more than six thousand years. Other architectural remains of this period also offer a glimpse into the social structure and political organization of the Iranian plateau and adjacent regions in Central Asia. Architectural remains varied from simple peasant huts, tea houses, and garden pavilions, to the most majestic structures reflecting power, personality, rivalries, taste, and status. The first major monumental structures were mountain-shaped temples such as the Temple of Chugha Zanbil near Susa, and royal funerary sites, such as Scythian Kurgans at Pazyrik. The first dynastic capital was built by Medes in 612 B.C.E. in Ecbatana (Hamadan) in present day western Iran, after they overthrew Assyria.

The Achaemenid Empire established its first capital in Pasargade, in Fars province, in modern day southern Iran. A huge artificial platform with enormous stone pieces and tall slender stone columns signified the beginning of an era known as the megalithic period in architecture. In Pasargade, there are three palaces, each enclosed by its own large masonry walls. The central room of the main audience hall covers an area of 230 by 131 feet. Initially, precious metal plating partially covered the painted columns. The columns were painted green, blue, red, and yellow. Cyrus was buried in Pasargade, and his megalithic style tomb crowns six stages that decrease in height as they progress upward.[4]

The Achaemenid capital was moved to Persepolis by Darius in 518 B.C.E. Persepolis was a ceremonial capital, composed primarily of a group of palaces and possibly temples, intended to celebrate festivities, especially Nowruz, or the Persian New Year. Its scale, visible still today, exhibits the magnitude, power, and wealth of the first superpower of the ancient world. In order to have access to the Persepolis platform, one has to climb up a majestic double stairway twenty-two feet wide, diverging and returning on itself. The stairs were carved from enormous single blocks that sometimes even included a part of the side wall, and wide enough for horse riders to incline to the upper platform, without dismounting the horse, and facing the "Gate of All Nations" guarded by colossal human-headed winged bulls. On the platform, spaces between buildings formed courts, each with its own garden. Across the court stood the so-called "Hall of a Hundred Columns," and the name of the two other palaces beyond Apadana palace as indicated on their entrance walls, were Tachara and Hadesh.

The walls of the buildings were polished to mirror brightness, and relief sculptures as sharp as if cut in metal, were decorated the interior and exterior walls. The Persepolis sculptural wall friezes are grouped, and spacing is planned, controlled, and rhythmical. The rows of sculptures depict representatives of twenty-eight satrapys (states) of the Achaemenid Empire, from the Nile to the Oxus, from the Aegean to the Ganges, in full-figure profile bringing a variety of gifts on the occasion of Nowruz, to their emperor. The emperor is seated on the throne supported by representatives of all the nations of the Achaemenid Empire. Thousands of rosette ornaments decorate the edging of the friezes. Persepolis covers an area of 1,300,000 square feet, larger than any Egyptian temple or medieval cathedral.[5]

The construction of Persepolis took more than one hundred years, but the style is unified and consistent. The Apadana palace of Xerxes I (486–465 B.C.E.), son of Darius, in Persepolis is two hundred fifty feet square, with a central room of one hundred ninety-five feet square with thirty-six fluted columns, elegantly tapered, seven feet thick, sixty feet high, and crowned by ten foot capitals. The reception hall is large enough to hold ten thousand people. Persepolis remains one of the wonders of the ancient world: a remarkable structure, unparalleled in any other part of the world.

NOWRUZ IN PERSEPOLIS AND INNER EURASIA (CENTRAL ASIA)

One of the sculptural reliefs repeated on the walls of Persepolis is the symbol of the lion (Leo) slaying the bull (Taurus). The moment that these constellations were at their zenith coincided with the Spring Equinox on March 21. The Persian New Year signaled the beginning of Spring. Today, Nowruz is celebrated in many different countries both in Inner Eurasia (Central Asia) and the Middle East.

SCULPTURES & SCULPTURAL RELIEFS

The giant terrace of Persepolis, one of the wonders of the ancient world, measures 125,000 square meters. The terrace or platform wall was reached from the flat ground below by twin returning staircases of 111 steps, 23 feet wide and shallow enough for riders to ascend. What is attributed to Darius I, is the earlier parts of treasury, the palace of Tachara, and the main structure of Apadana palace. Apadana palace is a large ceremonial audience hall, 1,000 square meters, 72 columns (only 14 standing), and 24 meters high. The columns are fluted more delicately than any Doric or Ionic style entity, with highly impressive capitals of animal style art of twin headed bulls, horses, eagles or lions. A. Godard thought the platform surface was deliberately divided into three functional areas—reception halls, treasury, and barracks.

Persepolis carries good deal of originality, including Dariush's Tachara palace, with its polished dark stone frames of doors and windows, which rose high and overlooked the plain. Apadana, with 36 interior columns, and another 36 in its porticoes, was grand. In the south-east of the platform was the treasury, built by 509 B.C.E. and enlarged about 493 by Dariush, then added to by Xerxes. The carving of the sculptured friezes of podium and staircases was completed under Xerxes. The Gate of All Nations with its colossal pairs of half human and half beasts faces the head of the stairway of the terrace. South-west of this area, Xerxea built the palace of Hadish on a high podium. His son, Artaxerxes I, completed after his father's death the Hall of Hundred Columns or Throne Hall, 255 square feet, larger than Apadana Hall. Here the sculptural decorations are on the doorjambs, with the king enthroned with guards and subject peoples lending him support. All evidences at Persepolis complex shows that the palaces on the platform served for formal receptions and ceremonial purposes.[6]

The main vehicle of Achaemenid art was its relief sculptures. The relief sculpture begins with Cyrus. One unique aspect of Cyrus' palace at Pasargad is its sculptures showing drapery folds that are repeated in sculptural relief of Persepolis. Although, there is an attempt by few to compare Achaemenid sculptural relief to Assyrian sculptures, however, one has to remember that there is no imitation of Assyrian battles and hunting scenes in Persepolis sculptural reliefs. On the contrary, there is sign of unity and friendship, reflected by representatives of all satrapys (provinces), hand in hand participating in festivities. For the first time in history, the delegations from Central Asia satrapys, including Sogdians, Parthians, Bactrans (people of Bakhtaran), Khwarazmians, and Scythian/Saka Tigrahuda (with pointed hats), are participants in Nowruz festivities.

The special qualities that made Achaemenid art impressive seem to be the clarity, composure, and timelessness. The range of the sculptural reliefs of the court themes begins where the king Darius is shown enthroned with Xerxes, the crown prince behind him and his court officials and commanders of his military at his back, and the subject people approaching him with gifts. Achaemenid sculptural reliefs display a fair degree of originality and realistic and symbolic detail, including various animals, especially horses, and also the dress, equipment, and hair styles of different peoples, offerings including gold vases, metalwork, and cloth from different regions. J. A. Becker states that some scholars have discussed the possibility that Persian relief sculpture from Persepolis may have influenced Athenian sculptors of the fifth century B. C. E., who were tasked with creating the Ionic frieze of Parthenon in Athens. The court art was attractive, and it served the purposes for which it was invented.

DECORATIVE AND UTILITARIAN ARTS OF ACHAEMENID EMPIRE

Decorative and Utilitarian arts flourished in the Achaemenid Empire as they were long done by their ancestors, Cimmerians, Scythians/Saka, Sarmathians, and Tokharians in Eurasia. Among the works of fine craftsmanship that were most prized were vessels in the precious metals such as rhytons, jars with animal handles, cups, bowls, jugs, gold discs and plaques, gold torques and penannular armlets with animal endings, gems and seals of different kinds, jewelry with bright colored inlay of lapis lazuli, garnet, and turquoise. These were prestigious objects such as might be given to high officials, as for instance, the cylinder seal of Dariush was found in Egypt. Achaemenid art style, and its special idioms, including Scythian/Saka animal style, was overlaid with other wonderful ideas and motifs, with the prestige that they carried, created, and invented in other satrapys of the empire for the next two centuries, and affecting the art of the next powerhouses and surrounding entities.

The third capital of the Achaemenid Empire was Susa, built by Darius.[7] The palace of Darius I (522–486 B.C.E.) in Susa is built around a central court, 116 by 118 feet. Susa was a powerful fort and a flourishing administrative city with a large civilian population, in the heart of the satrapy of Khuzestan. Many of the art objects discovered from the Achaemenid excavation sites have synthesized the motif of animals, and are either naturalistic or stylized animal forms.

The first systematic excavation of Susa took place in 1884, led by French archeologist, J. deMorgan. There was no conservation or preservation involved by the team. On the contrary, the Apadana Palace of Dariush at Susa was severely reduced to a rubble. Its animal style column capitals displaying bulls, horses, and lions, the walls of the site with some of the first glazed bricks and figural images of humans and animals, were taken apart from the site and stored in a newly being built fortress. Although they were excavating and working to preserve the site of ancient Susa, however, they used the ancient bricks with cuneiform writings, from the ancient site, to construct a new building, now known as Susa Castle. Apadana palace of Dariush was built on a platform of 820 by 490 feet, in 521 B.C.E., and was the center of a complex. While a large number of the scholars, including many archeologists, have condemned the vandalism of the site. One of the articles on the topic suggests that 800 eighteen-wheelers from Susa were taken to Louvre Museum in Paris. Although this may be an exaggerated statement, however, looking up "Susa at Louvre" may give a bit of clue that there was a large collection of artifacts taken from Susa, leaving a rubble behind.

NOTES

1. Herzfeld, E. *The Persian Empire*, Franz Steiner Verlag GMBH, Wiesbaden, 1968.

2. Dandamayev, M. A., *Media and Achaemenid Iran*, History of Civilizations of Central Asia, V. II, UNESCO Publishing, 1996, 35–66. Also, see: Muscarella, O. S., Caubet, A., and Tallon, F., *Susa in Achaemenid Period*, in The Royal City of Susa, The Metropolitan Museum of Art, Harry N. Abrams, New York, 1993, 215–52.

3. King, L. W. and Thompson, R. C., *The Sculptures and Inscription of Darius the Great on the rock of Bisutun in Persia,* London, 1907.

4. Stierlin, H., *Splendors of the Persian Empire* (Timeless Treasures), White Star, 2006. Also, see: Yamauchi, E., *Persia and The Bible*, Baker Book House, Grand Rapids, Michigan, 1990, 65–92.

5. Curtis, J. E. and Tallis, N. *Forgotten Empire*: The World of Ancient Persia, Published in Association with The British Museum, 2005, 18–49.

6. Schmidt, E. F. *Persepolis* 3 v. Chicago: University of Chicago Press, 1953–1970.

7. Muscarella, O. S., Caubet, A., and Tallon, F., *Susa in Achaemenid Period*, in The Royal City of Susa, The Metropolitan Museum of Art, Harry N. Abrams, New York,

1993, 215–52. On the fall of the Achaemenid Empire see: Davis, P. K. *One Hundred Decisive Battles from Ancient Times to the Present*: *The World Major Battles and how they Shaped History*, Oxford University Press, Oxford, 1999, 27. The rebellion that starts in Macedonia, one of the satrapys of the Achaemenid Empire, follows the defeat of Athenians at the Battle of Chaeronea (338 B.C.) by Phillip the Macedonian, and puts an end to the golden age of Athenian kingdom and the classical period (480 B.C.E. –331 B.C.E.) in Greece. The military expedition of Alexander of Macedonia, Philips' son continues for ten years and mysteriously he died at the age of thirty-three in Mesopotamia. Also, see: Curtis. J. E. and Tallis, N. *Forgotten Empire: The World of Ancient Persia*, Published in Association with The British Museum, 2005, 18–49. Also, see: E. Herzfeld, *The Persian Empire*, Franz Steiner Verlag GMBH, Wiesbaden, 1968. Also, see: Dandamayev, M. A., *Media and Achaemenid Iran*, History of Civilizations of Central Asia, V. II, UNESCO Publishing, 1996, 35–66. Also, see: Muscarella, O. S., Caubet, A., and Tallon, F., *Susa in Achaemenid Period*, in The Royal City of Susa, The Metropolitan Museum of Art, Harry N. Abrams, New York, 1993, 215–52.

Recent DNA tests (Lalueza-Fox [2004]) study suggest that, during the Bronze/Iron Age period, the majority of the population of present day Kazakhstan was an extension of Andronovo culture, and prior to the thirteenth to seventh century B.C.E., all samples from present day Kazakhstan belong to proto Andronovo culture. Keyser (2009), conducted test on ten human remains of the Bronze Age of various regions of Kazakhstan; nine possessed the R1a Y-chromosome Haplogroup and one Haplogroup C (Y-DNA) (xC3). On the issue of cultures and history of Central Asia, also, see: Kia A., Kia M., Bedunah D., Graetz R., Gunya A., Hampson S., Hendrix M. S. Klaits A., and Sears W. S., *Discovering Central Asia*, The University of Montana Press, 2012. Also, see: Kia A., Central Asia: *Rediscovering a Cultural Treasury*, Central & Southwest Asian Studies Program, Anthropology Department, the twelfth monograph in the contributions to Anthropology Series, (three articles), The University of Montana Press, 2010. Let's hope that the above-mentioned studies, conducted by various scholars in the field, although still very incomplete, will be instrumental to serve the reconstruction of the history and cultures of Central Asia and beyond, and not as a tool in the hands of extremists and fanatics to ignite conflicts.

Chapter Nine

Satrapy of Khwarazmia
Cultures and Arts

This chapter includes an analysis of the cultures and arts of the region of Khwarazmia as one of the oldest urbanized centers of Inner Eurasia (Central Asia). The chapter elaborates some of the significant historical, cultural, and artistic contributions of this region to Central Asia and the world.

NEOLITHIC CULTURES

Khwarazmia excavation at Toprak Kala, began under supervision of P. Preobzhensky, in 1929. As the leading archeologist of the Museum of Ethnography of the Peoples, S. P. Tolstov resumed the excavation of Toprak Kala between 1932 and 1934. Although Tolstov returned briefly to Toprak Kala in 1938, it was after WWII, between the years of 1951 and 1957, that he became fully committed to the Khwarazmia. S. P. Tolstov, a renowned archeologist and ethnographer by using aerial photography discovered hundreds of ancient sites, and mapped the roads and settlements.[1]

Kalteminar Culture: Pottery with Stamped and Incised Decorations

The Neolithic culture of Khwarazm is known as the Kalteminar culture, a term introduced by Tolstov, from the name of a village near the site. The first Neolithic occupation site to be investigated in Khwarazm is Dzhanbas-Kala. The animal remains found show that the main occupations of the inhabitants were hunting and fishing. They lived in large huts with an area of approximately 3000 square feet, roofed with rushes, each of which could accommodate a large family unit of over one hundred people. Varied material found on the site included stone tools and bones and fragments of pottery with stamped and incised decorations. Similar constructions from the same period were found in southern Xinjiang and recently in western Kazakhstan and in the lower Volga region.

Khwarazmian Bronze Age Cultures and Arts

The most informative Bronze Age site in Khwarazmia is the site of Kokcha III, where a tomb was excavated which yielded interesting anthropological and cultural material. The dead were frequently buried in couples, a man and a woman lying face to face. Various objects were buried along with the dead. The pottery consisted mainly of cooking pots decorated with simple patterns, usually incised, in the form of straight or zigzag lines or simple geometric motifs. The bronze articles included awls, pendants, and bracelets. The inhabitants of these settlements were farming, based on artificial irrigation, and stock rearing including horses and other domesticated animals.[2] The process of assimilation between the different cultures of Central Asia which can be observed at the end of the Bronze Age intensified.

Ancient Cultures and Arts of Khwarazmia

Tolstov discovered a great many remains of ancient irrigation systems of the middle of the first millennium B.C.E. Some of the major irrigation works discovered by Tolstov in Khwarazmia date back as far as the first half of the first millennium B.C.E., especially when Khwarazmia became the sixteenth satrapy (province) of the Achaemenid Empire.[3] At this time Khwarazmia was dominated by Massagetae Scythians/Saka. Prosperity and urbanization of Khwarazmia continues through the Parthian Empire era (247 B.C.E. –224 C.E.), Kushan Empire (30–320 C.E.), and Sassanid Empire (224–651 C.E.).

Hephtelites Invasion: Devastation of Cultures and Arts

Khwarazmia irrigation systems, however, underwent a substantial reduction in the fourth to the sixth centuries, following the collapse of the Kushan Empire and Hephtalites invasion and occupation of Central Asia (484–557 C.E.). Consequently, because of the breakdown of efficient government, the region entered a period of severe economic and social crisis.[4] From 1958, the Historical Institute of the Uzbek Academy of Sciences took over the expedition of the northern Amu-Darya delta.[5] The Khwarazmia expedition led by Gudkova in 1960 to 1962 entered a new stage, yielding spectacular results in Tok-Kala. As a result of Arab invasion of the eighth and ninth centuries C.E., the irrigation system of Khwarazmia was further reduced,[6] but it made a remarkable recovery, accompanied by the setting up of a strong authority of the Samanid Dynasty in the ninth and tenth centuries. There were series of mass migrations of very powerful tribes through Central Asia between the eleventh and thirteenth centuries, but the Mongol invasion, however, destroyed the whole irrigation system.

Khwarazmia was the area where successive waves of sedentary farming people from the Indus valley, Bactra, Parthia, Margiana, Soghdiana, and neighboring lands met and intermingled with similar movements from the pastoral societies of the Eurasian steppes. This Iranian-speaking population gave rise to the civilizations of Central Asia's sedentary and nomadic peoples. There was a gradual transition from a tribal society to the formation of social hierarchy in the context of statehood, which involved introduction and intensification of farming economy, urbanization, consolidation of ethnic communities, and emergence of historical regions with a sedentary culture through first millennium B.C.E.[7]

The transition phase, in which Central Asia advanced from its primeval condition to the formation of an agricultural and pastoral economy, is reflected in the oldest Central Asian text, the Avesta. Khwarazm was the first region in which Zoroaster's teachings spread. "Greater Khwarazmia" social-cultural character includes the entire Aral and Syr Darya belt of the northern Central Asia, which was then a zone of sedentary farming and nomadic pastoral people, stretching from Khwarazmia through Chach and Usrushana to Ferghana in the east.[8] Incidentally, Khwarazmians are also mentioned by Herodotus and Hecataeus of Miletus.

Khwarazmian Iron Age: Urbanization and Fortification

In Khwarazmia during the Iron Age a rapid growth of towns and their fortifications, the construction of city citadels and the development of agriculture by artificial irrigation works are discovered. The most interesting Early Iron Age culture of ancient Khwarazmia was that of Amirabad in the tenth to the eight centuries B.C.E. Dozens more settlements were found in the lower reaches of the former channels of Akcha Darya, the ancient delta of the Amu Darya. The most interesting was Yakka-Parsan II, alongside which were found ancient fields, and the remnants of Amirabad period irrigation system. The old channel passed nearby its banks being reinforced with dykes. More than twenty houses were found in the Yakka-Parsan II settlement.

Large numbers of storage pits were found around the houses, and the entire site is rich in animal bones, pottery, grain-querns, and so on. The houses stood between two canals that merged to the south, all the doors open on to the canals. Rectangular in ground plan, the houses were 90 to 110 square meters in area and had two or three rooms.

The interiors contained many storage pits and post-holes, each with a long fireplace in the center. The major finds were pottery, hand-made with a darkish brown, red, or grayish slip, the shoulders of the bowls being decorated with small crosses, lattice-work, or fir trees. According to S. P. Tolstov, the Amirabad culture dates from the tenth to eighth centuries B.C.E. Other finds include bronze artifacts—a needle with an eye, a sickle with a shaped handle, a bronze arrowhead with a shaft—and stone molds for casting shaft-hole arrowheads and sickles. A bronze sickle, large numbers of grain-querns and the advanced irrigation network and fields together show that agriculture was widely practiced, while the bone finds further indicate that the population was engaged in stock breeding.[9]

Amirabad Culture and Arts

The sedentary farmers and pastoralists of Khwarazmia represent the late Bronze Age Amirabad cultural pattern seen in the Dzhanbas and Yakka-Parsan settlements. At that time Khwarazmians were master craftsmen with settled houses.[10] Khwarazmia develops new forms of economy based on sedentary farming and urban culture with strong central authority and is included in the Achaemenid Empire at the height of its prosperity in the sixth and fifth centuries B.C.E.[11]

The oldest Khwarazmian city, and the key monument of the Achaemenid period, was Kyuzeli-gir. It lay on the left bank of the Amu Darya (Oxus) delta in the Sariamish region. Standing on a natural elevation, roughly triangular in ground-plan, it occupied an area of 25 ha. The city was surrounded by a powerful defensive wall with oval bastions. Its residential district was densely packed with buildings of rectangular unbaked brick and pakhsa. It had an advanced pottery industry, based on the wheel, and art objects of a type common in Scythian/Saka burial complexes of the period have been found.[12] Another early city of the same date, Kalali-gir, was surrounded by triple walls with bastions and had four gates with entrance barbicans and a hill-top palace.[13]

In Khwarazmia, in the eastern part of the south Akcha Darya delta, the agricultural oasis of Dingildzhe dates from the fifth century B.C.E. The eastern part of the site was occupied by a large house with many rooms and the western part by a large courtyard. The site was surrounded by an outer wall 2 meters thick, built of large rectangular unbaked bricks of archaic type. The archeologist who studied the farmstead suggests that it might have been a home for extended family of the district governor. Its inhabitants were engaged in agriculture and cattle breeding, pottery, metal work, and making farm products. Dingildzhe points to the relatively high standard of architecture, building techniques, and design that prevailed in ancient Khwarazmia.[14]

Walled Cities of Ancient Khorazmia—Toprak Kala, Urganj, and Khiva

Centers of Cultural and Artistic Activities & Silk Road Trade

Between the fourth and second centuries B.C.E., initiating stage of the silk road, Khwarazmia had a series of walled cities with strong moats, complex fortifications, and gateway barbicans. They defended farming districts that lay along the silk road caravan routes, and served as centers of crafts, trade, and culture. They include Dzhanbas-kala and Bazar-kala, with precise and regular ground-plans, on the right bank of Hazarasp and Dzhingirbent on the left bank of Amu Darya.[15]

Khwarazmia's ancient cities and fortresses have several characteristic features. They were either built on marshland where the farming population met the steppe, or stood on the major trade routes. Fortresses on the plains, such as Hazarasp, had a regular rectangular ground-plan; smaller fortresses stood on high ground, such as Kalali-gir II, Lesser Kirkkiz, and Burli-kala; and at the foot lay undefended secondary settlements, such as Guldursun, Akcha Gelin, Kunya-uaz, and Toprak-kala. Their size and strength contrasted sharply with the mass of small unfortified settlements in the farming oases.[16]

Fortress of Koy Krylgan Kala

Excavations of one of the ancient capitals of Khwarazmia led to the discovery of the ancient fortress of Koy Krylgan Kala (400 B.C.E.–400 C.E.), which was centered around a circle-shaped castle.[17] The castle was identified as one of the earliest ancient centers for astronomical observations and studies. The town was built in a circle around the fortress. Ancient documents found in the area suggest that the town played a central role in the life of the region in ancient times.

The outstanding structure of ancient Khwarazmia was the great fortified sanctuary of Koy Krylgan Kala of the fourth century B.C.E. to the fourth century C.E. in the southern Akcha Darya delta, on the right bank of Amu Darya. Circular in ground-plan with a diameter of about ninety meters, it consists of a large cylindrical building surrounded at a distance of fifteen meter by a fortress wall. The site has two periods of occupation. The lower floor was divided into two identical halves, suggesting that the structure may have been used as an astronomical observatory, as is suggested by its alignment. The lower floor excavation contained an assemblage of well-formed vessels with red slip, small-stepped altars, and terracotta figurines representing deities of the Khwarazmian pantheon. The upper strata, however, yielded a different series of pottery with light colored slips similar to Kushan-style vessels and coins.[18]

DISTINCTIVE, COMPLEX CULTURE AND ARTS WITH ADVANCED AGRICULTURE AND PASTORAL ECONOMY

The walls of cities, fortresses, and settlements in ancient Khwarazmia were ten to twenty meters high and five to eight meters thick. To strengthen the defenses, supplementary outer walls were built five to twenty meters from the fortress walls, with open ground intervening. Particular attention was given to the gates, which sometimes had additional projecting bastions at the entry, on the corners, and along the sides.[19] There is a striking variety of burial sites in Khwarazmia at this period and a growing influence of the Zoroasterian rite with its ossuary type of burial is clearly discernible. The rich mausoleum complexes from the late second and early first millennia B.C.E. with their monumental architecture and pottery, made by skilled craftsmen at Uygarak, Chirik-Rabat, and Babish-Molla, and continuation of unique architectural entities from the first century B.C.E. to the early Middle Ages suggest a distinctive, complex culture and arts with advanced pastoral economy alongside agriculture.

There were large cities, smaller settlements, a system of fortress strongholds with thick walls and towers, and enormous burial grounds. The irrigation system, using mountain streams and springs, helped develop the agriculture economy. Craftsmen also played an important role in the city life. The powerful defenses of the town, its complex architecture and planning structure, and fine pottery are evidence of the advanced social life and cultural level of the city.[20]

Khwarazmian Calendars and Book Art

Khwarazmia was also famous for its calendars, which were created based on the daily movement of the sun and the moon.[21] Keeping such calendars necessitated stationary observations of the daily movements of the moon and sun and the position of the stars at the vernal and autumnal equinoxes and the summer and winter solstices, which in turn presupposed a thorough knowledge of astronomy. Biruni provides us some information about astronomy in ancient Khwarazmia. He mentions that an astronomer was called akhtar-venik in ancient Khwarazmia. Of course, more extensive information has been preserved about astronomy in the pre-Islamic Persian world beyond Khwarazm.

To clarify this point, one of the very first significant contributors to the development of Arabic literature was Ibn Muqaffa. He was born in Firuzabad to a Zoroasterian family and knew knowledge of Middle Persian (Pahlavi), and went to study Arabic in Basra. He translated from Pahlavi into Arabic such works as the "Khowaday-namak" (Book of Lords), "Ayin-nama," "Mazdak-nama," "Kitab Taj," "Kalila va Dimna," "Risalat al-sahaba" (on the structure of ruling institution), "al-Adab al-Kabir" (on politics and the rules of communication), and "al-Adab al-Sahir" (on morality and ethics).[22]

Migration of Scholars and Artists from Inner Eurasia (Central Asia)

During the reign of Abbasid Caliph al-Mamun (813–833), many scholars from Khwarazm and the rest of Central Asia were forced to move to Baytal Hikma (house of wisdom) in the Shammasiyya district of Baghdad. Abbasid were building their new capital a few miles from Cetisphon, the last Capital of Persian Parthian Empire and Persian Sassanid Empire (231–651). The al Mamun capital in Khorasan was the city of Marv (813–819). While staying for six years in Marv, al Mamun gathered astronomers, mathematicians, and scientists of Central Asia including Khwarazm, Chach, Ferghana, and Khurasan.[23]

One of the most impressive scholars leaving Khwarazm and Central Asia for Baghdad was Muhammad b. Musa Khwarazmi. (Other scholars included Yahya b. Mansur, Khalid b. Abd al-Malik Marwarrudhi, Abbas b. Said Jawaheri, Abu Tayyib Sanadb. Ali, Ahmad b. Muhhamad b. Kathir Farghani, Ahmad b. abd Allah Habash Hasib, and Abd al-Hamid Ibn Turk Khuttali.)

The Shammasiyya district of Baghdad had also a high concentration of translators including Nirizi, Battani, Hajjaj b. Qurra, Ibrahim b. Sami, Husayn b. Ishaq, Umarb. Farrukhan, and Thabit b. Qurra.[24] Central Asia in general and Khwarazm in particular enjoyed a large number of extraordinary, high level educated scholars in early medieval times. Following is a brief analysis of only two of these scholars.

Khwarazmi

M. M. Khwarazmi was a Persian scientist, mathematician, geographer, and cartographer who was born in 780 in Khiva, Khwarazmia. In the field of mathematical geography, his "Kitab Surat al-arz" (Book of the map of the earth) is one of his earliest works creating map of the earth based on seven climes, with additional information on the subject.

He wrote a book on calculations involving restoration and confrontation "al-Mukhtasar fi hisab al-jabr wa moqabala." During the reign of Abbasid caliph al-Mamun, in Bayt al-Hikma, Baghdad, Khwarazmi composed the oldest astronomical tables and the oldest astronomical work which was translated into Latin in medieval Europe. His work focused on lunar anomalies, eclipses, parallaxes, the inclination of the elliptic length of the tropic, and on the sidereal year. He was the first scholar in history to discard the idea of the static universe and strongly upheld the idea of a dynamic universe.

Khwarazmi's Algebra was twice translated into Latin in the twelfth century, by Robert of Chester and then by Gerard of Cremona, and influenced medieval European algebra.[25]

Biruni

The life of the world-renowned Persian historian, geographer, and astronomer, A. R. Biruni (973–1048), reflects the historical events of the late tenth and eleventh centuries in the region. Biruni was born in the city of Kath (Biruni today), Khwarazmia. Eighty of his more than 150 books were devoted to astronomy. Astronomers played a central role in old Khwarazmia during the Sassanian era because they designed calendars and identified the most important days and festivities of the coming year. Central Asia in general and Khwarazmia in particular in the early seventh century was ethnically still largely an Iranian land whose people used various Middle Iranian languages.[26]

During the ninth and tenth centuries a remarkable development of civilization took place in Central Asia, including Khwarazmia. Not only Bokhara the capital of Samanid but also Gurgandzh (Kunya-Urgang) and Khiva were famous centers of sciences, cultures, and arts. By the end of tenth century Khwarazmia was one of the states of Samanid Empire. The Samanid capital was the city of Bokhara. Khwarazmia and Central Asia were enjoying the golden age of the Samanid Empire (815–999) when Biruni was a young man. Meanwhile, Ziyarids State from its capital Gorgan to the south and south-east of the Caspian Sea and Buwayid Empire to the south-west of the Caspian Sea was extending its territory to the shores of the Persian Gulf and Mesopotamia.

There was a military coup against Samanid by one of their slave warriors Mahmud Qaznavi in 999. Because of the turbulences within the region, Biruni left Khwarazmia and Central Asia. Biruni, while wondering and seeking a safe haven, at one point stopped at Ray (an ancient city to the south of Tehran today that had one of the largest libraries in the world). In Ray, Biruni visited Khojandi, an exceptional astronomer who was working with a very large instrument he had built on the mountain above the city. By the year 1000, Biruni was at Gorgan, the capital of Qabus, the king of Ziyarid. Biruni dedicated his book "Chronology" to the king. In his book "Chronology," Biruni refers to seven earlier books which he had written—one on the decimal system, one on astronomical observations, three on astronomy, one on astrolabe, and two on history. In June 1004 Biruni returned to Khwarazmia.

Khwarazmian Music and Dance

Khwarazmia was, in general renowned for its art—its distinctive music and interesting dances.[27] In the eleventh century Khwarazm had a local ruler, Abulabbas Mamun, who was highly educated, he held scholars, poets, and performers in great esteem and loved to play a stringed instrument called "rud." Biruni worked for seven years in Mamun's circle, respected by the local king.[28] Biruni built an instrument at Jurjanniya to observe solar meridian transit and made fifteen observations with the instrument in 1016.

In summer of 1017, Mahmud Qaznavi marched his army into Khwarazmia and took Biruni to his capital Qazna (in Afghanistan today). In Qazna, Biruni made observations which allowed him an accurate determination of its latitude. Biruni observed a lunar eclipse in Qazna, in September 17, 1019. One of the fascinating books written by Biruni is called "Shadows" which he wrote in 1021.

The book includes theoretical and practical arithmetic, summation of series, combinatorial analysis, the rule of three, irrational numbers, ratio theory, algebraic definition, method of solving algebraic equations, geometry, trisection of the angle and other problems which cannot be solved with ruler and compass alone, conic sections, the sine theorem in the plane, and spherical triangle. "Shadows" is an extremely important source for our knowledge of the history of mathematics, astronomy, and physics. Biruni had great contribution to geodesy and geography by introducing the techniques to measure the earth and distances on it, using triangulations. Biruni calculated the radius of earth in the eleventh century, while Europe obtained that in the sixteenth century. Biruni contributions to hydrostatics included some of the first measurements of specific weights and ratios between densities of metals including gold, mercury, lead, silver, bronze, copper, brass, iron, and tin.

Mahmoud Qaznavi invaded India in 1022. Mahmoud took Biruni with to India, and while in India Biruni determined the latitudes of eleven towns in Punjab and Kashmir. Biruni wrote a book, a master piece called "India." The book included Philosophy, religions, customs, systems of writing, mathematics, astronomy, astrology, and the calendar of India.

Mahmud Qaznavi died in 1030 and he was succeeded by his son Masud Qaznavi. Biruni died in Qazna, the capital of Qaznavids, in 1048. Biruni wrote 146 books in his life time. Biruni corresponded with Abu-ali Sina (Avicenna). The eighteen letters that were exchanged between Biruni and Sina included topics on philosophy, astronomy, physics, and discussions on the nature of heat and light. The rule of Qaznavids was relatively short lived. The penetration of the Seljuks from north put an end to Qaznavid rule in 1040.

The Golden Age of Khiva: 1511–1920

As indicated earlier, after parts of Central Asia were massacred by Timur in 1379 and 1388, he decided to rebuild Samarkand as his capital. The golden age of the Timurids emerged, in early fifteenth century, from the city of Samarkand, which was filled with great architecture, art, and literature brought by force from conquered lands especially from Shiraz. The Uzbek Shaibanids occupied large portions of Central Asia in the sixteenth century, and by the end of the seventeenth century three small Uzbek khanates were ruling parts of Central Asia from the cities of Khiva, Bukhara, and Kokand.

The town of Khiva in Khwarazmia was chosen as the capital of the khanate of Khiva and would remain that until 1920. In Khiva, one of the most popular destinations of newly wed couples was (and still is), the Pahlavan Mahmoud Khaneqah and mausoleum.[29] It was a relatively small architectural structure which dominated by brick construction and an intense centralized green-blue ceramic tile dome (1247–1325). One of the major districts of Khiva, known as Ishan Kala, was built in 1788, and another district known as Dishan Kala was added to the town in 1842. By 1804, the descendants of Qongrats, who had ruled the area after the Mongol invasion, once again emerged to rule Khiva.[30]

One of the most influential khans of Khiva was Allah Quli Khan (1825–1842), who ordered the construction of Tash Kauli Palace. The iwan of the palace housed some of the most attractive wood carving in the world. The tall columns, from top to the bottom, were carved with highly detailed and skillful wood working, a variety of curvilinear lines, and abstract patterns.[31] The extensive use of various shades and grades of blue ceramic tiles, enough to cover all the walls of the Tash Kauli Palace, created a strong contrast between warm and cool colors, and contributed more depth to the space. Another impressive construction of the first half of the nineteenth century was the Madraseh of Allah Quli Khan. Symmetrical in structure, with a central arcade entrance, it held two floors of rooms on either side of the central entrance. Pinpointed arches were used extensively throughout the building.

The last series of constructions in Khiva appeared at the time of the Mohamad Rahim Khan II (1863–1873). Mohamad Rahim Khan also built a school, and a hammam (public bath house). The architectural style he chose followed the existing traditions of the area. Dominated by brick construction as it utilizes ceramic tile compositions as the dominant source of decoration, introducing and adding colors, shapes, lines, and creating decorative elements. Located in ancient Khwarazmia, which is presently divided into the Karakalpak region of Uzbekistan and the Tashauz region of Turkmenistan, the city of Khiva was renovated into a walking museum after the Soviet authorities ordered the people living in the old town to vacant their homes. The residents of modern Khiva live in the neighborhoods of the old town.

Khanate of Kokand

To the east of khanate of the Khiva, and khanate of Bokhara, the third small Uzbek khanate came into existence in the eighteenth century. This was Kokand, which throughout its history enjoyed a close relationship with China's Qing Empire. Alim and Umar, the two sons of Nar Buta Beg (1774–1789) established the Kokand khanate. Some of the famous Khans of Kokand include Shir Ali (1842–1842) and the two last independent khans Khudayar and Malla (1845–1875). Conflict within the ruling family and friction with other Uzbek Khanates within the region weakened the Kokand Khanate. In 1875, the Russian Czarist forces occupied Kokand and put an end to its kingdom.

This chapter included a historical analysis of the region of Khwarazmia as one of the oldest urbanized regions of Inner Eurasia (Central Asia) and some of its cultural contributions to the region.

NOTES

1. Mongait, A. L., *Archeology, On the Tracks of the Ancient Khorezmian Civilization of the U.S.S.R.*, Penguin Books, Baltimore, Maryland, 1955, 47.

2. Belenitsky, A., *Central Asia*, The World Publishing Company, Cleveland and New York, 1968, 45.

3. Tolstov, S. P., *Ancient Khorezm*, Moscow, 1948, 14–48.

4. Tolstov, S. P. *On the Tracks of the Ancient Khorezmian Civilization*, Berlin, 1953.

5. Gudkova, A. V., and Yagodin, V. N., *Delta of Amu Darya: Tok Kala*, Moscow, 1968. Also, see: Gudkova, A. V. and Livshitz, V. A., *Inscriptions at Tok Kala*, Moscow, 1967.

6. Tolstov, S. P. *Ancient Khorezm*, Moscow, 1948, 113.

7. Negmatov, N. N., *States in north-western Central Asia*, History of Civilizations of Central Asia, V. II, UNESCO Publishing, 1994, 446. Moscow, 1962, 96–104.

8. Itina, M. A., *The Farmers of Ancient Khorezm*, Moscow/Leningrad, 1968.

9. Tolstov, S. P., *At the Ancient Delta of the Oxus and Yaksarta: Documents found at Toprak Kala*, Moscow, 1962, 96–104.

10. Itina, M. A., *The Farmers of Ancient Khorezm*, Moscow/Leningrad, 1968.

11. Negmatov, N. N., *States in north-western Central Asia*, History of Civilizations of Central Asia, V. II, UNESCO Publishing, 1994, 447.

12. Ibid, 443.

13. Tolstov, S. P., *Scythians of Aral and Khorezm*, XXVth Congress, Vol. III, 1960. Also, See: Tolstov, S. P., and Itina M. A., and Vinogradov, A. V., *On New Exploratrion in Akcha Darya delta, Kokcha, Western Kizil Kum, Toprak Kala, and Syr Darya*, Moscow, 1967.

14. Negmatov, N. N., *States in north-western Central Asia*, History of Civilizations of Central Asia, V. II, UNESCO Publishing, 1994, 446.

15. Ibid, 447.

16. Tolstov, S. P., *Ancient Khorezm*, Moscow, 1948, 114.

17. Nerazik, E. E., *Some questions about the history and culture of ancient Khwarazmian cities in the light of excavations at the Topraq qala site*, Moscow, 1981, 219–27. Also, see: Nerazik, E. E., *Detailed survey of post-Kushan Khorezmian pottery*, Moscow, 1959.

18. Khodzhaniyazov, G., *Fortified cities of Khorezma*, Soviet Archeology, 2, Moscow, 1981, 43–56. Also, see: Nerazile, E. E., and Bulgakov, P. G., History of Civilization of Central Asia, V. III, Ch. 9, *Khwarazmia*, 2000, 209–26.

19. Negmatov, N. N., *States in north-western Central Asia*, History of Civilizations of Central Asia, V. II, UNESCO Publishing, 1994, 449.

20. Khodzhaniyazov, G., *Fortified cities of Khorezma*, Soviet Archeology, 2, Moscow, 1981, 43–56.

21. Akhmedov, A., *Astronomy, Astrology, Observatories and Calendars*, History of Civilizations of Central Asia, V. IV, UNESCO Publishing, 2000, 195–204. Also, see: Tolstov, S. P., *At the Ancient Delta of the Oxus and Yaksarta: Documents found at Toprak Kala*, Moscow, 1962, 136–86.

22. Mushtaq, Q. and Berggren, J. L., *Mathematical Sciences*, History of Civilizations of Central Asia, Vol. IV, UNESCO Publishing, 2000, 177–94. Also, see: Tolstov, P., *Ancient Khorezm—Retracing Ancient Civilizations*, Moscow, 1948.

23. Bosworth, C. E., *Legal and Political Sciences in the Eastern Iranian World and Central Asia in the Pre- Mongol Period*, History of Civilizations of Central Asia, Vol. IV, UNESCO Publishing, 2000, 133–41. Also, see: Mushtaq, Q. and Berggren, J. L., *Mathematical Sciences*, History of Civilizations of Central Asia, Vol. IV, UNESCO Publishing, 2000, 177–94.

24. Akhmedov, A., *Astronomy, Astrology, Observatories and Calendars*, History of Civilizations of Central Asia, V. IV, UNESCO Publishing, 2000, 195–204. Also, see: Bosworth, C. E., *Legal and Political Sciences in the Eastern Iranian World and Central Asia in the Pre- Mongol Period*, History of Civilizations of Central Asia, Vol. IV, UNESCO Publishing, 2000, 133–41.

25. Mushtaq, Q. and Berggren, J. L., *Mathematical Sciences*, History of Civilizations of Central Asia, Vol. IV, UNESCO Publishing, 2000, 177–94.

26. Samian, A.L., *Reason and Spirit in Biruni's Philosophy of Mathematics*, in Reason, Spirit and the Sacral in the New Enlightenment, Vol. 5, Netherlands: Springer, 2011, 137–46. Also, see: Mushtaq, Q. and Berggren, J. L., *Mathematical Sciences*, History of Civilizations of Central Asia, Vol. IV, UNESCO Publishing, 2000, 177–94.

27. Lawergren, B., Neubauer B. E. and Kadyrov M. H., *Music and Musiology, Theatre and Dance*, History of Civilizations of Central Asia, Vol. IV, UNESCO Publishing, 2000, 585–93.

28. Ibid, 585–93.
29. Knobloch, E. *Monuments of Central Asia*, I. B. Tauris Publishers, NY, 2001, p. 81. Also, see: Chuvin P. and Degeorge, G. *Samarkand, Bokhara, and Khiva*, Flummarion, Paris, 1999, pp. 163–222.
30. Knobloch, E. *Treasures of the Great Silk Road*, The History Press, London, 2012, pp. 73–89.
31. Chuvin P. and Degeorge, G. *Samarkand, Bokhara, and Khiva*, Flummarion, Paris, 1999, pp. 163–222.

Chapter Ten

Satrapy of Parthia & Parthian Empire Arts

This chapter includes an analysis of the emergence of the satrapy of Parthia to an empire in the third century B.C.E. Some of the important historical variables contributing to the cultures and arts of Central Asia within this period have been given special attention.

Arsaces, the founder of the Parthian Empire (247 B.C.E. –226 C.E.), proclaimed himself king and expanded his empire to Central Asia and the Near East. Prior to the establishment of the Parthian Empire, descendants of one of the Macedonians, Seleucus, known as Selucids, ruled small, scattered kingdoms in Central Asia for a short period of time. One of the successors of Arsaces was Mithradates I. In 171 B.C. Mithradates established his capital at Nisa outside Ashqabad in present-day Turkmenistan.[1]

Seven Power Houses of The Parthian Empire
The House of Ispahbudhan, of Gurgan
The House of Varaz, of Eastern Khorasan
The House of Karen, of Nahavand
The House of Mihran, of Semnan
The House of Spandiyadh, of Ray
The House of Zik, of Adurbadagan
The House of Suren, of Sakastan

PARTHIAN RETURN TO EURASIAN ART STYLES

The reconquest of Central Asia and the Middle East by Parthians initiated a return to Eurasian art, which was synthesized from Scythian/Saka, Sarmatians, Tokharians, Medes, and Achaemenids ancestors. This was in reaction to a movement imposed by Macedonian invaders imposing Hellenization of art in Central Asia (330 B.C.E. to 247 B.C.E., for 83 years). Hence, a profound modification of art forms, linearism, and realism of a special kind make their appearance in plastic arts and related fields with the return to "frontalism" in sculpture and painting. Many art pieces within this time segment testify to a drastic change of formula, whose success could have been only due to the impact of non-Mediterranean art coming from Eurasia. Parthian arts in Palmyra, Dura, Assur, Hatra, Nisa, and Kuh-i-Khawaja play an active role in recreating a Eurasian art both relying on and reforming its own traditions.[2]

NISA AND PARTHIAN ART

Nisa, the first Parthian capital city, contained a royal palace, necropolis, and several temples. One of the temples was built and supported by four large square piers and round pillars to support the roof. Larger-than-life-size statues of men and women were placed between the pillars. The Soviet scholars who excavated the area found many valuable objects from a royal house adjacent to the royal palace. The objects uncovered included silver gilt statues representing deities and mythological and imaginary beasts, bronze and iron weapons, painted pottery, fluted glass vessels, and ivory objects. The most interesting group of finds included the bronze legs of a throne in the form of a gryphon's claw holding a spray of leaves, and several magnificent rhytons. Rhytons were drinking cups in the shape of an animal horn made of metal or clay. The finest of these were embellished with jewels and polychrome glass incrustations, as well as with friezes depicting human and animal heads.[3] Their bases were made of silver or gold and were often given the shape of an animal's head.

The loveliest rhyton of all was assigned to the second century B.C.E. and included inscriptions in Middle Persian, which was one of the official languages of the Parthian Empire. The majority of the remaining art objects date back to the first century B.C.E. Besides the several Parthian statues found at Nisa, similar Parthian sculptures were found in Khorazmia in modern day Uzbekistan, the Kushan sanctuary of Surkh Kotal in northern Afghanistan, Hatra in northern Iraq, Nimrud in present day eastern Turkey, and Dur Europos and Palmyra in Syria. Statues of comparable size were nevertheless rare at that time. Many statues at Nisa depicted the early kings and queens of the Parthian dynasty.[4]

The Parthians chose Dara (Damghan) for their second capital, then transferred to Ecbatana (Hamadan), and finally settled in Ctesiphon, outside of modern-day Baghdad in central Iraq. The Parthians of Central Asia assimilated the beauty of motion from Scythian/Sakian animal and figurative style, and synthesized their art with Achaemenid elements and local traditions to create a new school of art.[5] A good example of this new Parthian art is a wall painting of a hunt from Dura Europos, in Syria of today, from the second century C.E.

Parthian Art at Palmyra, Dura, Assur, Nisa, and Kuh-i-Khwaja

M. Rostovtzeff was one of the first to bring it to our attention that the art monuments brought to light at Palmyra, Dura, Assur, Hatra, Nisa, and Kuh-i-Khwaja were none other than Parthian art.[6] It bridged the gap between Achaemenid art and that of Sassanian art. Parthian art (247 B.C.E. to 224 C.E.) marks an important stage in the evolution of the arts of Eurasia. Analyzing and interpreting Parthian art, H. Seyrig agrees with Rostovtzeff that the so-called indigenous Oriental art has nothing to do with the West. Because of the vastness of the Parthian Empire and decentralized nature of managing it by its rulers, the Parthian art of Palmyra, Dura, Assur, Nisa, and Kuh-iKhwaja each have their uniqueness, with some similarities and differences.

Parthian Architecture: Elements of Composition and Design

Parthian architecture made significant contributions to architectural design of Eurasia and beyond. These included the development of a dome on squinches and the development of vaulted *iwan* (porch) structures. The Parthian temple of Kangavar, in western Iran today, and the Parthian city complex of Hatra in northern Iraq, are two excellent examples of the new style. In Hatra the main façade of blocks of masonry was stories high and pierced by two large *iwans* roofed with high barrel vaults separated by two smaller rooms.

Parthian Iwan

An *iwan* is a barrel-vaulted rectangular space closed in the back and completely open in front to a courtyard. Since Parthian times *iwans* played an important role in Eurasian monumental and imperial architecture. Though barrel-vaulting had long been known in the region, it was not used to span monumental halls before the Parthian period. Some scholars believe that construction of the Parthian palace of Ashur influenced that of the later Sassanian palace of Ctesiphone (Iwan-e Madain or Taq Kasra) 22 miles southeast of the city of Baghdad, Iraq.

Even more important was the smaller square-vaulted chamber directly behind the southern *iwan*. A different use of *iwans* is seen at Hatra. There each *iwan* is an entity in itself to which others could be added if necessary.

Thus, the palace of Hatra consisted of two *iwans* and their side rooms, which the façade makes appear as a single, unified structure.

Parthian Dome

In Central Asia mudbrick domes have been documented as far back as the third millennium B.C.E. In Khorezm, fourth century B.C.E., domes made of un-fired bricks have been found at Koj Kryl Kala and Balabndy 2. A large domed circular hall 17 meters in diameter was discovered by Italian archeologists from Turin University in the first Parthian capital, Nisa, dated to the first century B.C.E. A domed temple dating from the early Parthian period, with a dome on four arches known as the Rabate Sefid, sits 28 miles southeast of Mashhad, in today's northeast Iran. It is an excellent example of the Parthian style. In Sassanian times, and after establishment of Islam, this design became the square-domed chamber so vital to Persian architecture.[7]

The Parthians made widespread use of stucco, both carved and painted, a technique that was to be more fully developed under the Sassanians and Islamic Persia.

Parthian Paintings from Kuh-I Kwadia, Dura Europos Palmyra and Nisa

Paintings from the famous site of Kuh-I Kwadja illustrate a simplified style but with a certain competence in the grouping and rendering of the human figures. The paintings portray a strong frontal view (one of the major characteristics of Parthian figurative art), with large eyes, and strong combination of contrasting, bright colors. Similar statements can also be made about the two Parthian Mithraic wall paintings in a cave at Dura Europas, on the upper Euphrates. One painting shows Mithra, the sun god, as a mounted hunter, galloping his horse, chasing deer and other animals, in the parade dress of the nobles. Mithra's head and upper body are seen in frontal view. Some scholars believe that the style is a return to a conventional and traditional indigenous art of the region. In the hunting scene, depth and movements are only suggested by the arrangement in diagonal rows of sharply outlined fleeing animals.

There is also a Parthian painting from Dura-Europos (in Syria today), depicting two priests wearing white robes with smaller figures to their sides, created based on the Parthian frontality concept. All human or divine figures face directly forward, with eyes fixed on the spectator. The priests are involved in a ritual; one of them is pouring incense into an incense burner. Strong organic and contour lines define the figurative bodies of the three individuals in the painting, while in contrast the background is dominated by horizontal and vertical lines, defining the structure of the architectural divisions of the interior. Director of the excavation at Dura, M. Rostovtzeff, realized that the art of the first centuries C.E. from Palmyra, Dura Europos, Nisa, and Buddhist art of north India followed the same principles. He called this art style Parthian art.

Parthian Sculpture

The oldest Parthian sculpture is that of four nobles paying homage to Mithradates II at the foot of a cliff in Bistun and dates to about 100 B.C.E. Choosing a site under the bust of Darius, (Achaemenid emperor; under his rule, the empire extended to the largest empire of the ancient world, including 44 percent of the people of the world), the Parthian monarch proclaimed his descent from the illustrious dynasty with which he wished to associate the new Parthian ruling house.

Parthian Queen Sculptures

One of the most impressive Parthian sculptures was excavated in Susa in 1939. It is a marble head of the queen of the Parthian Empire, wife of Emperor Farhad IV, from the first century B.C.E. The queen is wearing a crown with crenellations, resembling those worn in the Achaemenid era. The graceful bust of the queen of Parthia is skillfully created with strong classical characteristics. There are also a number of full figural sculptures of Queens of Hatra at the Bagdad Museum. The two Queen of Hatra sculptures in the Baghdad Museum date to the second century C.E. Parthian frontality style is implemented, combined with an extremely detailed rendering of the queen's costume. By the late first century C.E. and early second century C.E., the Parthian capital was moved to Mesopotamia and the capital of Ctesiphon.

The most impressive free-standing sculpture of the Parthian era is an oversized figure of a Parthian warrior-prince, which was found in the ruins of a temple at Shami on the plateau of Malamirin in the mountain region of Khuzestan. The broad-shouldered Prince is wearing a Parthian costume and standing in a frontal posture. The figure stands with legs slightly spread. The feet, in boots, act as a base for the legs. The rest of the body is proportionally heavy. The prince wears a jacket with smooth borders, probably of leather, and a belt accentuates the waist. Details such as the eyes, eyebrows, moustache, short beard, and hair were engraved. The date of the sculpture (second century C.E.) is indicated both by the posture and by the style of the figure. It almost seems as if the effectiveness of the pose was recognized as a good fit for the representation of a powerful personage.

Similarities, however, are noted with the head of two rulers from Hatra, which belong to the same period. The two Hatra ruler sculptures are both displayed at the Baghdad Museum. One of the men, with a crown or highly decorated hat, is a Parthian king. The other sculpture, possibly a young prince, has a beard and mustache, displaying also a peculiar hair style popular at his time. These two Parthian sculptures both display a taste for technical refinement. Besides strong facial expressions, there is a lingering influence of Achaemenid art. These sculptures, obviously the work of skillful professional sculptors, convey a sense of spiritual value and a strong notion of naturalism and realism.

The Treasure of Tilla Tepe

One of the most fascinating discoveries from the Parthian era was made in Tilla Tepe in northern Afghanistan in 1979. A collection of about 20,000 gold ornaments was found in six graves belonging to five women and one man. The ornaments dated back to the first century B.C.E. They included coins, necklaces set with gems, belts, medallions, and crowns made of gold, turquoise, and lapis lazuli.

The site was identified as a Scythian/Parthian royal burial ground, which contained silver coins from the reign of Parthian king Mithradates II (122–88 B.C.E.) and gold coins from the era of the Parthian king Gotarzes I (95–90 B.C.E.). These artifacts were interspersed with items originating from much farther away, including Chinese bronze mirrors, Indian decorated ivory plates, and gold coins (found in tomb number three) depicting the Roman emperor, Tiberius, in profile view. These finds demonstrate that the first intercontinental trade route, known as the Silk Road, was already active and thriving over two thousand years ago.[8]

Parthian Decorative and Applied Arts

One of the most common characteristics of Parthian decorative arts is the animal-shaped handle. Many objects have handles decorated in the shape of an animal, especially snow leopards or panthers. There is strong notion of a naturalism, expressed especially in creating the head of the animal. There are also series and sequences of small clay figurines and plaques of humans and animals that seem like descendants of prehistoric figurines covered in this text. The figurines' quality varies from some fairly naturalistic and elegant examples to some others not so appealing. Some of the small figurines discovered in tombs and funerary sites were identified as deities.

Nihavand Treasure

Nihavan Treasure, known as Treasure of Karen Pahlavs, was discovered in 1927. Karen family, centered in Nihavand, was the most powerful family within the Zagros Mountain area, and one of the strong allies of the Parthian royal family. A large portion of this treasury is at the British Museum.

Parthian Pottery

The Parthians took considerable interest in the decorative arts. The shapes of pottery varied from place to place. Parthian amphoras from Mesopotamia have large handles and a wealth of ornamentation. At Susa, decoration is replaced by incised designs, while the handles are reduced to small rings placed at the end of the Parthian era on the shoulders of the vessel. A special green glaze, largely composed of cupric oxide, made its appearance in Susa. It was used exclusively for the bowls resting on three small shell-shaped feet. Parthian ceramists manufacture glazed rhytons with molded ornaments and others in ordinary earthenware. [9]

Hellenistic Artifacts

Trade played a central role in the rise of the four ancient empires of Parthia, China, Rome, and Kushan, all of which enjoyed a great deal of prosperity through the exchange of goods and ideas. Many Central Asian cities were located at the heart and along the route of this intercontinental trade route—the Silk Road. By the year 79 C.E., however, the Roman forces led by Emperor Titus occupied the Holy Land, destroyed the temple of Jerusalem, and looted its treasury back to Rome. Since Augustus declared himself the premier emperor of Rome in the first century C.E., Roman forces expanded the borders of their empire from Scotland to the northern shore of Africa, annexing Spain, Gaul, Central Europe, Greece, Egypt, parts of the Near East, and all the islands of the Mediterranean Sea. The Roman Empire reached the zenith of its power under the leadership of the emperors Trajan and Hadrian in the second century C.E. The only force halting Roman military expansion was the Parthian Empire.

Roman forces suffered one of their major losses in the battle of Carrhae in 53 B.C.E.[10] The Roman commander, Crassus, and 20,000 Roman soldiers were killed in this battle. The Parthian forces led by their commander, Suren, took 10,000 Roman soldiers as prisoners of war and relocated them to the Parthian province of Margiana. This region corresponds to present-day southern Turkmenistan, Uzbekistan, Tajikestan, northeast of Iran, and northern Afghanistan.

The Roman prisoners were integrated into the Parthian culture, married native wives, and later served as Parthian soldiers, protecting the trade routes that traversed through Central Asia.[11] Apparently, these Romans built a city in the area. The ancient city of Merv had a concentration of Roman soldiers, and in a cave outside the city, Roman writings were found on a wall. A unit within the Roman army that fought in Carrhae originated in the Roman colonies of Syria and Greece. Some artifacts found from the excavations in the region have been identified as Greco-Roman or Hellenistic.

This chapter includes an analysis of the emergence of the satrapy of Parthia to an empire supporting decentralization and pluralism between the third century B.C.E. and third century C.E. Some of the important historical variables contributing to the cultures of Central Asia within this period are given special attention. The following chapter includes an analysis of a powerhouse named Sassanids to the south and south-west of Central Asia between the third and seventh centuries.

NOTES

1. Koshelenko, G. A. and Pilipko, V. N., *Parthia,* History of Civilizations of Central Asia, V. II, UNESCO Publishing, 1994, 131–50.

2. Hopkins, C. *The discovery of Dura-Europos*. New Haven: Yale University Press, 1979. Also, see: Cumont, F. Francis, E. D., ed., trans. (1975), The Dura Mithraeum, in Hinnells, John R. (ed.), Mithraic studies: Proceedings of the First International Congress of Mithraic Studies, Manchester UP, 1975, pp. I.151–214. Also, see: Francis, E. D., Mithraic graffiti from Dura-Europos, in Hinnells, John R. (ed.), Mithraic studies: Proceedings of the First International Congress of Mithraic Studies, Manchester University Press, 1975 pp. II.424–45.

3. Ghirshman, R., *Iran: Parthian and Sassanians*, London: Thames & Hudson, 1962, 15–118.

4. Koshelenko, G. A. and Pilipko, V. N. *Parthia*, History of Civilizations of Central Asia, V. II, UNESCO Publishing, 1994, 131–50.

5. Ibid, pp. 131–50.

6. Rostovtzeff, M. I., *Dura-Europos and Its Art* (Oxford University Press), 1938.

7. Ghirshman, R., *Iran: Parthian and Sassanians,* London: Thames & Hudson, 1962, 15–18.

8. Sarianidi, V. I., *The Treasure of Golden Hill*, American Journal of Archeology, V. No. 2, Apr. 1980, 125–31.

9. Ibid, pp. 125–31.

10. Kia, A., *Central Asia: Rediscovering a Cultural Treasury*, Central & Southwest Asian Studies Program, Anthropology Department, the twelfth monograph in the

contributions to Anthropology Series, (three articles), The University of Montana Press, 2010.

11. Plutarch, *Parallel Lives*, translated by Bernadotte Perrin, Loeb Classical Library, 1916, 12–35.

Chapter Eleven

Inner Eurasian Art Schools of the East

The following historical analysis reveals the unifying as well as differentiating factors and variables in the art centers and schools, as well as the successive phases and trends of painting within the eastern parts of the Central Asia.

The first phase of painting in Central Asia is clearly of Scythian/Saka inspiration. During 700 BC to 300 BC the whole of Central Asia formed a peripheral area within the Scythian/Saka-Tokharian sphere of influence.[1] This classical background synthesized ideas and elements from Achaemenid, and Hellenistic, traditions as well as the School of Gandhara (that flourished in northwest of India), and went on to play one of the major dimensions of the future evolution of Central Asian art. Following is an analysis of the rich variety of styles and iconography initiated by the artists who gave material embodiment to a spiritual world, in the midst of warrior and trading communities operating in the heart of Eurasia.

BACKGROUND

European scholars and explorers such as Sven Hedin,[2] Aural Stein,[3] and Albert von Le Coq[4] have written extensively on the prehistoric Indo-European mummified bodies discovered in the eastern parts of the Eurasian steppe and the western parts of the Altai Mountains. They did not, however, pay any attention to the mummies of Xinjiang.

In the late 1980s, Chinese scholars resumed excavation of some of the archaeological sites of Xinjiang province. Two experts, Dolkon Kamberi and Wang Binghua, conducted extensive field work in the area and discovered a number of additional mummies. Since the mid-1980s, hundreds of ancient mummies around the cities of Khotan, Niya, Qiemo, Kumul, Kroran, Turfan, and Loulan have been unearthed.

The C^{14} testing conducted by Chinese scholars has identified the origin of some of these mummies as ranging between 4,000 to 2,000 years ago. The Grande Dame of these ancient wonders is a female from 3800 B. C. E. known as "The Beauty of Loulan," a woman with reddish hair and unique fabric covering her body.[5] Another of the well-preserved mummies of the first group is known as "The Cherchen Man," distinguished by his long brown hair and sophisticated clothing.[6] This earliest group of mummies are all Caucasoid and their DNA matches closely with the Bronze age population of the Eurasian steppe who lived in a vast region extending from the Altai Mountains to the shores of the Black Sea. Han Kangxin, who has examined 302 of these mummies, has confirmed the similarities of the earliest mummies of Xinjiang with the other mummies unearthed in other regions of Eurasia.[7]

Most recently, in Yanbulaq, on the edge of the Taklemakan Desert, in an ancient cemetery, twenty-nine mummies were discovered. The C^{14} dating identified the origin of these mummies as between 1100 B. C. E. and 500 B. C. E. This second group of mummies included twenty-one Mongoloid mummies, and eight Caucasoid. This indicates that by this time, the Xinjiang region contained both Mongoloid and Caucasoid populations, and even a mixture of the two groups. The DNA from the second group confirms this conclusion.[8]

Xiang'nu & Yuezhi (Yueh-chih)

In his writings, Herodotus refers to a seventh century B. C. E. mass migration of the Scythians from the east, which resulted in their invasion and occupation of southern Russia. He refers to those Scythians who remained around the Altai Mountains as the Detached Scythians. Some scholars suggest that the Yuezhi (Yueh-chih) people mentioned in Chinese history books are the Scythians who emerged many centuries later as the ancestors of Tokharians and Kushanids.[9] The Chinese historian Sima Qian mentions that until the advent of the third century B. C. E., Yueh-chih and the Tung Hu tribes were the dominant powers of the eastern parts of Central Asia.[10]

Xiang'nu Empire and Chinese Historiography: Ban Gu & Sima Qian

Mongolia and Dzungaria in prehistoric times were inhabited by tribes such as Huns (Hsiung-nu), Hu, Tung Hu (Eastern Hu), Hsi Hu (western Hu), and Hsien-pi. According to two Chinese historians, Ban Gu[11] (d. A.D. 92) and Sima Qian[12] (d. 86 B. C. E.), a powerful confederation of twenty-four tribes was established to the northwest of China, known as Xiang'nu (Hsiang'nu or Huns). For over a century the emperors of China sent annual gifts of silk, fabrics, handicrafts, rice, gold, and money to Xiang'nu, as bribes to prevent the Huns from invading China.

In the second century B.C., Chinese Emperor Han Wudi (141 B. C. E. –87 B. C. E.) embarked on a series of campaigns against Xiang'nu. He sent an envoy to the king of the Yuezhi, to the northwest of China, to form an alliance against the Xiangnu.[13] Instead of an alliance, however, the emperor received a report that the king of Yuezhi had been killed in a war against the Xiangnu. According to Chinese sources, the Yuezhi tribe split into three groups: one group fled to Tibet, and the second group entered the Parthian Empire from northeast. The third group of the Yuezhi headed west toward Europe.[14]

In 93 A.D., the Chinese alliance with eight of the Xiang'nu southern tribes defeated the Hun tribes, and pushed them westward. Hunic tribes migrated from Central Asia to eastern and central Europe. Led by Attila in 445 A.D., they took Gaul and Rome. The death of Attila in 453 A.D., and the internal conflict that ignited following his death, weakened the Huns.[15]

The economy of the Huns was based on herding, and as with the other nomadic groups in Central Asia, their animals included horses, sheep, cows, goats, camels, and yaks. Trade played an important role in their everyday life, but some of the artifacts found in their kurgans are identified as war trophies.

Art of Bronze Age

The satrapy (state) of Bakhtaran (Bactra) merges to an empire in the first century A.D., supporting the birth of Mahayana Buddhism which had profound influences on the Central Asian cultures and arts. A branch of the Yeuzhi tribes composed partially of Tokharians or Asiani Scythians was pushed from northwest China, by the Huns, toward the southwestern regions of Central Asia.[16] Upon settling in the southern and south-western areas of Central Asia, and expanding into an empire, the mobile Scythian Empire emerged as the Kushan state.

The Kushan Empire (AD 30–AD 320)

The Kushan Empire was one of the four major powers of ancient times along with Parthia, China, and Rome. It included (present day) Afghanistan, northeastern Iran, southern Uzbekistan, Tajikestan, Turkmenistan, Pakistan, and northern India.[17] On the shores of the Yamura River in India, the Kushans established their southern-most cultural capital, Mathura. Surkh Kotal, Bagram—their summer capital—and Bamiyan in Afghanistan were among the empire's most important cities.

Surkh Kotal Art School

Surkh Kotal was located in the Kunduz Valley on the main road leading from Kabul to Mazar-e Sharif, in northern Afghanistan. Its buildings rose up a hill and were surrounded by two lines of defenses, which followed its contours. The most spectacular site within the enclosure was a complex temple, to which an immense stairway led. The temple faced an impressively large courtyard and included human figures rendered in a manner that recalled the Scytho-Parthian school of Mathura. The building's plan followed Achaemenid palaces built in Iran a few hundred years earlier.[18]

A French excavating team identified Surkh Kotal as an early Kushan complex, possibly a Zoroasterian temple, belonging to the first half of the second century A.D., prior to Emporor Kanishka's conversion to Buddhism.[19] Kushan royalty converted to Buddhism possibly in the second half of the second century, and Afghanistan remained one of the centers of this religion until the arrival of Islam in the seventh century C.A. Afghanistan was once a treasure of excavation sites. A large portion of the artifacts discovered, however, were destroyed during the many wars that have engulfed Afghanistan in the last four decades. In the late 1990s, during the Taliban occupation, 25,000 art objects were destroyed, including the large Buddha sculptures in Bamyan.

Buddhist Art of Central Asia: 32 Major and 80 Minor Artistic Figural Compositions of Buddha

Bamyan became the cultural capital of Buddhism in the fourth century C.A. Immense statues of Buddha representing him as Locatarra, the Lord of the World, were cut in the rock, at the eastern and western gates of this city in today's Afghanistan. Surrounding the statues were hundreds of caves, which at one point were used as the cells and sanctuaries for Buddhist monks. Some of the earliest Buddhist images were discovered in these caves. Thirty-two major and eighty minor figural compositions initiated in Bamyan, Begram, and Gandhara, to the southeast of this area, travelled eastward to China, Korea, and Japan, giving rise to major divisions of the religion, including Esoteric, Pure Land, and Zen Buddhism.

Buddhism moved across Central Asia to conquer the Far East. Siddhartha Gautama, the founder of Buddhism, was born in 560 B. C. E. among the foothills of the Himalayas. According to the Buddhist view, the center of the universe was a mountain, Meru, from the top of which rose the various levels of the heavens. This towering mountain was surrounded by seven circular, concentric chains of mountains, each separated by one of the seven oceans. Beyond these was the great ocean, containing the four island continents, one in each of the four regions of space, with the southernmost, the island of

Jumbudvipa, being the realm of humans. This entire universe was surrounded by a huge wall of rock. The heights of Mt. Meru included the residence of the four rulers of the cardinal points and the thirty-three principal gods.[20]

Buddhist temples and Christian churches were found in various parts of Central Asia. The Buddhist temple discovered at the town of Krasnaya Rechka, thirty-five kilometers from Bishkek, the capital of Kyrgyzstan today, was one of the best examples of the Buddhist architecture.[21]

The excavation conducted under the supervision of A. N. Bernshtam, P. N. Kozhemyako, K. M. Baipakov, and V. D. Goryacheva revealed Sogdian castles and urban settlements with interior frescoes and other art work. A twelve meter high statue of Buddha was found within the temple. In Ak Beshim town, eight kilometers south-west of Tokmak, excavations were conducted by L. R. Kyzlasov in 1953 and 1954, and A. P. Zyablin in 1955 through 1958. A seventh century church with a cemetery beside it was unearthed. In 1953, not too far from the church, a Buddhist temple from the same period was found with sitting statues of Buddha. In the seventh century writings of a Buddhist monk known as Tripitaka, there are references to the Ak Beshim, near Tokmak.

Khotanese Art School

To the east of Central Asia, in the present-day province of Xinjiang, the city of Khotan, which served as the capital of jade, was one of the major trade centers of the region.[22] Since early ancient times, Khotanese and Sogdian merchants transported the much-sought-after precious stone, jade, to the cities of China. Jade could be found in two dominant shades and grades of pastel white and light green. In Chinese shamanism, and Taoism, it was believed that anyone possessing or wearing jade would have long life.

Khotan was identified as one of the first cities in which silk was produced outside China. According to Chinese sources, the prince of Khotan, who married a Chinese princess, sent an envoy with a message to her, saying: "the kingdom to which you are traveling does not have any silk production. Bring some of the silk producing secrets when you come to Khotan." Hiding the cocoons in her clothing and crown, the young princess slipped them out of her home and introduced the wonders of the luxurious fabric to Khotan, which today has one of the oldest and most sophisticated silk industries in the world.[23]

In the third century B.C.E., when the son of the first Indian emperor to convert to Buddhism, Ashoka, was ruling Khotan, the Uyghurs settled in the Lake Balkhash area, to the north-east of the modern-day Xinjiang province of China. By the first century C.E., the Khotanese kingdom had expanded to include 13 smaller kingdoms, and was the dominating power in Central Asia.

Conquered by the Chinese in 61 C.E., the Uyghurs struggle for their independence continued. Ban Chao, the Chinese general, conquered Khotan and the kingdom remained under Chinese rule until 105 C.E. Struggling for independence, Khotan enjoyed autonomy until 127 C.E. Chinese forces occupied the kingdoms of Khotan, Kashgar, and Yarkand between the years 127 C.E. and 132 C.E. Meanwhile, in 220 C.E., Uyghurs, defeated by the Kyrghyz, entered Tarim Basin in the Xinjiang area.[24]

Chang Yen-yuan, a ninth-century Chinese historian, states that the influence of Sogdiana or Iran must have brought to China that remarkable painter, Ts'ao Chung-ta. His peculiar style was familiar to the Chinese. Essentially, in his paintings of figures, the clothes seemed to cling to the body as though they were bathing in them, or the figures had wet clothes on. The paintings of Khotan School gives evidence that they have absorbed Indian, Sassanian, Chinese, Sogdian, and Khwarazmian influences. Out of synthesizing a number of different influences, a new painting style emerged, which was implemented on the walls of many architectural entities, including Domoko group, to the east of Khotan. From this style derived the geometric simplifications of anatomical details noticeable at Kucha.

Some of the greatest Khotanese painters worked in China in the late Sui and Tang dynasties and left a deep impression on Chinese critics. According to Hsuan-tsang, the family name of the king of Khotan was Wei ch'ih. There were three painters in the family, one of whom, Wei ch'ih Chia-seng, remained at home. Po-chih-na arrived in China in the last years of the Sui dynasty (589 C.E. –617 C.E.) and was there ennobled. He painted Buddhist themes, flowers, an exotic composition in a free and expressive style. His son Wei ch'ih I-seng was sent to China by the king of Khotan. He became famous for his murals, scrolls, and flower combination pieces.

Khotan was a popular destination for Chinese monks, who stayed in the city and gathered up Buddhist documents and sources, writing extensively of the beauty of Khotan, its prosperity and diligent people.[25] Meanwhile, Mahayana Buddhism expanded from Khotan into Kucha, the capital of music and home to an astonishing variety of produce, and into Turfan, the largest city of the Silk Road.[26] By 744 C.E., the Uyghur court declared Manichaeism as the state religion of their kingdom. One intriguing and peculiar personality who tried to synthesize the teachings of Buddha, Christ, and Zoroaster in his gospel was Mani.

Miran Art School

A group of wall paintings discovered in Miran, on the southern route of the Silk Road in Xinjiang, may be considered a product of this classical formula of ancient times, especially as a product of the Gandhara School. (That school accounts for much of the iconography and certain points of style peculiar to the earliest wall paining at Dunhuang.) Classicizing trends were to a large extent the result of the spread of Buddhism eastward, along the Silk Road. The intensification of the influx of these trends took place at the time when the Kushan (30 C.E. –320 C.E.) Empire was dominant in Gandhara area.[27]

Miran paintings date to the third or fourth century C.E. The paintings are done by the same master, or a group of artists, possibly a master and his pupils. Miran paintings display unique classical technique, not only in treatment of drapery but also in the skillful use of chiaroscuro, done by means of applying a light clear coat of paint over the treatment of drapery. Graceful Miran portraits focus on reflecting classical poses and gestures with facial characteristics of large eyes, curved eyebrows, and unique hairstyles. This new wave of painting in Central Asia begins with a group of works remarkable for the skill with which perspective and illusionistic effects are handled.

Miran paintings introduce into Central Asia perspective techniques of sufficient complexity and refinement to leave their distinct mark on the subsequent evolution of painting. Effects of color and light here are used technically in the service of a complicated system of optical illusion. This Central Asian aesthetic conception treating light and color with its symbolic values and mystical speculations of Indian and Iranian origin derived largely from Buddhist thought.[28]

In works of that initial phase in Central Asia, the classical element, the extent to which it was transmitted by way of Iran and Gandhara, ensured the absolute pre-eminence of the human figure. Favored by the partiality of Buddhist art for edifying narrative themes, it was long maintained and does not disappear even when the scene changes from the story of Buddha's lives to a more complex plan of paradise and great miracles.[29] The Iranian element contributed, maintaining the primacy of the human figure, which held its ground even under the impact of Chinese influences. Inherent in Buddhist thought and inseparable from the art it inspired, that primacy remained a constant unifying characteristic, even in the western area of Central Asia. Unlike the Chinese tendency to reduce the role of the human figure, in Central Asian art, proportions given to figures have a symbolic value, the leading figure (e.g., Buddha), invariably is created larger than the others.

M. A. Stein was the first archaeologist to systematically study the ruins at Miran in 1907. The many artifacts found in Miran demonstrate the extensive and sophisticated trade connections these ancient towns had with places as far away as the Mediterranean Sea. Archaeological evidence from Miran shows the influence of Buddhism on artistic work as early as the first century B.C.E. Early Buddhist sculptures and murals excavated from the site show stylistic similarities to the traditions of Central Asia and North India.

Satrapy of Bakhtaran (Bactra) and Kushan Empire

Bamyan Art School

Bamyan was the most important religious and monastic center of Hinayana Buddhism,[30] which flourished from the first to the seventh century. It was a prosperous caravan town on the road from Bactra to Taxila, famous for its colossal statues of Buddha. The art of painting was practiced on a large scale at Bamyan and it was here that Mani received his education in the arts. The surviving painting works reveal a combination of various styles and trends. Classical traditions within Buddhism have been fused with considerable Iranian and Indian elements. Many scholars assume that Bamyan paintings are largely the result of a combination of Buddhism with Iranian art, produced by artist-monks of different schools. Bamyan paintings, often enriched by flowery twining around the figures, reflect the joy in floral decorations and a rich of variety of colors. The paintings are based on lively drawings, intelligent stylization, and a touch of refinement in the decorative structure.[31]

Bamyan rose to greater prominence when two immense statues of Buddha were built in the fourth century, representing him as Locatarra, the Lord of the World. Statues were cut in the rock, at the eastern and western approaches of the town.[32]

Kucha Art School

Artistic development of Kucha is closely connected with neighboring monasteries and rock-cut shrines of Kizil, Qumtura, Qarashahr, and Tumsuq, sites of caravan centers proper.[33] The autonomous nature of Kucha and its surroundings is identified to be based on the hospitality it extended to Iranian exiles fleeing the Arab invasion of Sassanian Empire (241 C.E. –651 C.E.) in the middle of the seventh century. Kucha became the capital of the exiled Sassanian royalty in 658 C.E., supported by the Tang (618 C.E. –906 C.E.) dynasty of China, with its capital in Chang'an (Xian, today). In spite of strong foreign influences from Iranian and Chinese parties, Kucha painting style remained distinct from the others in its conception and treatment of space.[34]

Three Distinct Styles Within Kucha Paintings

There are three distinct styles within Kucha paintings. Between the first and second styles of Kucha paintings, there is a real difference, a sort of bilingualism, not only in regard to the choice of colors, but also as far as treatment of space and volume are concerned. There is also a strong notion of symbolism, and movement away from reality in the direction of allegory, corresponding to the movement of Buddhist thought toward mysticism. Developments in religious thinking, social structure, and extension of Persian and Chinese influence reflect major modifications within the vocabulary of painting of Kucha. Another distinct aspect of the second style of Kucha figurative paintings is elongation of the figures, resulting in changing proportions of the body, idealized in the Indian manner.[35]

A third phase of Kucha painting is identified, which combined currents from Tang's China with earlier styles. Here, however, the palette with its forceful, brilliant colors, with greater liberties taken in portraying figures in front, three-quarters, or profile view and certain effects in perspective, all show how the taste of Kucha still persisted in creations of the new style.

Kucha paintings are one of the high points of all Central Asian art. Along with selected selection of other schools, they constitute some of the richest, most complex figurative art of the region.[36]

Kizil Art: Caves of One Thousand Buddhas

Seventy miles west of Kucha on the northern bank of the Muzat River, there are a set of over three hundred Buddhist rock-cut caves. More than half of the caves are still intact, while a new series of caves within the area were discovered only in the 1990s.[37]

The Kizil caves were first discovered and explored in 1902–1904, by the Otani expedition that included two Japanese scholars, T. Watanabe and K. Hori. A severe earthquake in the area disrupted the explorations.[38]

A. Grunwedel led a German expedition to the Kizil caves (1905–1907). Some of the Kizil mural paintings were moved to Berlin by the German team, and are now displayed at the Museum of Asian Art. Some of the murals moved from Kizil now can be found in museums in Russia, Japan, Korea, and the United States.

Kizil Different Styles of Mural Painting

Scholars have divided the mural paintings of Kizil into three general groups. The earliest cave paintings are identified with the Tokharian kingdom of Kucha and its so-called Indo-Iranian Style I.

A. Grunwedel's analysis concludes that the Indo-Iranian style derives from the art of Gandhara. Carbon-14 dating traces the first style of the Kizil caves to the years 300 C.E. to 500 C.E. The murals of this style have dark backgrounds, with green and orange colors and natural shading.

The second style of Kizil mural Indo-Iranian Style II, derives from Sassanian art and is identified by a strong contrast of light and dark, greens, browns, oranges, and lapis-lazuli blue pigments. Grunwedel's analysis concluded that the cultural and artistic activities of the Kizil area came to a halt by the year 800 A.D.[39]

The last or third style of Kizil mural paintings is Uyghur-Chinese style, which appears in only two caves in Kizil. Despite all the destruction, damages, and lootings, there are over five thousand square meters of wall painting remaining in this treasury of human creativity called Kizil.[40]

Turfan School of Art

Turfan came into direct contact with the rest of Central Asia in the first century C.E. It developed culturally when caravans ran through the region. It attracted some of the traffic in the earlier stages, later however, it became the main artery of communication with the west.[41]

The first painting style of Turfan, just like Kucha, was dominated by classical style, with Iranian and Indian characteristics. In the year 640 C.E., the Tang defeated K'iu, the ruling dynasty of the region. Tang realistic style left a deep imprint in the area. Then came Manichaeism and resumption of Iranian style of painting, particularly in the art of miniature painting.

With the introduction of Nestorian Christianity, there were additional Iranian, Syrian, and western elements added to the Turfan painting compositions. The second wave of Buddhism in the seventh and eighth centuries added harmonious iconographical and calligraphical elements to the paintings of the Turfan area. Brilliant works of art were created in the region, with various historical factors affecting them, and their various components mingling and being fused with fuller intensity than elsewhere. After a short Tibetan interlude, the whole area became part of the Uyghur Empire. The ancient capital of Kao-ch'ang (or Qoco), was now called Idiqut-shahri.[42]

Qoco offers the most complete evidence of Manichaean and Nestorian influences, and also of the various phases of the interaction of Chinese and Iranian cultures, especially in architecture. The areas various phases of complex paintings of the area are rendered differently from one locality to another. Monastic centers of the area such as Bazaklik and Muurtuq show different degrees of influence from some of the involved sources. From Bazaklik wall paintings, Uyghur princes and princesses are found in worshipping posture, each carrying in their hand a flower as an offering, with an inscription showing their identity. They are draped in loose-fitting garments.

In the Turfan area, the art of portraiture continued to be cultivated by some of the highly gifted artists, who carried it down to quite a late period. Landscape painting of the Turfan area reveals a different spirit. In general, the occasional rendering of landscape departs reality for fairyland, and the stylized mountains follow Sassanian models, possibly by way of Kucha. A little more realism sometimes appears in trees or rocks, most of all in animals.

It is undoubtedly Buddhist fantasy further developed in Central Asia, which inspired the creations in which typological and iconographic elements from many civilizations meet and mingle.[43]

Between 850 C.E. and the beginning of the thirteenth century, Uyghurs enjoyed a great deal of prosperity, expanding their kingdom into a large empire, from the shores of the Caspian Sea to the heart of China. Manichaeism was the dominating religion of the Uyghur kingdom in Xinjiang until the beginning of the eleventh century. In 1005, Yusef Qadr, Khan of the Karakhadids, forced Uyghurs and Khotanese to convert to Islam. The rise of the threatening Mongols in the Gobi Desert (1220s C.E. onward) forced Uyghurs to join their alliance under leadership of Ghenghiz Khan.

Some of the major art schools of the Eastern part of Eurasia were analyzed and discussed in this chapter. The emergence of Mahayana Buddhist Art in Central Asia and its domination to the south and east of this region was also analyzed in this chapter. Some of the significant historical events of the Kushans era and the consequences of events and their impact on Central Asian cultures and arts were also discussed. The following chapter includes an analysis of Central Asian Bronze Age and urban civilization boom in southern Central Asia.

NOTES

1. Beckwith, C. I., *Empires of the Silk Road: A History of Central Eurasia from the Bronze Age to the Present,* Princeton University Press, 2009.

2. For more information on Hedin S. and explorations in Central Asia, see: *Across the Gobi Desert,* New York, Greenwood, 1968; *Riddles of the Gobi Desert,* London: Routledge, 1933; and *My Life as an Explorer,* New York, Boni and Liveright, 1925.

3. For more information on Stein, M. A., Explorations in Central Asia, see: *Sand-buried Ruins of Khotan,* Asian Educational Services, 2000; *On Ancient Central Asian Tracks,* Chicago: University of Chicago Press, 1974; *Innermost Asia,* Oxford: Clarendon Press, 1928; *Ruins of Desert Cathay,* London, Macmillan And Co. 1912; *Ancient Khotan,* Oxford, Oxford University Press, 1907; *Preliminary Report on a Journey of Archeological and Topographical Explorations in Chinese Turkestan,* London: Eyre and Spottiswoode, 1901.

4. Le Coq, A. von, *Buried Treasures of Chinese Turkestan: An Account of the Activities and Adventures of the Second and Third German Turfan Expedition,* London: G. Allen, 1928.

5. Barber, E. W. *The Mummies of Urumchi,* W.W. Norton & Co., New York, 1999, 71–88.

6. Ibid, 57–68.

7. Mair, V. H. *Mummies of Tarim Basin,* Archeology, 48, 2, 1995, 28–35.

8. See: Sima Qian, *Shih chi,* Chapter 123, Vols. 46–48, B. Watson, New York, Columbia University Press, 1961.

9. Herodotus, The History of Herodotus, *The Fourth Book: Melpomene*, translated by G. Rawlinson, New York, Tudor Pub. Co., 1956, 204–11.

10. Enoki, K., Koshelenko, G. A. and Haidary Z., *The Yuech-chih and their migrations in History*, History of Civilization of Central Asia, UNESCO Publishing, Vol. II, 1994, 171–90.

11. Kangxin, H., *The Study of Human Skeletons from Xinjiang*, China, Sino-Platonic Papers, 1994, 51.

12. According to Chinese bone inscriptions, the famous shih-chi (historical record) by Sima Qian, Mongolia, and Dzungaria were inhabited by the tribes such as: Huns (Hsiung-nu), Hu, Tung Hu (Eastern Hu), Hsi Hu (western Hu), and Hsien-pi.

13. Ban Gau, *The History of the Former Han Dynasty*, translated by H. Dubbs, London, 1938, 27–42.

14. Yu, Y., *The Hsiung-nu*, The Cambridge History of Early Inner Asia, Cambridge University Press, 1994, 120–51.

15. Yong, M. and Yutang, S., *The Western Regions under the Hsiung-nu and the Han*, History of Civilization of Central Asia, UNESCO Publishing, Vol. II, 1994, 227–46.

16. Enoki, K., Koshelenko, G. A., and Z. Haidary, *The Yueh-chih and their migrations*, History of Civilization of Central Asia, UNESCO Publishing, Vol. II, 1994, 171–90.

17. Ibid, 171–90.

18. To consider the important Turkish factor in details, consult various chapters of Sinor, D. *The Cambridge History of Early Inner Asia*, Cambridge University Press, 1994.

19. Schlumberger, D., *Surkh Kotal,* Antiquity, Vol. 33, No. 130, 1959, 81–86. Also, see: Rawlinson, G., *The Sixth Oriental Monarchy*, Ch. XI, Longmans, Green and Co., London, 1873, 150–82. Also, see: Bivar, B. D. H., *The Kanishka Dating from Surkh Kotal*, BSOAS, 15, 1963, 488–502.

20. Enoki, K., Koshelenko, G. A., and Haidary, Z., *The Yueh-Chih*, History of Civilization of Central Asia, Vol. II, UNESCO Publishing, 1996, 171–89.

21. Sircar, D. C., *The Kushanas*, in The History and Culture of the Indian People, Ch. 9, A. D. Puusalkar, Bombay, 183–231.

22. Schlumberger, D., *Surkh Kotal,* Antiquity, Vol. 33, No. 130, 1959, 81–86.

23. Stein, M. A., Ancient Khotan, Oxford, 1907. Also, see: Bivar, B. D. H., *The Kanishka Dating from Surkh Kotal*, BSOAS, 15, 1963, 488–502.

24. Klimkeit, H. J., *Christians, Buddhists, and Manichaeans in Medieval Central Asia,* Buddhist-Christian Studies, 1, 1981, 46–50.

25. Calmard, J., *Cultural and Religious Cross-Fertilization between Central Asia and The Indo-Persian World*, in History of Civilizations of Central Asia, Vol. V, UNESCO Publishing, Turin, Italy, 2001, 812–20.

26. Goryacheva, V. D., *The Early Medieval Monuments of Buddhism in Northern Kirgizia*, Buddhist for Peace, No. 4, Ulan Bator, 1980, 35–44. Also, see: Kyzlasov,

L. R., *Archeological Explorations in Ak-Beshim Settlement*, Funze, 1953–1954. Also, see: Zyablin, L. P., *Second Buddhist Temple of Ak-Beshim*, Settlement, Funze, 1961.

27. Santoro, A. *Miran: The Visvantara Jataka on Visual Narration Along the Silk Road*, Rivista degli studi orientali, Published By: Sapienza Universita di Roma, 2006, pp. 31–45. Also, see: Tewinkle, K. *Miran, Xinjiang Uyghur Autonomous Region, Central Asian Archeological Landscapes*, 2020.

28. Tewinkle, K. *Miran, Xinjiang Uyghur Autonomous Region, Central Asian Archeological Landscapes*, 2020.

29. Rowland, B. *The Art of Central Asia*, p. 103, Crown Publishers, 1974.

30. Hammer, J. *Searching for Buddha in Afghanistan*, Smithsonian Magazine, Dec. 2010.

31. Falser, M. *The Bamiyan Buddhas*, performative iconoclasm and the "image" of heritage. In: Giometti, S. and Tomaszewski, A. (eds.), *The Image of Heritage. Changing Perception, Permanent Responsibilities*. Proceedings of the International Conference of the ICOMOS International Scientific Committee for the Theory and the Philosophy of Conservation and Restoration. 6–8 March 2009, Florence, Italy. Firenze 2011: 157–69.

32. Rowland, B. *The Art of Central Asia*, p. 103, Crown Publishers, 1974.

33. Lee, S. *Recent Articles on Art and Archaeology of Kucha: A Review Article*, Archives of Asian Art, 68 (2), 215–32, 2018.

34. Waugh, D. C. *Kucha and the Kizil Caves*, Silk Road Seattle. University of Washington, 2014.

35. Zhang, G. "*The city-states of the Tarim Basin*," Chapters 11, 12, in History of Civilizations of Central Asia. Vol. III. The crossroads of civilizations: A.D. 250 to 750, B. A. Litvinsky et al., eds. Paris: UNESCO, pp. 281–314, 1996.

36. Ghose, R. *Kizil on the Silk Road: Crossroads of Commerce and Meeting of Minds*, Marg Publication, 2008.

37. Morita, M. *The Kizil Paintings in the Metropolitan* in The Metropolitan Museum Journal, Vol. 50, pp. 115–36, 2015.

38. Ghose, R. *Kizil on the Silk Road: Crossroads of Commerce and Meeting of Minds*, Marg Publication, 2008.

39. Howard, A. F. *In Support of a New Chronology for the Kizil Mural Paintings*, Archives of Asian Art, XLIV, pp. 68–83, 1991.

40. Zin, M. *The Identification of the Kizil Paintings II* [3. Sudåya, 4. Brhaddyuti] in Indo-Asiatische Zeitschrift (Berlin) 11: 43–45, 2007.

41. Dabbs, J. A. *History of the Discovery and Exploration of Chinese Turkestan*, The Hague, 1963.

42. Le Coq, A. V. *Buried Treasures of Chinese Turkestan*. George Allen & Unwin Ltd. 1928. Paperback with introduction, Hong Kong, Oxford University Press, 1985.

43. Rowland, B. The Art of Central Asia, p. 103, Crown Publishers, 1974.

Chapter Twelve

Sassanid Empire Arts

This chapter includes an analysis of the emergence of the Sassanid kingdom to an Empire in the third century C. E. Imposition of certain values on Central Asian cultures, including a state religion, within this time has been given special attention.

One of the dramatic events of the ancient era was the rise of the Sassanian Empire (226–651) that ruled a large area of today's Middle East, Central Asia, and the Caucasus. The new dynasty ended the domination of the Parthian Empire and ushered in a new era in the political and cultural history of the region.[1] Migrating from Central Asia, the Sassanians were a prominent family who settled in the Fars (Pars) province in present day southern Iran. At its zenith, the Sassanian dynasty ruled a vast empire stretching from the river Oxus in the north-east to the gates of Jerusalem in the west. Under the Sassanian rule, Zoroastrianism was established as the state religion of the Persian empire.

SASSANID ARCHITECTURAL ENTITIES

Sassanian art synthesizes art of Achaemenids and Parthian traditions. Sassanian architecture's characteristics includes: the vault, the dome, and the *iwan* for palaces and temples. Its architectural decorations take the form of revetments and use stucco, wall paintings, and mosaic art in interior decorations like those at Ctesiphon or Iwan-e Karkheh. Scenes of royal feasting and bow and arrow hunting on the horseback are among the iconographic themes that reoccur in applied and decorative arts, especially exquisite metal arts. Sculptural reliefs and decorations on the walls and enamel drinking vessels rank as the masterpieces of Sassanian gold-smiths' work. In the seventh century C. E.., ceramics are enriched with the enamel glaze, and Sassanian textile art is travelling on the Silk Road, while an indigenous glass industry flourishes in some parts of the region, including Susa. The Sassanian kings created an administration so efficient that it permitted them to carry out programs of irrigation, town building, and industrialization on an unprecedented scale.²

Palace of Firuzabad and Palace of Ctesiphon

The Sassanian palace at Firuzabad is a remarkable achievement, and the focus of a new epoch. The façade was 180 feet long, the vault of the large central *iwan* spanned 42 feet. Inherited from Parthian times, it is now combined with one domed immense *talar* (hall). Beyond this central *iwan*, which was flanked on either side by two rectangular *iwans*, were three square-domed chambers supported by walls 13 feet thick. The walls of the city palace of Firuzabad were covered with plaster. The largest Sassanian architectural entity was the palace complex of Taqe Kasra at Ctesiphon, in Iraq. Its *iwan*, a great open vault, spans 75 feet (wider than any vault in Europe), is 90 feet high, and 150 feet deep.³ The layout of Ctesiphon palace is basically the same architectural element as the smaller *iwans* of the Parthian palace at Ashur. The façade of the Ctesiphon, like that of the palace at Ashur, is divided into horizontal registers, which are articulated by niches and engages columns.

Popular Arts

The royal art of the Sassanid court included prestigious monuments and exceptional artifacts. The luxury art of Sassanid Empire traveled near and far because of trade, conquest, and diplomacy. Some of the popular art of the time included silver plates and gold trays decorated with scenes of the emperor on horses, hunting rams, deer, and boars. Some of the monumental rock reliefs within various parts of the empire have similar scenes repeated. The most famous of the hunting scenes can be found in Bistun near Kermanshah. The rock reliefs of the Sassanid Empire era could also be found in Nagsh-e Rustam, near Shiraz and outside Ctesiphon, the capital of the Sassanid Empire (today in Iraq). The royal art of Sassanid Empire also includes seals made of precious stones and textiles including silk, glass, and ceramic vessels.⁴

Crowns

The stylistic changes from one Sassanian emperor to the next are more easily recognizable from the shape of their crowns, which were brought about by different choices and combinations of emblems. Some of these emblems were symbols of gods intended to show the close relation of the god and the king. They include the rays which were taken over from the radiance of Mithra (the sun god) or several emblems that were ascribed to Anahita, (deity and guardian of waters) such as a pair of wings with the head of an eagle or falcon, which holds a pearl in its beak.[5]

Sculptural Reliefs/Rock Reliefs

Some of the best-known works of Sassanian art are the sculptural reliefs (or rock reliefs), of which more than thirty are known, most of them from the first two centuries of Sassanian rule. A large number of reliefs can be found in Fars province, in the majestic valley of Naqsh-I Rustem, in small bay of rocks at Naqsh-I Rajab, and in the steep inclines of the gorge at Bishapur. One of the reliefs on the left bank of the river of Bishapur commemorates the triumphs of Shapur I (241–272) over three Roman emperors, Gordian III (238–244), Philip the Arab (244–249), and Valerian (253–260). At the relief's center is Shapur I on horseback; in front of him is Philip the Arab on bended knee suing for peace. Emperor Valerian stands behind the conqueror, who holds him by wrist, while the body of Gordian III is lying on the ground. The sculptural relief of Shapur I's triumphs against three Roman emperors was reproduced at different locations, at Naqsh-I Rustem, in Fars province and at Darab, and also in Fars province. Shapur I commemorated his victories over Rome in narrative scenes well calculated to the imagination of his subjects. Under Bahram I, son of Shapur I, Sassanian art reached its highest point in Bishapur bas-reliefs. Two other popular Sassanian sculptural relief subject matters are coronation of the monarchs and hunting scenes.[6]

The royal hunting relief to the left of the entrance on the side walls of the *iwan* at Taq-I Bustan (590–628) is a boar hunt in a swamp, more precisely, in a lake overgrown with rushes through which elephants drive a herd of boars to pass in solid formation before the royal huntsman's boat. In a dramatic move, one of the boars breaks out of the herd and turns in the direction of the king. Female musicians accompany the king in the midst of the hunt and also at the end where he is shown smaller, standing in the boat. The hunting scene in a landscape presents a unified picture, elephants and boars lead the eye of the viewer around the king and over the entire picture surface.

Mosaic Art

Bishapur, to the west of the province of Fars, lies at the foot of a mountain on which a fortress with an elaborate network of high defensive walls and small forts defended it from attacks. In the middle of the third century C.E., Shapur I decided to build a royal city there. One sector of the city was reserved for the royal buildings. Here stood a palace with a great hall whose plan and technique conformed to the best tradition of Eurasian architecture. A central room 72 feet square, flanked by four triple vaulted *iwans*, supported a cupola over

80 feet high. This layout is the same as that of the Parthian courts surrounded by *iwans* at Nisa and Assur. Sixty-four recesses are let into the walls of this room. The floor of a triple *iwan* opening on a large court east of the great hall was paved with slabs of stone and bordered with mosaic panels. There are portraits representing members of the royal family, nobility, and aristocracy. Women are dancing, playing the harp, or making garlands. The figurative mosaics are either full body or close-up portraits. The mosaic compositions are all dominated by cool blues in contrast with warm colors of burnt sienna and ochre brown. The background of the pieces are pastel white, while there are suggestions of shading and grading of faces or bodies with lighter or darker neutralized colors. The palace of Bishapur was excavated by French archeologists in the late 1930s.[7]

Metal Art Works

There are more than a hundred bowls, plates, and trays of precious metals of silver and gold excavated and discovered from Sassanian courts. One of the finest examples of these pieces is a silver plate with partial gilding in the Metropolitan Museum of Art in New York. The plate depicts king Peroz (457–484), identified by his crown, hunting on horseback. Two Argali bucks, which are represented in a second rendering where they appear already transfixed by the king's arrows, lay lifeless under the hooves of his horse. This imagery indicates the symbolic character of the hunting scene, which is also stressed by the representation of the king in full regalia including the crown worn in official occasions. The silver plate in the Metropolitan Museum belongs to a group of plates that show the king hunting. These hunting plates belong to the fourth and partly to the fifth century. The figures are small and numerous and the composition is free and stylized by each goldsmith or silversmith.

A silver plate in the Hermitage Museum at Saint Petersburg, shows a royal hero with elegant ram's horns on his helmet, engaged in a dangerous boar hunt. The representation is quite dramatic. The figures are large, and the principal figure is calm in contrast to the violent movement of the animals. The composition favors acute angles formed by the lines of action. The silversmith of this plate has a totally different style of materializing a hunt scene. The figures remain mostly within the plane of the plate, and only single parts are applied in low relief.[8]

A different type of metal vessel with figural decoration comprises tall silver ewers with flattened bodies and projecting narrow spouts. An interesting ewer from Bibliotheque Nationale, Paris, displays two pairs of lions with crossed bodies on either side of a flowering tree. The lions have eight-pointed stars on their shoulders and manifest a relation with even earlier metal works of Eurasian art discussed previously from Ziwiye, Hasanlu, Kalardasht, and Taq-I Bustan.

Sassanian Silk Making

Sassanian silk woven with elaborate patterns came to the churches and monasteries of the West as wrappings of Christian relics. There are many fragments of Sassanid silk preserved in European collections, which gives some ideas of the brilliantly colored and effectively patterned garments worn by Sassanians. After the fall of the Sassanian empire, Byzantine silk weavers continued the Sassanian tradition for centuries with few changes in pattern, but with drastic changes in colors. Patterns are frequently composed of birds, ducks, fowl, parrots, or eagles, which are combined with other elements such as floral medallions or borders of hearts, to form a clearly organized pattern in which each retains its individual value.

Zoroaster and Zoroastrianism

The prophet Zoroaster initiated one of the earliest Central Asian religions. Many scholars identify Zoroaster as a prophet who originally came from the shamanistic tradition (3500–3000 years ago). He is often identified as a wise man or a healer.[9] Zoroaster introduced the idea of monotheism to the world, and his concepts and ideas left a profound impact on many other world religions and cults.

Zoroastrianism was declared the state religion of the Persian Sassanid Empire, which ruled a large part of Central Asia and the Near East for over four hundred years (226–651). After the fall of the Sassanian Empire, hundreds of Pahlavi texts were translated from Middle Persian, the official language of the Persian Empire, into Arabic and modern Persian, which emerged after the introduction of Islam. A few of the literary sources translated from Middle Persian included: Ayadgari Zareran (Memories of Prince Zarir); Hazar Afsan (The Thousand Tales); Sindbud-namag (Book of Sindbud or Sindbud Bahri); Vis and Ramin (a famous love story); Ayen Ewen-namag (etiquette, manners, ceremonies, backgammon, and horsemanship); Madigan-i hazar Dadestan (Book of a Thousand Judicial Decisions by Farrukhmard, son of Bahram); and Kweskarihi-i Redagan (Education of Children).

Three Supreme Fire Templess: Azar Goshnasb, Azar Faranbagh, Azar Borzinmehr

Fire symbolized Mithra, the sun god, who was worshiped as a deity by followers of Zoroaster. Mithra also had its own cult, which had already developed into a distinct sect under the Parthian rule. There were three major and hundreds of minor fire temples in Central Asia at the time of the Sassanian Empire. The most important was the Fire Temple of Azar Goshnasb in the Iranian province of Azarbijan. The temple complex, a fortified fortress surrounded by high massive walls with numerous gates, was built around a volcanic lake on top of a mountain. Azar Goshnasb was the fire temple of the kings and the top warriors of Sassanian Empire in a place today called Takhte Solaiman. In ancient texts, the area is identified as Ganjak, and in the Middle Ages the area was identified as Sheez.

The second most important fire temple was the Azar Faranbagh, or the temple of priests. It was believed that this temple was originally located in Khwarazm to the south of the Aral Sea and was then relocated to the Fars Province near the Persian Gulf.

W. A. V. Jackson[10] writes that the Azar Borzin Mehr fire temple of the farmers is close to the village of Mihr between Miandasht and Sabzevar, near the ancient city of Neyshabur, in Khorasan province, in Iran today. The fire temple of Azar Borzin Mehr, the third most important, was dedicated to Mithra, the sun god and the deity of love. It was located near the city of Nishabur, in the state of Khorasan, in Iran, and was devastated by the Mongols in the thirteenth century.[11]

Fire Temple of Surakhany

In the northern part of the ancient city of Baku, on the western shore of the Caspian Sea stands the well-preserved fire temple of Surakhany. The temple is surrounded by thick outer walls 120x102 feet. The central shrine stands nearly in the middle of a court. A square-towered building, approached by a steep flight of steps, rises toward the northeast corner. The walls of the precinct are very thick, as they consist of separate cells or cloistered chambers running all the way around and entered by arched doors. The whole is solidly built and covered with plaster. The structure in the middle is a square fabric of brick, stone, and mortar and is 25 feet in height and 20 feet in length. In the middle of the floor is a square well measuring forty and one-half inches in each direction. Pipes that once transported oil or gas to the temple are visible. The top of the shrine is surmounted by four chimneys at the corners from which the flaming gases once rose.

Mani and Manichaeism

The prophet who tried to synthesize the teachings of Buddha, Christ, and Zoroaster in his gospel was Mani (216–276), the founder of a religion that came to be known as Manichaeanism. His teachings were influenced by his mother Maryam who was related to the Parthian royal family and came from a Judeo-Christian background. Mani's father Patik was born in Hamedan and moved to Ctesiphon, the capital of the Persian Sassanid Empire. Mani was only 24 years old when he started preaching. Unlike the Sassanids and the Roman Empires that persecuted Manichaeans, Central Asia tolerated the religion and provided it with a safe haven.[12]

Mani and Book Art

Manuscript Illuminations as Educational Sources

Manichaeism was always identified with the ancient tradition of book making. In one of his own passages, St. Augustine described Manichaeism and its exquisite book art. It was in Turfan, on the northern route of the Silk Road in Central Asia, that A. von Le Coq discovered several illustrated manuscripts that dated back to the eighth and ninth centuries.[13] The significance of these miniature paintings lie in the fact that they were some of the oldest surviving book paintings in the world. The illustrations were closely associated with the surrounding text. Rich red, purple, white, green, and gold colors illuminated landscape elements of trees and floral scrolls. Enlightened figures drawn in outline wore elaborate and simple dress patterns. Under the Abbasid caliphs, who ruled a vast empire from Baghdad, the Manichaeans were persecuted and their books and manuscripts were burned. According to sources who witnessed this, streams of molten gold and silver ran out of the bonfires.[14] (Also, see: Appendix III of this book.)

Despite suppression by the Sassanid Empire, Manichaeism rapidly spread from Egypt and North Africa into the Roman Empire through missionary activities. Over the next several centuries Manichaean missionaries converted many in Armenia, Bulgaria, and France.

According to Chinese sources, Manichaeism reached the Chinese court in 694 C. E., and its teachings were freely preached in eighth century China. In 762 C. E., Uyghurs, who ruled large parts of Central Asia, declared Manichaeism as their state religion.[15] The systematic and continued persecutions of Manichaeans in the Sassanid Empire forced them to move to Central Asia, North Africa, and even Europe. The defeat of Uyghurs by the Kyrghyz in 840 C. E. forced Uyghurs to migrate from the shores of Yenisei River to the Tarim Basin. Here the Uyghurs converted to Manichaeism, inherited the traditions of eastern Iranians or Tokharians, and adopted the script of northern Iranians or Sogdians. Following the persecution of Manichaeans by the Caliphs of Baghdad in the tenth century, the city of Samarkand in today's Uzbekistan, became a Manichaean center.

The next chapter includes an analysis of the region of Soghdia, one of the earliest urbanized centers of cultural and trade activities in Central Asia.

NOTES

1. Knobloch, E., *Monuments of Central Asia*, A Guide to the Archeology, Art and Architecture of Turkestan, I. B. Tauris Publishers, New York, 2001, 167–84.
2. Christensen, A. E., *L'empire des Sassanides*: Le people, l'etet, la cour, Levin and Munksgaard, Copenhagen, 1944.
3. Ghirshman, R., *Iran: Parthian and Sassanian*, London: Thames & Hudson, 1962, 119–253.
4. Christensen, A. E., *L'empire des Sassanides*: Le people, l'etet, la cour, Levin and Munksgaard, Copenhagen, 1944.
5. Ghirshman, R., *Iran: Parthian and Sassanian*, London: Thames & Hudson, 1962 Also, see: Christensen, A. E., *L'empire des Sassanides*: Le people, l'etet, la cour, Levin and Munksgaard, Copenhagen, 1944.
6. Christensen, A. E., *L'empire des Sassanides*: Le people, l'etet, la cour, Levin and Munksgaard, Copenhagen, 1944.
7. Ghirshman, R., *Iran: Parthian and Sassanian*, London: Thames & Hudson.
8. Litvinsky, B. A., Shah, M. H., and Samghabadi, R. S., *The Rise of Sasanian Iran*, History of Civilizations of Central Asia, V. II, UNESCO Publishing, 1994, 473–84.
9. For more information on ancient religions of the region, particularly Zoroasterianism, see: Duchesne-Guillemin, J. Religions of Ancient Iran, Bombay, 1973.
10. W. A. V., Jackson, *From Constantinople to the Home of Omar Khayyam*, Ch. IV, Macmillan Co., 1911, pp. 73–82.
11. Muller, F. M., *The Sacred Books of the East*: Vol. 23, The Zend Avesta, Adamant Media Corporation, Oxford, 2000. Yashts include a pantheon of twenty-one supernatural forces: 1. Ormazd Yasht (Hymn to Ahura Mazda); 2. Haft Amshaspands Yasht (Haptan Yasht), (Hymn to Seven Archangels); 3. (Bahman Yasht); 4. Ardibehisht Yasht; 5. Khordad Yasht; 6. Aban Yasht (Hymn to the Waters); 7. Khorshed Yasht (Hymn to the Sun); 8. Mah Yasht (Hymn to the Moon); 9. Tir Yasht; 10. Mihr Yasht (Hymn to Mithra); 11. Gos Yasht; 12. Srosh Yasht Hadokht (Serosh); 13. Rash Yasht; 14. Farvardin Yasht (Hymn to Guardian Angels); 15. Bahram Yasht; 16. Ram Yasht; 17. Din Yasht; 18. Ashi Yasht; 19. Ashtad Yasht; 20. Zamyad Yasht (Hymn to the Earth); 21. Vanant Yasht (Hymn to the Vega). For more detailed analysis of Sassanids implication of Zoroasterinism as their state religion, see: Ghirshman, R., *Iran: Parthian and Sassanians*, London: Thames & Hudson, 1962. Also, see: Jackson, W. A. V., *From Constantinople to the Home of Omar Khayyam*, Ch. IV, Macmillan Co., 1911, 73–82.
12. For more information on Manichaeism in the region, see Widengren, G., *Mani and Manichaeism*, translated by Charles Kessler, Upsala, 1965.
13. Browder, M. H., Biruni Manichaean Sources, in P. Bryder, ed. Manichaean Studies, 1982, 9–12.

14. Klimkei, H. J., *Gnosis on the Silk Road* (Gnostic Texts from Central Asia), Harper, San Francisco, 1993, 1–26. Fragments of Manichean manuscripts written by Mani have survived: 1. Living Gospel; 2. Treasure of Life; 3. Treatise; 4. Book of Secrets; 5. Book of Giants; 6. Palms; and 7. Prayers. The social formation of Manichaeian communities was composed of two major groups, the elect (the few) and the hearers (the masses). Fragments of Manichean manuscripts written by Mani have survived.

15. LeCoq, A. von., *A Buried Treasures of Chinese Turkestan*, London, 1928. Fragments of Manichean literature in a variety of languages were found in Kan-tcheou and Qoco, within the Uighur lands. Also, see: Widengren, G., *Mani and Manichaeism*, translated by Charles Kessler, Upsala, 1965. Also, see: Tongerloo, A. van., *Notes on the Iranian Elements in the Uygur Manichaean Texts*, in P. Bryder, ed., Manichaean Studies, Lund, 1987, 213–19. Also, see: Arnold, T. W., *Survival of Sasanian and Manichaean Art* in Persian Painting, Oxford: Oxford Press, 1924, 52. On the complicated issue of the ancient believe systems of the region, the cult of Mithra or Mithraism has to be indicated here: The cult of Mithra, known as Mithraism, was conveyed from Central Asia and Persia to Rome. Before the declaration of Christianity as the state religion of Rome in the fourth century C. E., Mithraism was an influential and popular cult, especially in the second and third centuries C. E. The Mithra cult in Rome included seven ranks that marked the spiritual progress of an individual toward ever higher ranks. The seven ranks were: 1. Corax: Raven, 2. Nymphus: Bridegroom, 3. Miles: Soldier, 4. Leo: Lion, 5. Perses: Persian, 6. Heliodromus: Sun courier, 7. Pater: Father. Also, see: M. J. Vermaseren, M. J., *Mithra*: The Secret God, Uppsala: Chatto and Windus, 1963, 53.

Chapter Thirteen

Satrapy of Sogdia and its Art Schools

PREHISTORIC & EARLY ANCIENT CULTURES & ARTS

Satrapy (state) of Soghdia is one of the earliest and most urbanized centers of cultural and trade activities in Central Asia. Soghdia was the eighteenth satrapy of the Achaemenid Empire in the sixth and fifth centuries B.C.E. The Soghdian satrapy lay north of Bakhtaran (Bactra) and east of Khwarazmia between the Oxus River (Amu Darya) and the Jaxartes River (Syr Darya). In Avesta, the holy book of Zoroastrians, Soghdia is identified as the second-best land on earth. In this section, the most active urbanized centers of Soghdia— their arts and cultural activities—are given special attention.

Settlement of Sarazm

One of the oldest settlements of Central Asia is Sarazm, which dates to 4000 B. C. E. Since 1976 and after fifteen seasons of work, only one hectare of the 100 ha. of this city on the shore of Zarafshan River has been excavated. A temple with a round altar, palaces, public buildings, and residential homes has been excavated. Jewelry, armor, and objects made of gold, silver, bronze, and copper have been discovered. In fact, Sarazm has been identified as one of the earliest mining and agricultural centers of the region.[1]

Capital City of Varakhsha

The fortified capital of Varakhsh, close to Bokhara and two hundred miles west of Samarkand, was partially excavated between 1947 and 1953. The central hall of the palace of Varakhsh was decorated with paintings of human beings, animals, birds, fish, trees, geometric decorations, and amazing mythological species. The next hall of the palace includes an image of a king sitting on a throne surrounded by two rows of decorations. The upper row of the mural includes a variety of animals. The lower row of this mural displays hunting scenes with dynamic animals like leopards. The murals were identified as the sixth and seventh century C.E. paintings. The palace belonged to one of the local rulers of the area and lasted into the eleventh century C.E. The site of Varakhsha has not been fully excavated, and as with so many other Soviet Union archeological sites, after a few years of incomplete research and excavation, the team of excavators was assigned to a different location.[2]

Art School of Panjkent: Background

Soghdians are one of the major eastern Iranian groups. Full-size profile figures of Soghdians appear for the first time as high relief sculptural pieces on the walls of Apadana audience hall in Persepolis, the capital of the Achaemenid Empire (550–330 B.C.E.) in the sixth century B.C.E. The reliefs portray Soghdians offering the Persian Emperor Darius I, a pair of gold bracelets, a pair of rams, some fabric cloth, an animal skin, cups, and vessels. Soghdia was the sixteenth satrapy of the Achaemenid Empire. Apadana reliefs portray representatives of all provinces offering a variety of gifts to their emperor, including representatives from the other Central Asian satrapies of Kharazm (Kharazmia) and Bakhtaran (Bactra).[3] The disintegration and fall of the Achamenid Empire in the fourth century and the resistance of the Soghdians to foreign rule prevented the invading Macedonians from establishing any firm authority over Soghdia. It forced some of the Soghdians, however, to pursue commercial and business interests with traders and merchants sponsored by the Chinese court.

The history of the Chinese court and production of silk is over four thousand years old. Queen Leizu, the wife of Emperor Huangdi (The Yellow Emperor, 2674–2575 B.C.), was known as the goddess of silk. She was also identified as the founder of silk production. She taught her people how to breed the silkworms and unwind the cocoons. In 1958 archeologists excavating a Neolithic site in the province of Zhejiang discovered a silk belt, some silk felt, and raw silk. Subsequent C^{14} dating identified them as 4,750 years old. It was, however, Shi Huang Di of the Chin dynasty (221–206 B. C. E.) who decided to export silk for the first time. Previously, silk was made exclusively for Chinese royalty and only in limited amounts.

To stop tribal invasions from the north and to provide safety and security for trade and commerce to the west, the Chin emperor initiated the construction of the Great Wall. That first intercontinental route of trade and commerce was later named the Silk Road. In 1974, the tomb complex of the Chin emperor, Shi Huang Di, was discovered accidentally by a farmer digging a well in a farm in the Shaanxi Province. Over six thousand life size terracotta warriors and over two thousand terracotta horses were found in the outlying areas of the tomb.

The Chin Empire was short-lived, and many of Shi Huang Di's dreams did not materialize. In fulfilling the dreams of the Chin emperor, in 138 B.C. Emperor Wudi of the Han Dynasty (206 B.C.E. –220 C.E.) ordered an officer, named Zhang Qian, from the palace guards to lead ninety-nine soldiers to embark on a mission of diplomacy. The central objective of the mission was to establish diplomatic and commercial strategy alliances with China's neighboring states. The delegation headed for the north-west through the Gansu province and Hexi corridor to the west of the Yellow River, where they encountered the Xiongnu tribe warriors. The Xiongnu tribe, which dominated the area, imprisoned the members of the Chinese delegation, including Zhang Qian, who remained in prison for eleven years. Zhang Qian managed to flee from the prison and traveled for two more years visiting eight different kingdoms. Only in the land of Dayuan (Ferghana Valley) did Zhang Qian receive a warm welcome. On his return to China, he took Central Asian horses, grapes, garlic, carrots, sesame, and alfalfa to the Chinese capital, Chang'an, and the court of Emperor Han Wudi.

Upon his return to the Han court, Zhang Qian was declared a high dignitary by the emperor Han Wudi. Shortly afterward, he was assigned to his second mission. The second, which began in 126 B.C., included a visit to Bakhtaran (Bactra) and Shengdu (Northern India). Zhang Qian was sent on a third mission with three hundred warriors in 115 B.C.E.[4] The Chinese delegation passed through the northern Tianshan Mountains, continued its way westward, and entered the Empire of Anxi (Parthian Empire, 226 B.C.E. –206 C.E.) in 105 B.C.E. The Chinese delegation was met by twenty thousand Parthian horsemen warriors in the heart of Soghdia. Zhang Qian was surprised to discover that the Parthian warriors were sent by the Parthian Emperor Mithradates II (124–91 B.C.E.) not to murder him and his men, but to welcome them. The systematic flow of capital and goods in both directions between the Parthian and Han empires brought prosperity to both states as well as the surrounding countries.

Soghdian merchants played a central role in linking the Parthian state to the Chinese Empire. Soghdian merchants provided their western neighbors with Chinese, Indian (Kushanids 30–320 A.D.), and Persian products including silk, cotton, wool, spices, plants, medicine, perfume, glassware, ceramics, gold, silver, gemstones, and jewelry.[5]

The prosperity of many Soghdian cities and towns was the result of expanding trade and exchange between the Parthian and Han empires. Parthian, Soghdian, Khotanis, and Kuchan musicians, acrobats, jugglers, magicians, and dancers traveled to and performed in Chang'an, the old capital of China. A bundle of documents and letters from 313 C.E. was unearthed in a watchtower in the far western end of the Great Wall of China, indicating extensive trade between Soghdia and China in ancient times.[6] For eight hundred years (105 B.C.E.–722) intense trade and exchange of goods, technologies, and ideas continued between Central Asia and China with a number of dramatic interruptions.

One of the dramatic events of the ancient era was the rise of the Sassanian Empire (226–651 A.D.) that ruled a large area of today's Middle East, Central Asia, and Caucasus, ending the domination of the Parthian Empire and ushering in a new era of political and cultural history of the region.[7] Sassanians, a prominent family from Fars (Pars) province in present day Iran, expanded their kingdom into Central Asia.

At its zenith, the Sassanian dynasty ruled a vast empire stretching from the river Oxus in the north-east to the gates of Jerusalem in the west. Under their rule, Zoroastrianism was established as the state religion of the Persian Empire. By the mid-fifth century Central Asia was invaded by the Hephthalites (Ephtalites or the White Huns). Hephtalites occupied Khotan, Koche, Kashgar, Samarkand, Balkh, and Badakhshan and expanded into northern India. In 484, the Sassanian Emperor Piruz was killed fighting Hephtalites in Central Asia. Piruz's grandson, Emperor Khosrow (Chosrow), made an alliance with the Turkish leader, Qaghan Sinjibu, ending the Hephtalites rule of the area in 557.

From 557, some parts of Central Asia, including Panjkent, were ruled by the members of the Sassanid royalty and members of Qaghan Sinjibu family, who enjoyed a close alliance with the Sassanian dynasty. Some of the murals of Panjkent painted between 557 and 722 portray members of the Qaghan Sinjibu family as they hosted their royal guests. The prosperity of Panjkent lasted another one hundred sixty-five years. In 722, the region was devastated by an Arab army, forcing the last ruler of Panjkent, Divastich, to flee to Mount Mugh fortress where he died shortly thereafter. In 1933, shepherds digging the fortress floor accidentally found the treasury of the last ruler of Panjkent, with a significant number of Soghdian documents. During the golden age of Panjkent from 105 B.C.E. to 722, especially in the seventh to the eight centuries, Soghdian communities expanded their trade not only with China and India, but also with Japan, Rome, and the Byzantine Empires.

The Old City of Panjkent & Its Art Treasury

The climax of Soghdia's prosperity was reflected in Panjkent's power and influence dating back to 105 B. C. E. when a trade agreement was concluded between Emperor Mithradates II of the Parthian Empire and Emperor

Han Wudi of China. Central Asia suffered from the disruption of trade on the Silk Road in 722 when Panjkent was devastated by the Arab invasion. Central Asia and the surrounding regions, however, began to enjoy another golden age of prosperity and cultural revival under the leadership of the Samanids (815–999), who established their capital in Bokhara. The ancient city of Panjkent had already re-emerged as an affluent urban center prior to this period.

The modern town of Panjkent, with a population of over fifty thousand, is less than two kilometers from the old city on the shore of the Zarafshan River, between the town of Aini in north-west Tajikistan and the city of Samarkand in present day Uzbekistan. The excavation of the old city of Panjkent, begun in 1946, was led by the Tajik scholar and academician B.G. Ghaffurov. Some of the best Tajik and Russian archeologists, numismatists, and scientists of the Soviet Union were involved in different phases of excavation and research until 1991.

Excavation and research in the area was interrupted because of the fall of the Soviet Union in 1991 and the civil war in Tajikistan that erupted shortly after the fall. The members of three institutions (the Institute of History in Dushanbe [A.I. Isakov], the Museum of Regional Sciences and History [I. Rahmatuulaev], and the Saint Petersburg Archaeological Institute [A.M. Belenitsky]), played prominent roles in the Panjkent excavation project. Only one-third of old Panjkent's fourteen hectares was excavated by 1981. The excavation of the old city of Panjkent continued until 1991; however, a large section of the old city remains unexcavated.

On the extreme western side of the ancient city of Panjkent were the royal palaces, and on the same side, closer to the center of the city, there was a temple. A Zoroastrian fire temple with a symmetrical centralized fire altar in the middle was the largest architectural monument of this section. To the north-east of the city, a Hindu temple was unearthed. Over one hundred and sixty houses to the east of the city were excavated. The majority of the houses had two floors and belonged to rich aristocrats and merchants who traded with China, India, Persia, and Rome. At least one third of the homes were painted with a variety of murals.[8] Toward the center of the city, excavators discovered a bazaar with a number of shops. The large quantities of coins discovered in this area suggest that the town was a prosperous center for trade and commerce.

The cultural artifacts portray a relatively peaceful and prosperous urban center before it was devastated in 722 by Arab invaders. According to the Soviet scholars, the coins found in Panjkent belonged to Vagoman and Chakin Chur Bilga, the two rulers of the seventh century. A group of coins from the beginning of the eighth century belonged to Turgar the ruler of Samarkand. Some Arab coins belonging to the latter part of the eighth century were also found. Their existence demonstrated that even after the Arab invasion of 722, city life continued until the year 770.

The major building materials used to construct the walls, arches, and ceilings were mud bricks of hard clay. As far as space and structure are concerned, the residential houses in the eastern portion of Panjkent appeared dense compared to the western section of the city, which offered more open space and included palaces and temples. Besides coins, a variety of pottery (e.g., plates, dishes, jugs); iron tools; glassware objects; mirrors; belts; bronze, silver and gold bracelets, rings, and earrings; and toys were unearthed during the Panjkent excavation. Some of the jewelry pieces found included precious stones, turquoise, pearls, agates, and corals. Some of the most peculiar and unique art pieces in Panjkent are woodworks. Wooden doors, door frames, columns, and even ceiling beams with exceptional carvings decorated with organic and geometric patterns were discovered in Panjkent.

These art pieces, including most of the woodworks and paintings, were moved to the Hermitage Museum in St. Petersburg and other museums and institutions in Moscow for further analysis. Today, few of these art pieces can be found at the museum next to the excavation site of the old city of Panjkent, the museum of the new city of Panjkent, and the National Museum of Tajikistan in Dushanbe.

One way of saving the ancient city of Panjkent from total disintegration is rebuilding, preserving, and recreating it, including replacing all the murals on the walls where they belonged. United Nations affiliated institutions and some international private and public firms may be willing to collaborate in saving the old city. A new excavation season is planned to begin soon, and with the consultation and help of Tajik experts who have worked at the site, and contribution and help from other international specialists, Panjkent could turn into one of the most fascinating and educational archeological sites in the world.

Two Sogdian Golden Ages of Culture and Arts

Soghdia enjoyed two golden ages in the Middle Ages. The first of the two golden ages was centered in Bokhara[9] in the ninth and tenth centuries. The city of Bokhara in the ninth and tenth centuries was the capital of Samanid Kingdom. By the second half of the ninth century, a genuine Persian renaissance was developing in Khorasan, north-east of Iran, under the patronage of the Samanid dynasty, which claimed Sassanian ancestry.

Starr suggests the cultural accomplishments of the ancient era had a crucial and profound impact on the medieval golden ages of Central Asia that began in Bokhara (corresponding to the Dark Ages in Europe). Of course, there were other variables and factors contributing to the golden age of Bokhara itself, like the Samanid leadership, which created an atmosphere of support and tolerance, and the establishment of educational institutions, which attracted talented individuals from near and far. After severe interruptions, the golden age of Central Asia continued in Samarkand and Khiva.

The Golden Age of Bokhara: Samanids 814–999 A.D.

The following analysis includes some of the accomplishments of one of the cultural capitals of Central Asia, Bokhara, in the ninth and tenth centuries. Throughout the tenth century in Bokhara, (present day Uzbekistan), a new yet characteristically Persian culture emerged. Bokhara was an ancient city, and since the time of the Persian Achaemenid dynasty it had been one of the major urban centers of the region.

The old city of Bokhara or Qohandiz (Qala) was one of the oldest cities in Central Asia. An extension of the Zarafshan River, the Shahrud, flowed through the city. The city retained its place as one of the main centers of Persian civilization until the imposition of Russian rule over the region and the assignment of the city to a new Uzbek Republic in the late 1920s. The Bokhara of Parthian and Sassanid times included the ark (citadel) and the surrounding suburbs known as shahristan. The ark was destroyed by the invading Arabs in 722 C. E. The revival of Bokhara began during the reign of the Persian Samanids (815–999 C. E.). The Persian Samanid dynasty traced its roots to Saman Khoda, a recent convert from Zoroastrianism to Islam who claimed lineage from a Persian Sassanian general.[10]

Saman was a nobleman and landowner who was born and raised near the city of Balkh in a district in present-day northern Afghanistan. After serving as the representative of the Abbasid caliphs in the province of Khorasan (northeastern Iran and northwestern Afghanistan today), the family of Saman achieved great power and prominence Four of Saman's grandsons were appointed governors of Chach (Tashkent). Ustrushana, Samarqand, Ferghana, and Herat. Under the leadership of Saman's great grandson, Ismail Samani (892–907), the Samanid dynasty reached the zenith of its power. Now, Bokhara with a population of many hundreds of thousands, was the capital of Central Asia, including Khorasan, Khwarazm, the Fergana Valley, and surrounding regions.

It is under the leadership of Shah Ismail that the system of central and local state administration (diwans) was established.[11] The army as well as internal and external security of the country was given especial attention. Opportunities for agricultural, economical, and commercial activities were increased. Cultural, scientific, literary, and artistic traditions were revived and appreciated. New canals and hydro-technical installations were constructed. Wheat, barley, rice, millet, and oilseeds were cultivated. Vineyards were expanded and orchards of apricots, cherries, plums, grapes, pomegranates, figs, walnuts, and almonds were created.

Samanid's Model of Patronage and Support System for Educational, Cultural, and Artistic Activities

Concerning the affairs of the Samanid Empire, Maqdasi writes, "The character of the Samanids, their appearance and their respect for people of learning make them the best rulers."[12]

It was during Samanid rule that Rudaki Samarkandi, (858–941), one of the greatest of all Persian poets and the first literary giant of new Persian literature, composed his poems. Rudaki was born in 858 A.D. and served as the court poet during the reign of the Samanid ruler, Nasr 914–943). Samanid monarch, Nuh II, asked the poet, Daqiqi, to compose Shahnameh in verse in modern Persian. Daqiqi was murdered after a relatively short period of time working on the text. It was Ferdowsi, who, after thirty years of labor, finished in 1010.[13]

Other giants of the Samanid era included the prominent physician and scholar Avicenna (d. 1037), who wrote a book on medicine, Qanun, which was used as a medical text for over five hundred years at European universities. The historian, geographer, and astronomer Biruni, (d. 1048) described ways of determining the specific gravities of the minerals. Narshakhi (d. 959), wrote The History of Bokhara. Balkhi recounted Marvels of the Lands, and the scholar and mathematician, Khwarazmi, wrote extensively on mathematics, especially on logarithm and algebra.

The city of Bokhara in the ninth and tenth centuries was the capital of the Samanid Kingdom. By the second half of the ninth century a genuine Persian renaissance was developing in Khorasan, north-east of Iran, under the patronage of the Samanid dynasty, which claimed Sassanian ancestry.

Under the influence of the Samanid monarchs who supported the revival of Persian culture and language, another giant of Persian poetry, the epic poet Ferdowsi (935–1020), composed the Shahnameh (Book of Kings), which still serves as the national epic of all Persian/Tajik/Dari speakers of the world today. It recounts the history of ancient Iranians from the dawn of history to the fall of the Persian Sassanian dynasty in the seventh century. Epics of pre-historic and ancient monarchs, warriors, and heroes, recalling their struggles and the glories of their victories, had been handed down for centuries. It was during the enlightened reign of the Sassasnian emperor Khusro Anushervan (531–579) that a systematic attempt was made to collect pieces of literature and historical documents from all over the empire.

A group of scholars synthesized the material, collected, and presented it as the "Khvatai namak" in Pahlavi, or Middle Persian. The book was translated into Arabic in the ninth century. In 976, the mausoleum of Ismail Samani in Bokhara, both in its structural development and brilliant use of decorative elements, exerted a strong influence on subsequent Islamic architecture. Simple yet impressive in scale, the dome-centered mausoleum's harmonious and thoroughly studied proportions, along with its vigorous and inventive ornamentation, combined to rank it among the masterpieces of Persian architecture. Brick was used with a vivacity and intensity that had no precedent.[14]

Samanids played a crucial role reviving some of the cultural institutions of Central Asia, by establishing Bokhara not only as a strong political capital, but also as a safe haven for the talented and gifted from the region to seek education and conduct cultural and artistic creativities. The stability and wealth of Samanids allowed them to maintain and patronize a rich cultural life, and it is through patronage that Samanids left their mark on all subsequent Central Asian history. Samanids model of patronage and support for education, cultural, and artistic activities was utilized by some of the following dynasties, namely Ghaznavids and Seljuks, ruling the area. After the fall of the Samanids in 999, Persian continued to be the language of the educated class. Persian dialects were spoken by the craftsmen, peasants, and the educated class, but the rulers and their soldiers were Turks.[15]

Bokhara and other urban centers of Central Asia were devastated by the Turkic and Mongol invasions of the region, which started with the arrival of the Seljuks in the eleventh century and culminated in the destruction of urban life across Central Asia by the Mongols in the thirteenth century.

Seljuks, Kara Khitaeyes, and Mongols in Central Asia

The Seljuk Turks occupied Central Asia between 1040 and 1141. Central Asia was ruled by Seljuk sultans Arsalan (1156–1172) and Takish (1172–1200) and the Sufi dynasty, Qongrat, independently by the mid-thirteenth century. Sufi Lord Yusuf and Sufi Lord Sulayman were two of the famous local rulers of this period. By the beginning of the thirteenth century, Gurganj became the capital of the powerful Khwarazmshahian Empire. The economic situation of the area had greatly improved. Towns were revived and irrigation farms were reclaimed. Crafts, especially pottery, had also recovered. This era is identified by new forms of richly decorated and elaborated jars that were glazed ceramics decorated in diverse colors of red, ochre, yellow, and cinnamon, on white or yellowish backgrounds. Silk Road trade was once again revived on all routes.

Depopulation of Central Asian Cities

In 1220 and again in 1273, 1276, 1279, and 1316, Central Asia was devastated by the Mongol army and their destruction of dams on the Amu Darya resulting in the flooding of the low lands of Central Asia. A study by Russian and Chinese scholars concludes that between AD 1220 and 1316, seventeen million people were massacred by Mongols in Eurasia and beyond, depopulating many cities of the time. There are, however, sources that conclude more that 40 million people were massacred by Mongols, in the territories they occupied. After a series of bloody invasions during the reign of Timur (1336–1405), particularly in the second half of the fourteenth century, some of the region's most culturally significant urban centers were rebuilt.[16]

During Timurid rule, in the early fifteenth century, a school was built in Bokhara by the Timurid prince Ulug Beg. In the early sixteenth century, however, Bokhara was declared the capital of the Shaibanids (1503–1598 A.D.), an Uzbek dynasty who managed to expel the Timurids out of the western Central Asia. Timur's great grandson, Babur, went on to establish the Mughul dynasty in India. A famous sixteenth century construction, which has survived in Bokhara, and became a popular Sufi gathering place, was Khaneghah-e Khoja Zaynadin, built in 1544.

Khanate of Bokhara

The Janaid dynasty (1599–1785 A.D.), ruled from Bokhara, and their influential Khan, Imam Quli Khan (1619–1636 A.D.) ordered the construction of the Lab-e Hawz complex (1620–1623), in the heart of the city. He also finished the construction of the Shirdar School of Samarkand. One of his descendants, Abdulaziz Khan (1647–1680), built the Telakari School in Samarkand. During the rule of Mangits (1785–1920), however, Bokhara came under Russian protection in 1868. A few years later, General Konstantine Petrovich von Kaufmann was appointed as the first Russian Governor General of the Turkestan region, and the age of Russian rule in Bokhara began.

SOGHDIANA AND TIMURID'S GOLDEN AGE

Old Samarkand (Afrasiab)

On the northern side of the present-day city of Samarkand is the old city of Afrasiab, one of the largest excavation sites in Central Asia. The excavation site of Afrasiab covers an area over 550 acres. By the fall of the Soviet Union in 1991, only 5 percent of the old city was excavated. The old Samarkand,

Afrasiab, was a prosperous city from 500 B.C.E to 1220 C.E. when the area was devastated by the Mongolian army. Some of the inhabitants of the city fled the area and the others were massacred by the Mongols.

A new team of excavators, including a group of Uzbek scholars and French archeologists, have been conducting a new season of excavation that started a few years ago. The discovery of a collection of high-quality pottery, glass artifacts, terracotta statues, and other objects is reported by the new excavation team. Besides Zoroastrianism and a number of other religions and cults, the discovery of a number of statues of Anahita, the goddess of beauty and the guardian of waters, suggests that the cult of Anahita was practiced in this area and was one of the popular cults of the area. Samarkand has been an important cultural capital of Soghdia since ancient times. The city of Samarkand has played a key role in the social, political, and cultural affairs of urban life of Central Asia.

Rebuilding Samarkand

The city of Samarkand is located in the fertile Zerafshan Valley in what is today Uzbekistan. Samarkand is the ideal city in which to study the architecture and extensive ceramic art of the fourteenth and fifteenth centuries in the context of impressive interiors and exterior decorations. The ancient city of Afrasiab (old Samarkand), located to the north of the present city, was one of the most important ancient cities on the Silk Road. It was demolished and its inhabitants massacred by the Mongols in the thirteenth century. Masson in 1919 and Vyatkin in 1925 visited the ancient site and conducted brief archeological surveys on it. In 1989 a Franco Uzbek team reopened the excavation of the ancient city of Afrasiab, one of the largest excavation sites in Central Asia. A small percentage of the ancient city of Afrasiab has been excavated. Two palaces and one temple belonging to the eighth century have been identified.

Afrasiab was destroyed by Mongols in the thirteenth century and by Timur in fourteenth century. Timur (1336–1405), however, decided to rebuild the city and designated it as his new capital in the second half of the fourteenth century.[17] One of Timur's most famous buildings is the Gur-e Amir, which was designated as the ruler's tomb. The dome of Gur-e Amir is 112 feet high, enriched by sixty-four round flutes, and flanked by minarets 83 feet high. It is set on a high but narrow cylindrical drum at the base of the dome. The dome is covered with bright blue tiles and a high drum ornamented with inscription. The interior holds a superb mosaic portal built in 1454 by the Persian artist Mohamad Mahmud Isfahani.

Golden Age of Samrkand and Timurid Arts

During his reconstruction of Samarkand, Timur carried out other superb construction works. He built a citadel in 1370, and within its walls included a residence, a guardhouse, and administrative and military buildings. He then set about redesigning the city and planning other new buildings. Bibi Khanum complex, named after the queen of the empire, was the largest Timurid architectural project. It was never completed by Timur and his successors.[18] Only in 1975 did the Soviet authorities decide to finish the building. Several years after the fall of the Soviet Union, the Uzbek government declared the completion of the building.

Bibi Khanum complex stood within a high wall. Its rectangular plan measured 110 by 170 meters. In typical Persian fashion, it contained a courtyard of 65 by 75 meters and four *iwans*, one in the center of each façade. At the four corners of the great enclosing wall, four polygonal minarets in pairs flanked a monumental *pishtaq* and framed the principal *iwan* that led to the room containing the *mihrab* or a great central hall. A forty-meter-high dome covered with blue-green ceramic tiles stands next to two shorter domes. The tallest dome included thirty-six thick ribs enlivened by blue, white, and orange ceramic tiles.

Of course, there were other architectural structures built in Samarkand in the second half of the fifteenth century, including Ak Saray (White House), built in the 1470s. Sixteen relatively small architectural monuments covered with ceramic tiles were built at the Shah Zinda, where a number of Timur's relatives were buried.[19] The next golden age of Central Asia culture and arts would occur in the sixteenth and seventeenth centuries, after Shah Ismail Safavi founded the Safavid Empire in Iran.

This chapter included an analysis of the region of Soghdia, one of the earliest urbanized centers of cultural and trade activities in Central Asia. Some of the most active urbanized centers of Soghdia including Sarazm, Varakhsha, Panjikent, Bokhara, and Samarkand were given special attention. The next chapter includes an analysis of some of the artistic traditions of Central Asia as ceramic art, wood working, metal works, jewelry making, book making, miniature panting, and fabric arts.

NOTES

1. Izakov, A. I., *Excavations of the Bronze Age Settlement of Sarazm*. In: The Bronze Age civilization of Central Asia: Recent Soviet Discoveries, edited by P. L. Kohl, Armonk, N.Y., 1981. Also, see: Isakov, Kohl, Lamberg-Karlovsky and Maddin, *Mettallurgical Analysis from Sarazm,* Tadjikistan SSR, Archeology 29, Feb. 1987.

2. Shishkin, V. A. *Varakhsha*. Moscow: Izdatel'stvo Akademii Nauk, 1963. Also, see: Marshak, B. I. *The Ceilings of the Varakhsha Palace*, In Parthica. Incontri di culture nel mondo antico. Issue 2. Pisa-Rome: Istituti editoriali e poligrafici internazionali, 2000.

3. Belenitskii, A. M. and Marshak, B. I. *The Paintings of Sogdiana* (in G.Azarpay, Soghdian Painting—The Pictorial Epic in Oriental Art). Berkeley: University of California Press, 1981, pp. 11–77. Also, see: Azarpay, G. *Soghdian Painting—The Pictorial Epic in Oriental Art*. Berkeley: University of California Press, 1981, pp. 81–203

4. Ban Gu. *The History of the Former Han Dynasty* (translated by H. Dubs). London: Kegan Paul, Trubner, 1938, p. 32.

5. Boulnois L. *Silk Road—Monks Warriors & Merchants on the Silk Road*. New York: W. W. Norton & Company, 2005, p. 54.

6. Tucker, J. *The Silk Road: Art and History*. Chicago: Art Media Resources, 2003.

7. Ghrishman, R. Iran: Parthians and Sassanians. The Arts of Mankind Series, London: Thames & Hudson, 1962, pp. 119–408.

8. Belenitskii, A. M. and Marshak, B. I. *The Paintings of Sogdiana* (in G. Azarpay, Soghdian Painting—The Pictorial Epic in Oriental Art). Berkeley: University of California Press, 1981, pp. 11–77.

9. Vambery, A. *History of Bokhara from the Earliest Period down to the Present*, Eliborn Classsics, London, 2005, pp. 88–392.

10. Frye, R. *The Heritage of Central Asia - From Antiquity to the Turkish Expansion*, Markus Wiener Publishers, Princeton, 1996. Frye's concluding chapter suggests that the ancient accomplishment of the power houses of the region had profound impact on the golden age of Bokhara and Central Asia in the ninth and tenth centuries and continued it existence in Samarkand.

11. Chuvin P. and Degeorge, G. *Samarkant, Bokhara and Khiva*, Flummarion, Paris, 1999, 89–162.

12. Starr, S. F. *Lost Enlightenment*, Princeton University Press, 2015. Starr's Lost Enlightenment suggests that the golden age of Central Asia begins in Bokhara in the ninth and tenth centuries after number of interruptions continued in Samarkand in the fourteenth and fifteenth centuries.

13. Knobloch, E. *Monuments of Central Asia*, I. B. Tauris Publishers, New York, 2001.

14. Chuvin P. and Degeorge, G. *Samarkant, Bokhara and Khiva*, Flummarion, Paris, 1999.

15. Starr, S. F. *Lost Enlightenment*, Princeton University Press, 2015.

16. Lenz T. W. and Glenn, D. L. *Timur and Princely Vision*, Persian Art and Culture in the Fifteenth Century, Washington, D. C., 1989, pp. 17–66. Also, see: Appendix V of this book on what formula that was utilized by master Behzad creating some of the manuscript illuminations of Timurid era.

17. Hookham, H. *Tamburlaine the Conqueror*, London, 1962, pp. 37–58.

18. Chuvin P. and Degeorge, G. *Samarkant, Bokhara and Khiva*, Flummarion, Paris, 1999.

19. Lenz T. W. and Glenn, D. L. *Timur and Princely Vision*, Persian Art and Culture in the Fifteenth Century, Washington, D. C., 1989.

Chapter Fourteen

Artistic Traditions of Middle Ages
Ceramics, Metal Works, Jewelry, Wood Working, Suzani, and Rug Making

This chapter includes an analysis of some of the traditional intellectual and artistic impulses of Inner Eurasian (Central Asian) People in the form and shape of arts. Some of the artistic traditions of Central Asia as ceramic art, wood working, metal works, jewelry making, book making, miniature panting, and fabric arts are given special attention in this chapter.

CERAMICS

There were many cultural and artistic centers in Central Asia including Bokhara, Khiva, Afrasiab (Samarkand), Chach (Tashkand), Herat, Urganj, Merv, Khotan, Kashgar, Kucha, Turfan, and Nishapur. These cities were among the most active cities in pottery production. Potters occupied large quarters in each city. The pottery of the ninth century to the beginning of the thirteenth century was divided into the two major categories of glazed and unglazed ware. Stamped ware became widespread in the twelfth century, offering a particular wealth of inscriptions and organic and geometric decorative patterns or abstractions. The pottery pieces were elaborated by decorative motives of birds, including doves, pheasants, and ducks; animals such as mountain goats, horses, cheetahs, and lions; mythical creatures such as phoenixes; plants, pomegranates, and flowers; and even scenes from royal receptions. The geometric patterns included squares, triangles, and varieties of lines. Inscriptions occupied the rim of the plates, while the remaining surface was usually undecorated. One glazing technique with particular appeal was a lead glaze that resulted in a particular gloss to the ware.[1] After the Mongol invasion of the thirteenth century and the massacre of many of the inhabitants of cities in the region, particularly artisans and craftsmen, we witness a sharp decline in the quality of ceramic products. Ceramic production regained some of its quality after Timur decided to rebuild Samarkand as his capital and brought artisans from all parts of his empire especially from the city of Shiraz. The city of Shiraz was not affected by the Mongol invasion. The architects and tile makers who were brought from Shiraz to Central Asia left a profound impact on the architectural styles of the fourteenth and fifteenth centuries, especially on the obsessive fashion with which some of the interiors and exteriors of the buildings were covered with ceramic tile works.[2]

As a result of the drastic changes of the fourteenth century, the color of the ceramic tiles and their style of decorative motives changed. By the fifteenth century these tiles were among the most outstanding achievements of ceramic art in the world. Under khanate rule in Khiva, Bokhara, and Kokand the styles and techniques of the Timurid fourteenth and fifteenth centuries continued in Central Asia until the Russian Bolshevik revolution of 1917.

METAL WORKS & JEWELRY

Prior to the Mongol invasion the metal art of Khwarazmia and the rest of Central Asia included magnificent silver gilt artifacts created in the manner and style of Sassanian and Soghdian ancient metal works.[3] These included well proportioned jugs with narrow necks and wide pear-shaped bodies, spoon-shaped hemispheric cups, round flat plates, and small jugs of various shapes decorated with relief, embossed, and engraved ornamentation. Many of the themes of this period resembled the compositions of Sassanian and Soghdian subject matter. Some of the medieval metal works included inscriptions that distinguished them from the ancient pieces they were modeled on. New types of bronze and copper spherical jugs were created during this time. Engraving was the dominant technique of ornamentation. Carpet-like patterns were created through engraving. Popular motives of engraving of the eleventh and twelfth centuries included winged sphinxes and goats, griffins, human-headed birds, hunting scenes, and enthronements.[4] The use of motives of animals such as deer, dog, leopard, hare, bird, and fish were extremely popular. Some of the engravings included medallion shaped rings on the body of the jug.

The pre-Mongol period bronze pieces from Marv and Herat reflected mastery of the technique of the period. Incrustation with silver thread began to be practiced at this time. Sixty artifacts intended for variety of uses from the fourteenth and fifteenth centuries were found near Registan in Samarkand. They included pots, cups, and jugs with vegetal geometric patterns.

Exceptional jewelry pieces, dating from the eighth century through the twelfth century and then fourteenth century through the sixteenth century, made of gold, silver, and other metals, with insets of emerald, turquoise, cornelian, diamonds, rubies, sapphires, pearls, chalcedony, garnet, and crystal, reflected the richness of the material culture of the region.[5] Thousands of Central Asian silver coins from this era have been found in Russia, Poland, Sweden, and Denmark, which exhibits the close commercial ties among these countries. Khwarazmian and Central Asian artisans also produced rare sophisticated silver, copper, and brass besides jewelry, pottery, and metal works, other artifacts made of glass, wood, bone, and paper were also produced within the region. In the ninth and tenth centuries, decorative glass figures of birds, animals, fish, and medallions were manufactured in Termez and Afrasiab. Bone carvings, produced between the eighth and sixteenth centuries were also found, and they included pieces of a chess set from Samarkand as well as decorative spoons.

WOOD WORKING

Wood panels frequently embellished the walls of the buildings at this time. Interiors of homes and palaces from the fourteenth through sixteenth century bear witness to the high artistic quality of wood carvers. Two masterpieces of wood carving included the fourteenth century mausoleum of Sayf al Din Bakharzi in Bokhara and the fifteenth century mausoleum of Shams al din Kulyal in Shahre Sabz. Both of these wood carvings are highly symmetrical and included stylized inscriptions, as well as geometric and organic ornamentations.[6]

SUZANI AND RUG MANUFACTURING

During the pre-Mongol period, wool, cotton, linen, silk, and even blended fabrics were produced in Khwarazmia and the cities of Samarkand, Bukhara, Nishapour, and Merv and exported to other regions and countries.[7] The variety of textile and carpet designs of the ninth and tenth centuries included decorative motifs of rosettes, spirals, garlands, buds, and floral patterns. Many carpets were created either for wall decoration or floor cover. Gold embroidery was used for a variety of purposes including horse cloth and cover, cushions and pillows, robes, and other clothing items.[8]

Rugs have a special place in the social and cultural history of Central Asia. Soviet archaeologists discovered the earliest knotted rug in a frozen grave, in Pazyryk Kurgan, in Altai mountains, in Southern Siberia. It pre-dates all other known knotted rugs by over a thousand years. Medieval Persian literature contains quite a few references to Persian rugs. A number of different Central Asian and Iranian regions and towns remain famous today for their high-quality rugs, which utilize appealing color combinations, along with distinctive design and patterns. These include, Khiva, Tabriz, Isfahan, Bokhara, Kashghar, Kashan, Khotan, Kerman, and Naiin.[9] Turkmen rugs, however, had a particular place and appeal amongst rug admirers. The production of Turkmen weaving included a variety of utilitarian and decorative items, that were created with the same material, and in the same colors, but took different shapes and forms, including khorjin (bag), javal, saddle bags and a variety of bands, and decorative rugs for the interior and exterior of the yurt.

The main elements of traditional Turkman knotted rug design were known as guls (flowers). Turkman rugs were composed of repeated geometric shapes and forms; hence, although initially the motif of a flower was borrowed from nature, it was abstracted into geometric motifs. The semi-diamond shaped guls repeated on Turkman rugs were woven across different tribal regions, and the shape and details of the gul varied from one tribe to another. Traditionally, maroon, black, and pastel white colors were favored for Turkmen rugs. There are twenty-eight major Turkman tribes; however, many of the Turkman rugs are identified by the name of Salor, Tekke, Saryk, Yomud, Ogurjali, Chaudor, or Ersari tribes. The more recent wave of rugs woven in the region included some green and blue colors. Khiva in Khwarazmia is one of the major markets for Turkmen rugs.

BOOK MAKING AND MINIATURE PAINTING REFLECTING THE POPULAR MODE OF LIVING

Khwarazmians in particular, and in general the people of Central Asia, Afghanistan, and Iran have always been artistic, poetic, and nature loving. The qualities and characteristics of the people's feelings and thoughts were reflected in various styles of painting throughout many centuries. Epics, romances, histories, and fables provided artists with subjects to paint in exquisite detail. Clarity, quality of color, and elegance of composition were the common characteristics of the Persian and Central Asian paintings. Gardens, orchards, and landscapes in spring were included in paintings that depicted poetry reading, story-telling, and outdoor entertainment with music, dance, and wine drinking scenes. Elegant court banquets, as well as chess and polo matches were popular subject matters and often decorated and illuminated different kinds of manuscripts.

Masterpieces of book making, particularly those produced in the courts of Khiva, Samarkand, Herat, Shiraz, Tabriz, and Bokhara, were appealing, artistic, and highly prized. Many illustrative artists of the time initially were trained and educated by the master artist Behzad.[10] He originally lived in Samarkand, but moved to a number of other major cities. Behzad was in charge of Herat School, during the reign of Shahrokh, son of Timur. He then moved to Tabriz and continued his education and training of young artists at the court of Shah Ismail, the founder of Safavid dynasty of Iran. Behzad's formula for creating manuscript illuminations included cityscapes with multi-figure subjects, and a variety of contrasting cool and warm toned colors, alternating with extensive use of earth tones and neutralized colors. In countless examples of book making from this time, Behzad's techniques and training may be reflected in the stamped and gilded decorations of the book's cover, to the elegant calligraphy of the manuscript, to the diverse ornamentation and bright colors and illuminations and illustrative miniature themselves.

Many manuscript illuminations created by the royal atelier were images created for popular books on literature, poetry, and history, which were commissioned by princes and princesses of the royal family. The similarity of images from Khiva, Samarkand, Bokhara, Herat, Shiraz, and Tabriz can be attributed to the influence of Behzad, since many of them were designed and produced by Behzad's students, who were now residing at different courts, and were trying to follow his earlier formula. By the late sixteenth and early seventeenth century the Iranian city of Isfahan was chosen by the Safavid dynasty as the new capital of their powerful empire. The School of Isfahan led by a new master, Abbasi offers a new vocabulary and formula materializing painting compositions. The new formula concentrated on single portraits of young men and women, often reflecting leisure time, or melancholy, in the face, body language, or impressions.

The School of Isfahan, led by Abbasi, produced many masterpieces with strong monochromatic tendencies. In book art, however, the climax of miniature illumination that started over a century before in Samarkand, and expanded into Khiva, Herat, Bokhara, Shiraz, and Tabriz, continued in Isfahan, with new elegant and exquisite accomplishments in the late sixteenth and early seventeenth century. The styles of Persian miniature illumination continued in Central Asia until the Bolshivik Revolution of 1917.

Russians took control of the region in the nineteenth century and after years of civil war (1917–1924), Soviet rule was established. A state sponsored cultural and artistic school "Social Realism" was imposed on the people of Central Asia and the rest of the Soviet Union as the only choice to conduct cultural and artistic activities within their society. Shortly after its establishment in 1924, the highly politically motivated school of Social Realism became a tool in the hand of the state to conduct propaganda art, promoting the state and its ideology. Furthermore, based on no historical or cultural foundations, Stalin fabricated five new Soviet states (1924–1936), which since 1991, are the independent republics of Uzbekistan, Kazakhstan, Tajikistan, Kyrgyzstan, and Turkmenistan.

The eastern part of Central Asia was occupied by twenty-five thousand Chinese Qing Empire (1644–1911) forces in 1760. Despite the resistance of the ancient Turks, Uyghurs, and other ethnicities to this invasion, Chinese occupation in the east, continued throughout the era of the Republic of China 1911–1949. In 1949, the region was once again invaded by Mao's Red Army and was devastated during the Cultural Revolution (1966–1976).

It is only after the fall of the Soviet Union in 1991 to the west of Central Asia, and a relative opening to the east of Central Asia from 1989, that some of the historical, cultural, and artistic accomplishments of Central Asians in the past were allowed to be paid attention to.

For over seven thousand years, Central Asian people have left a record of distinguished cultural artifacts. Like creators and innovators of any age or period, they sought to respond as creatively as possible to the necessities of their societies as a whole, and those of their individual patrons. In doing so they have given us a timeless source through which we can detect the dynamic stages of their creativity throughout history, and also the breadth of our own rich cultural and artistic heritage.

This chapter included an analysis of some of the artistic traditions of Central Asia as ceramic art, wood working, metal works, jewelry making, book making, miniature panting, and fabric arts.

NOTES

1. Ettinghausen, R., *Medieval Near Eastern Ceramics*, Freer Gallery of Art and Smithsonian Institute, Washington D. C., 1960, 7–54.

2. Allen, J. W., *Nishapur: Metalwork of the Early Islamic Period*, New York, 1982, 23–84.

3. Melikian-Chirvani, A. S., *Islamic Metalwork from Iranian World*, eighth to eighteen Centuries, London, 1982, 21–73.

4. Komomaroff, L., *The Golden Disk of Heaven: Metal Work of Timurid Iran*, Cosa Mesa, California, and New York, 1992, 31–132. Also, see: Sykhova, N., *Traditional Jewellery from Soviet Central Asia and Kazakhstan*, Museum of Oriental Art, Moscow, 1984, 14–79.

5. Chuvin P. and Degeorge, G., *Samarkand, Bokhara, and Khiva*, Flummarion, Paris, 1999, 163–222.

6. Blackwel, B., *Ikats: Woven Silk from Central Asia*, Oxford, 1988, pp. 34–73.

7. Kennedy, A., *Central Asian Ikats*, Philadelphia, 1980, 14–67.

8. Bode, W. von and E. Kuhnel, E., *Antique Rugs from the Near East*, 4th revised ed., trans. C. G. Ellis, Berlin, 1958, 35–83.

9. Erdmann, K., *Oriental Carpets*, second edition, trans. By C. G. Ellis, London, 1960, 9–58.

10. Arnold, T. W., *Behzad and His Paintings in Zafarnamah*, London, 1930, 7–4.

Conclusion

This book has explored the cultural heritage of Inner Eurasia (Central Asia) through the arts, from prehistoric times to ancient and medieval golden ages. The strongest features are inclusion and analysis of so many cultural groups and their artistic traditions and their development through the history of Inner Eurasia.

This analysis is based on research of a wide range of appropriate sources: both archeological reports on numerous excavations and research projects conducted by experts throughout the twentieth century, as well as ancient and medieval manuscripts on the topics. While many books focus more specifically on one era, region, site, site type, cultural group, or specific material type or motif group, they do not attempt the scope of this macro-analysis, and there is a good reason for that. As one of the pioneers of teaching cultures and arts of Inner Eurasia in the United States for the past twenty-eight years, the author has always had to draw on different books and articles to teach classes, since no single source addressed all the arts, cultures, and civilizations of the region in one volume. Hence, this was one of the main reasons the book is composed as it is, to contribute a synthetic overview of artistic and cultural traditions of prehistory, ancient, and medieval golden ages of Inner Eurasia.

The time periods: Paleolithic, Mesolithic, Neolithic, Copper, Bronze, and Iron Ages, as well as prehistoric, ancient, and medieval eras, are defined in both the text itself, as well as a glossary following this conclusion. Within the context of these time periods, related artistic activities are linked to the places involved in cultural creativity for a holistic analysis by readers.

The arts of Inner Eurasia since prehistoric times including petroglyphs, paintings, drawings, etching, pottery, figurines, statues, sculptures, sculptural reliefs, glazed brick compositions, mosaic art, metal art (copper, bronze, and iron), jewelry (gold, silver, and precious stones), crowns, book art, mural painting, calligraphical writing, manuscript illumination, silk making, fabric design, wood working, suzani (embroidery), rug making, and architectural projects are a legacy of the peoples of Central Asia, and occupy a brilliant page in the universal genius of humanity's arts. These regions deserve to be studied and appreciated by all who seek in the arts not simply aesthetic enjoyment, but meaningful expression of humanity's cultural achievements.

Appendix I
Prehistoric Pottery Stages According to R. Ghirshman and G. Contenau

SUMMARY OF SIALK ARCHEOLOGICAL EXCAVATIONS ANALYSIS

Neolithic Period
Farming
Villages & Towns
Indigenous population
Sialk I
6000–5000 B.C.
Plain Pottery

Late Neolithic Period
5000–4000 B.C.
Sialk II
Copper tools/Silver artifacts
Stamp seal
Geometric period

Late Neolithic Period
4000–3500 B.C.
Silver products
Sialk III
Urbanization
Potter's wheel
"Animal Style Art"

Bronze Age
3500–1500 B.C.
Sialk IV
City States
Animal Style pottery

R. Ghirshman and G. Contenau found at least 9 (and possibly 11) layers of civilizations in Sialk.
The fifth layer of Sialk pottery includes human figure motifs.
(Iron Age: 1500–1000 B.C.)

The sixth layer of Sialk (A & B) is identified as the "Organic Style Pottery," which includes all organic motifs, forms, and shapes.

There are transitionary periods between the upper named stages
(There are at least three additional layers of civilizations in Sialk—ancient & medieval)

Appendix II
Avesta's Yasht Twenty-one Chapters

YASHT	TITLE	RESPECT & GRATITUDE FOR	INCLUDES
I.	Ormazd Yasht	Ahura Mazda	33 verses
II.	Haptan Yasht	The seven Amesh Spentas	15 verses
III.	Ardibehisht Yasht	Asha Vahishta of "Best Truth"	19 verses
IV.	Khordad Yasht	Haurvatat of "Wholeness" and "Perfection"	11 verses
V.	Aban Yasht	Aredvi Sura Anahita of the waters	132 verses
VI.	Khorshed Yasht	Hvare-khshaeta of the "Radiant Sun"	7 verses
VII.	Mah Yasht	Maonghah of the "Moon"	7 verses
VIII.	Tir Yasht	Tishtrya, the star Sirius	62 verses
IX.	Drvasp Yasht	Drvaspa, guardian of horses	33 verses
X.	Mehr Yasht	Mithra of "Covenant"	145 verses
XI.	Srosh Yasht	Sraosha of "Obedience"	23 verses
XII.	Rashn Yasht	Rashnu of "Justice"	47 verses
XIII.	Fravardin Yasht	the Fravashis	158 verses
XIV.	Bahram Yasht	Verethragna, "Smiter of resistance"	64 verses
XV.	Ram Yasht	the "good" Vayu	58 verses
XVI.	Din Yasht	Chista, "Wisdom"	20 verses
XVII.	Ashi Yasht	Ashi of "Recompense"	62 verses
XVIII.	Ashtad Yasht	khvarenah, the "(divine) glory"	9 verses
XIX.	Zamyad Yasht		97 verses
XX.	Hom Yasht	Haoma	3 verses
XXI.	Vanant Yasht	Vanant, the star Vega	2 verses

The Zend Avesta, Part II
Sacred Books of the East, Vol. 23
Translated by James Darmesteter, 1882

Appendix III

MANI AND MANICHAEISM MANUSCRIPTS

Fragments of manuscripts written by Mani demonstrate that he wrote several books. These include:

Living Gospel,
Treasure of Life,
Treatise,
Book of Secrets,
Book of Giants,
Epistles, and
Psalms and Prayers.

Manicheans were found as far north as Armenia and Bulgaria, and in the twelfth century C. E., they had established themselves as Cathars or Albigensians in France.

Widengren, G. (1965). *Mani and Manichaeism.* London: Weidenfeld & Nicolson.
Foltz, R. (2010). *Religions of the Silk Road.* New York: Palgrave Macmillan.

Appendix IV

SOME OF THE BOOKS TRANSLATED FROM MIDDLE PERSIAN INTO ARABIC AND MODERN PERSIAN

After the fall of the Sassanian Empire, hundreds of Pahlavi texts were translated from Middle Persian, which was the official language of the Persian Sassanian Empire, into Arabic and modern Persian, which emerged after the introduction of Islam. A selection of the literary sources translated from Middle Persian include:

Hazar Afsan (The Thousand Tales);

Sindbud-namag (Book of Sindbud or Sindbud Bahri);

Vis and Ramin (a famous love story);

Ayen Ewen-namag (etiquette, manners, ceremonies, backgammon, horsemanship);

Madigan-i Hazar Dadestan (Book of a Thousand Judicial Decisions by Farrukhmard son of Bahram); and

Kweskarihi-i Redagan (Education of Children).

Ayadgar-i Zariran, the "Memorial or Zarer," is the only surviving specimen of Iranian epic poetry composed in Middle Persian.

Shahrestaniha i Eranshahr is a catalogue of the four regions of the Sassanid empire with mythical and/or historical stories related to their founding.

Andarz-namag texts, the type of wisdom literature containing advice and injunctions for proper behavior.

Wizarishn i Chatrang, "Explanation of Chess," also known as the Chatrang Namag, is a humorous story of how an Indian king sent a game of chess to the Sassanid court to test Iranian wits, in response to which a priest invented backgammon to challenge the Indian king.

Abdih ud Sahigih i Sagistan is a description of the "Wonders and Remarkable Features of Sistan."

Mah Farvardin ruz khordad is a book that described all the events which historically or mythically occurred on the sixth day of the Persian month of Farvardin.

Madayan i Hazar Dadestan, "Book of a Thousand Judgements," a seventh-century compilation of actual and hypothetical case histories collected from Sassanian court records and transcripts. Only a single manuscript of this unique text survives.

Khwaday Namag ("Book of Kings"), a legendary genealogy of the Sassanid kings in which the Sassanians were dynastically linked to Vishtaspa, i.e., Zoroaster's patron and the legendary founder of the mythological Kianian Dynasty. The original Middle Persian version of the chronicle has been lost, and the contents survive only through Arabic translations and in a versified New Persian version, the Shahnameh by Firdausi, finished around 1000.

Letter of Tansar, a rationale for Ardashir's seizure of the throne. The letter was translated into Arabic in the ninth century by Ibn al-Muqaffa, and from Arabic into New Persian in the thirteenth century History of Tabaristan by Ibn Isfandiar.

Ayyatkar-i Anushirvan, which has survived as an Arabic translation in a section of Ibn Meskavayh's Tajarib al-Umam.

During the reign of Abbasid Caliph al-Mamun (813–833), many scholars from Khwarazm and the rest of Central Asia were forced to move to Baytal Hikma (house of wisdom) in the Shammasiyya district of Baghdad. Abbasid were building their new capital few miles from Ctesiphon the last Capital of Persian Parthian Empire (247 B.C.–226 A.D.) and Persian Sassanid Empire (231 A.D.–651 A.D.). Al Mamun capital in Khorasan was the city of Merv (813–819). While staying for six years in Merv, al Mamun gathered astronomers, mathematicians, and scientists of Central Asia including Khwarazm, Chach, Ferghana, and Khurasan. One of the most impressive scholars leaving Khwarazm and Central Asia for Baghdad was Muhammad b. Musa Khwarazmi. Other scholars leaving Central Asia for Baghdad included Yahya b. Mansur, Khalid b. Abd al-Malik al-Marwarrudhi, Abbas

b. Said Jawaheri, Abu Tayyib Sanadb. Ali, Ahmad b. Muhhamad b. Kathir al-Farghani, Ahmad b. abd Allah Habash al-Hasib, and Abd al-Hamid Ibn Turk al-Khuttali). The Shammasiyya district of Baghdad had also a high concentration of translators including Nirizi, Battani, Hajjaj b. Qurra, Ibrahim b. al-Sami, Husayn b. Ishaq, Umarb. Farrukhan, and Thabit b. Qurra.

Appendix V

THE FORMULA UTILIZED BY MASTER K. BEHZAD TO COMPOSE HIS MANUSCRIPT ILLUMINATIONS

Behzad, the master, initiated an idea materializing the landscape (or cityscape) paintings. Based on the new formula, composing a landscape, the horizon line is moved up, hence, the detail of the landscape occupies (approximately) more than 80 percent of the composition, while the skyline takes the rest of the composition, less than 20 percent of it. Therefore, there is a slanted view of the events within the composition (not a bird's-eye view). Hence, the artist is looking down at a landscape in an angle, elaborating more details of the overall picture, and each of the components of the composition. One popular subject matter, chosen by Behzad and his students, is banquet (*bazm*). Often, the banquet is occurring, at the presence of the royalty, with foreign and domestic guesses, with musicians and dancers, and variety of food dishes. Although, some of the events appear to be an outdoor scene, yet there is a component of the composition that includes an architectural entity merging in, suggests that the allegorical event is happening on the edge of town, or in an orchard with a royal palace or complex.

Many of the compositions are surrounded by polychromatic spring flowers and fruit-tree blossoms, symbolically, suggesting the event is happening, in an early spring day (*Nowruz*), or early summer with many figurative elements, human and animal. Although, there is a centrality to the composition, around one or few of the human figures, who may be recognizable, however, that centrality is challenged by other figurative components in the periphery, involving other tasks. The colors of the compositions are mixed with bright, contrasting, complimentary colors, combined with earth tone, neutralized colors, masterfully elaborating organic naturalistic elements at time mixed with fabric or mosaic geometric or organic patterns of the objects within, adding to the complexity of the composition.

Appendix VI
The Golden Age of the Safavid Empire

ISFAHAN 1491–1722

Chardin (1988 Dover edition of Chardin's travels) reports that in 1666, Isfahan, the capital of Safavids (1491–1722), had 48 schools, 173 public bath houses, and 182 caravanserais.[1] The great Maydan Shah of Isfahan, scene of maeuvers, processions and games, especially polo, is surrounded by two storied arcades which focus on the recessed portal of the Masjid-e Shah. Opposite, at the north end of the Maydan is the royal caravanserai and bazaar, at the middle of the west side in the palace of Ali Qapu, the seat of the government, and facing it, across the Maydan, is the mosque of Shaykh Lutf Allah. With Shah Abbas I (1589–1627), the great period of Safavid architecture opened. Isfahan, was reconstituted with so many palaces, schools, bridges, parks, avenues, and public bath houses that the European travelers referred to it as "half of the world" and wrote extensively of its beauty.[2]

The Isfahan palaces, of which two have survived, are exceedingly modest, in comparison to ancient Achaemenid and Sassanian royal palaces and constructions. The Chehel Sutun palace includes a talar, or a columnar porch (1647), a form used in palaces and temples for centuries. At its simplest it is only a roof high porch constituting the façade. When it is attached to the royal building, it provides a huge outdoor reception hall, and it susceptible to lavish embellishments which have included mirror plated columns, panels and stalactites, and polychrome mosaic ceilings. The interior of this palace is covered with painted ornament of both figurative and abstract designs and capped with ceiling vaults of intense harmonious colors.

The palace of the Ali Qapu, constructed in early seventeenth century, on the Maydan Shah of Isfahan, was the center of political power. It is seven floors tall, square in plan. It has a huge reception hall capable of holding more than two hundred courtiers.[3] The talar of the palace of Ali Qapu commands a fine view over the city with mosques, domes, and minarates, and particularly over the activities of the maydan below. The interior is covered with delicate polychrome reliefs. Many rooms for private entertainment have fireplaces and open on one side, evidencing again the Persian technique of bringing the out of doors into their houses.

In fact, the remodeling of Isfahan began with a great north south avenue named Chahar Bagh. Chahar Bagh was a very wide tree lined avenue, leading directly to the river Zayandeh Rud. Then the avenue continued over the famous bridge of "Seyu Se Pol" (thirty-three arches), also known as "Alaverdi Khan" bridge (over 900 feet long and 40 feet wide), named after the Georgian general of the Safavid, who later became the governor of Fars province. Downstream from Alaverdi Khan bridge, another bridge called "Pol e Khaju" Khaju Bridge is 4500 feet was built in the mid seventeenth century by the Safavids. On the other bank lay the attractive Armenian suburb of Julfa, with its historical museum, church, and complexes.[4]

By the late sixteenth and early seventeenth century the city of Isfahan was chosen by the Safavid dynasty as the new capital of their powerful empire. The School of Isfahan led by a new master, R. Abbasi offers a new vocabulary and formula materializing painting compositions. The new formula concentrated on single portraits of young men and women, often reflecting leisure time, or melancholy, in the face, body language, or impressions.

The School of Isfahan, led by Abbasi, produced many masterpieces with strong monochromatic tendencies. In book art, however, the climax of miniature illumination that started over a century before in Samarkand, and expanded into Khiva, Herat, Bokhara, Shiraz, and Tabriz, continued in Isfahan, with new elegant and exquisite accomplishments in the late sixteenth and early seventeenth century. The styles of Persian miniature illumination continued in Central Asia until the Bolshivik Revolution of 1917.[5]

NOTES

1. Chardin, J. *Travels in Persia* 1673 – 1677, Dover Publications, 2012, pp. 73–132.

2. Savory, R. *Iran under Safavids*, Cambridge University Press, 1980, pp. 154–76, 5.

3. Newman, A. J. *Safavid Iran: Rebirth of a Persian Empire*, St. Martin Press, N.Y., 2006, pp. 50–72.

4. Blake, S. P. *Half the World*: Social Architecture of Safavids Isfahan 1590–1722.

5. Taylor, A. *Diversity and Identity in Seventeenth Century Persia*, Getty Publications, 1995.

Glossary

Animal Style Art: A term referring to the characteristic of artifacts worn and carried by peoples of Inner Eurasia for over two millennia, utilizing realistic, naturalistic, or imaginary animal motives symbolizing powers of nature for the purpose of artistic ornamentation and decorations.

Anahita: Inner Eurasian goddess of fertility and waters.

Apadana: The great audience hall in ancient Achaemenid palaces.

Artifact: Is a general term for an item made or given shape by humans, such as a tool or a work of art, especially an object of archaeological interest.

Bronze Age: A prehistoric period in the Old World, dating roughly from 3000 B. C. E.–1000 B. C. E., following the Copper Age, defined by the widespread use of bronze as a material for tools, weapons, and ornaments.

Capital: The head or crowning feature of a column.

Caravanserai: A lodging place for travelers including merchants, with provision for securing people, animals, and goods.

Copper Age: Also known as the Chalcolithic Age, (also known Eneolithic or Aeneolithic) is an archaeological period which researchers now regard as part of the broader Neolithic period, succeeded the Stone Age with the introduction of copper tools to replace the tools made by stone. This age began at different times throughout the world but it approximately lasted one thousand years followed by Bronze Age.

Earthenware: A type of pottery made from common clay and fired at a temperature of less than 1000 C. The resulting vessel is soft and requires a glaze to render it waterproof.

Fluting: Vertical channeling, roughly semicircular in cross-section and used principally on columns.

Glazed brick: Bricks painted and then kiln fired to fuse the color with the baked clay.

Hellenistic period: The era between the destruction of the Golden Age of the Athenian Kingdom by Alexander of Macedonia in 338 (Battle of Chaeronea), and the rise of the Roman Empire (27 B. C. E.).

Iron Age: The prehistoric period in the Old World that followed the Bronze Age, characterized by the use of iron implements in place of bronze tools.

Iwan: A vault closed at one end and open at the other, a kind of open porch, usually opening onto a courtyard, a standard feature in particular started in Hatra, the Parthian city in the first/second century C. E.

Kala: Town

Kitabkhana: A library and scriptorium, where books were both stored and produced

Kurgan: A burial mound, a raised mass of earth or debris within or below which deceased individuals are placed.

Mosaic Tilework: A decorative technique in which large ceramic panels are fired, cut into smaller pieces, and set in plaster.

Neolithic: The New Stone Age, approximately 7000 B. C. E.–3000 B. C. E. when many areas were developing a lifestyle and material culture associated with farming as it developed in different parts of the world.

Madrasa: A school for the teaching of foundations.

Mesolithic: The period between the Paleolithic (Old Stone Age) and the Neolithic (New Stone Age), beginning around 10,000 years ago.

Mithra: Sun god.

Monochromatic: Consisting of single color.

Paleolithic: The Old Stone Age, the archaeological period before 10,000 B.C., during which humankind produced the first art objects around 30,000 B.C.

Petroglyph: Engravings or incising in rock.

Pictograph: Painting on rock.

Pishtaq: A portal or high arch framing an iwan.

Polychrome: Done in several colors.

Pottery: The most commonly found categories of archaeological find. It is used widely for the dating of archaeological deposits. Different regions produce different types of pottery, it can also be studied to identify trade contacts and communication routes between different cultures.

Prehistory: The study of the cultures and events which occurred in any given region prior to the time for written records are available. Consequently, history begins at different times in different places.

Preservation: Actions or processes aimed at protecting a resource from change, deterioration, or destruction in order to maintain the object in an intact state or to prevent its decay or decomposition.

Rock Art: A general term for figures or designs painted or engraved on rock.

Satrapy: A province or state of the ancient Achaemenid Empire.

Scythian Animal Style Jewelry Art: Highly skillful gold pieces featuring animals including horses, stags, birds, snow leopards, and mythical beasts (included Cimmerian and Sarmatian cultures). The species represented seemed to many scholars intended merely for decoration, but some of them initially had their roots in early supernatural beliefs.

Shaman: A man or a woman thought to have direct contact with supernatural powers, which he or she uses to help people.

Stone Age: The time during which the implements that have survived were made of stone. It has traditionally been subdivided into Paleolithic (Old), Mesolithic (Middle), and Neolithic (New) ages.

Style: Characteristics of appearance used to classify objects into groups. Style helps to identify cultural and chronological changes and connections.

Talar: A columned hall.
Tepe: Artificial mound.

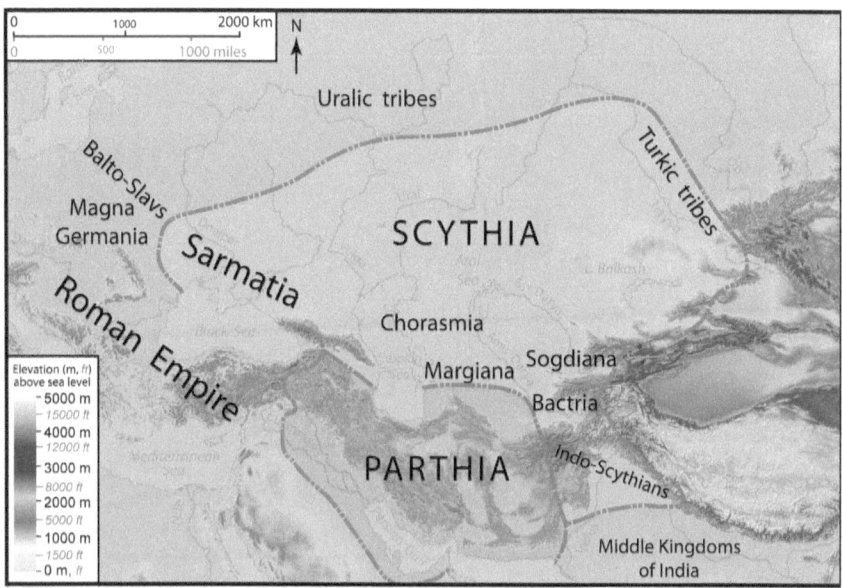

Map of Scythia

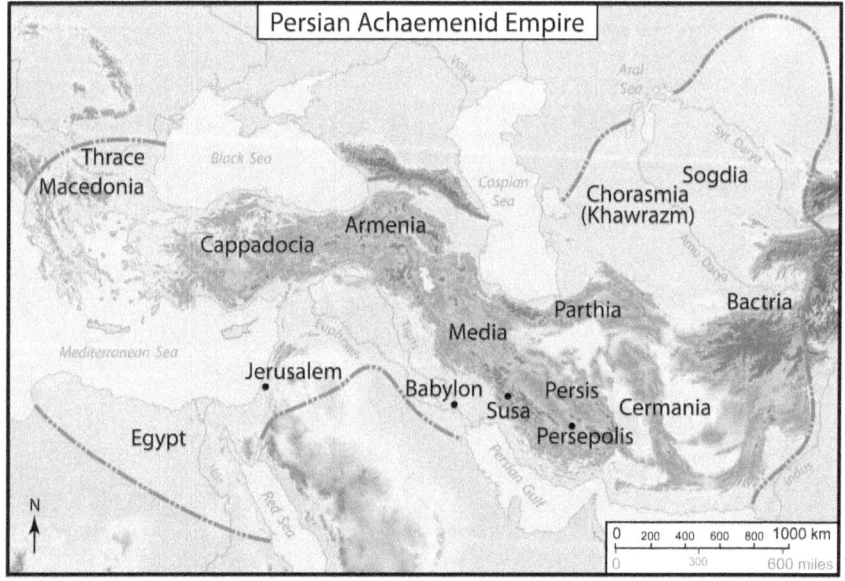

Map of Achaemenid Empire

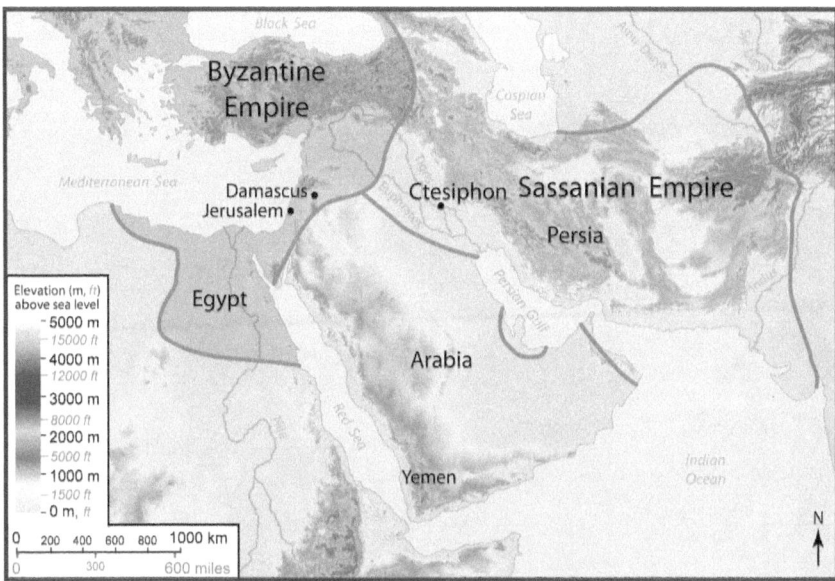

Map of Sassanian Empire

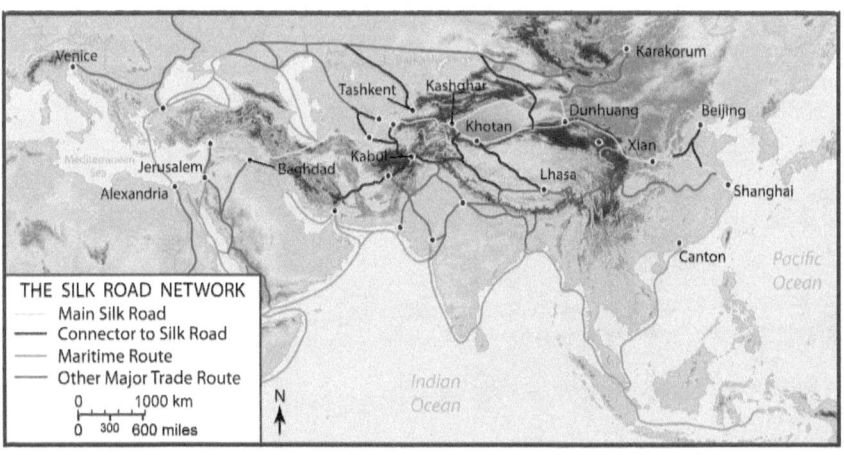

Map of Silk Road

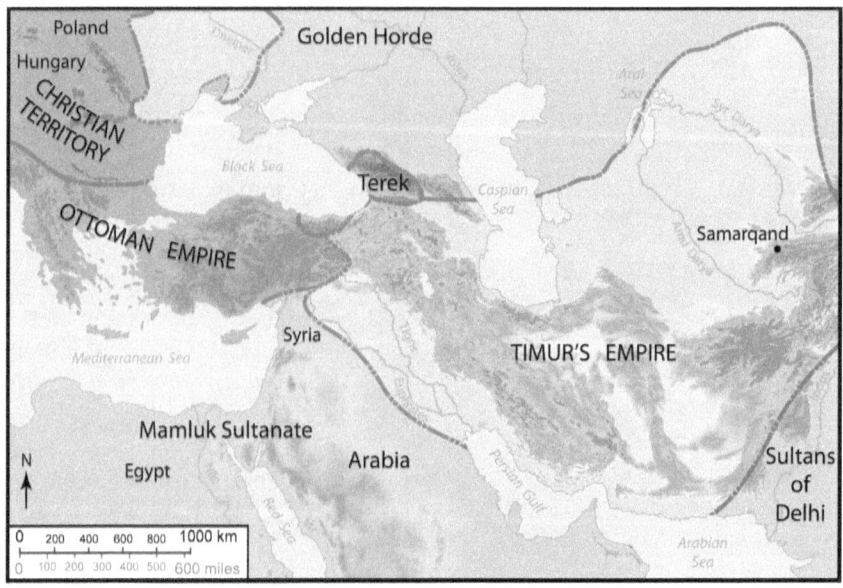

Map of Timurid Empire

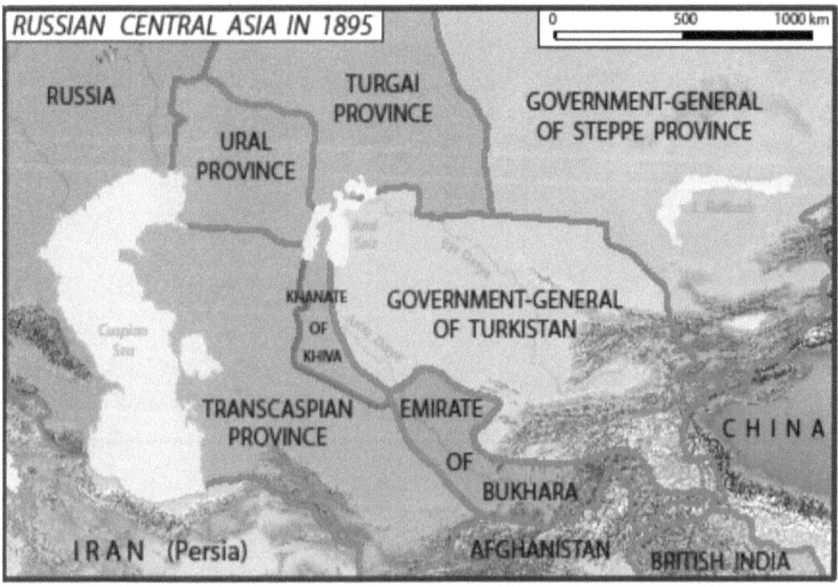

Map of Russian Central Asia in 1895

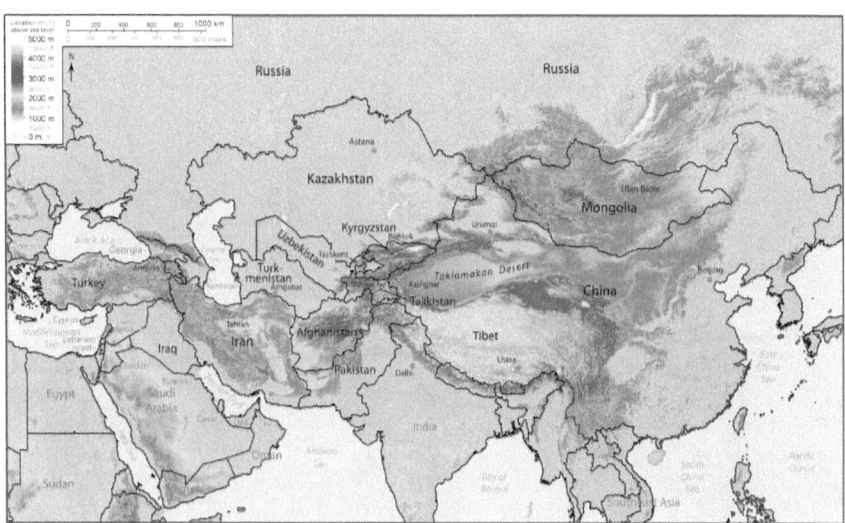

Map of Contemporary Inner Eurasia (Central Asia)

Bibliography

Abetekov, A. and Yusupov, H., *Ancient Iranian Nomads in Western Central Asia*, History of Civilization of Central Asia, Vol. II, UNESCO Publishing, 1994.
Akhmedov, A., *Astronomy, Astrology, Observatories and Calendars*, History of Civilizations of Central Asia, Vol. IV, UNESCO Publishing, 2000.
Akishev, K., *Ancient gold of Kazakhstan*, Alma-Ata, 1983.
Akishev, K. A., *Andronovo Cultures of Central Kazakhstan*, 1966.
Akishev, K. A., *South Kazakhstan: Ili Basin, Gigantic Saka Kurgans*, Bes-Shatyr, 1959.
Akishev, K. A., *General Survey: Stone and Bronze Ages*, Izviestiya Academy of Sciences, Kazakhstan SSR, 1958.
Akishev, K., *Art and mythology of Sakas*, Alma Ata, Science, 1984.
Allen, J. W., *Nishapur: Metalwork of the Early Islamic Period*, New York, 1982.
Alpysbayev, Kh. A., *Bostandy Rock Engravings*, Trudy Instituta Arkheologii i Etnograffii, 1956.
Alpysbayev, Kh. A., *Palaeolithic in South Kazakhstan*, Sovietskaya Arkheologiya, 1959.
Marshak B. I. and V. I. Raspopova, *A Hunting Scene from Panjikent*, Bulletin of the Asia Institute 4, 1990b.
Sarianidi V. I., *Cult building of a settlement of the Anau culture*. SA 1, 1962.
Anthony, D. and N. Vinogradov, *Birth of the Chariot*, Archaeology, 48(2), 1995.
Anthony, D. W., *The Horse, The Wheel and Language: How Bronze Age Riders from Eurasia Steppes Shaped the Modern World*, Princeton University Press, 2007.
Arnold, T. W., *Behzad and His Paintings in Zafarnamah*, London, 1930.
Arnold, T. W., *Survival of Sasanian and Manichaean Art* in Persian Painting, Oxford Press, 1924.
Artamonov, M. I., *The Splendor of Scythian Art: Treasures from Scythian tombs*, F. A. Praeger Publishers, New York, 1969.
Excavation of a monumental temple at Jarkutan. Tashkent, 1985.
Askrov, A., *Sites of Andronovo Culture in the Lower Basin of the Zarafshan*, Istoriya material'noi kul'tury Uzbekistana, Vol. 3, Tashkent, 1962.
Azarpay, G., *Soghdian Painting—The Pictorial Epic in Oriental Art*. Berkeley, 1981.
Azarpay, G., *Some Classical and Near Eastern Motifs in the Art of Pazyryk*. Artibus Asiae XXII/4, 1959
Baipakov, K. M., A. N. Maryashev, and S. A. Potapov, *Petroglify Tamgaly*, Almaty, 2006.
Ban Gau, *The History of the Former Han Dynasty*, translated by H. Dubbs, London, 1938.
Barber, E. W., *The Mummies of Urumchi*, W. W. Norton & Co., New York, 1999.
Barthold, V. V., *Turkestan Down to the Mongol Invasion*, Luzac & Co., London, 1928.

Beckwith, Christopher I., *Empires of the Silk Road: A History of Central Eurasia from the Bronze Age to the Present*, Princeton University Press, 2009.

Bednarik, R. G., *Dating Rock Art in Xinjiang*, AURA Newsletter 32(1): 2015.

Belenitskii, A. M. and Marshak, B. I., *The Paintings of Sogdiana*, in Azarpay, G., the Pictorial Epic in Oriental Art, 1981.

Belenitskii, A. M., *Excavations of ancient Panjikent*, ART, No. 16, 1982.

Belenitskiĭ, M. B. I. Marshak, V. I. Raspopova, and A. I. Isakov, "Raskopki gorodishcha drevnego Pendzhikenta v 1977 g." *Excavations of ancient Panjikant in 1977*, Arkheologicheskie raboty v Tadzhikistane (Archaeological works in Tajikistan), Vol. XVII (1977), Dushanbe, 1984.

Belenitsky, A., *Central Asia*, The World Publishing Company, Cleveland and New York, 1968.

Berdyiev, O. K., *Chagilli Depe, A new Site of the Neolithic Djeitun Cultures*, Moscow, 1966.

Berghe, L. V., *La Necropole de Khurvin*, Nederlands Historisch Archaeologisch Instituut in het Nabije te Istanbul, XVII, 1964.

Berghe, L.V., *Les Bronze du Luristan*, Archeologie, 1959.

Bernshtam, A. N., *Reports of the Semirechye Archeological Expedition: The Chu Valley*, MIA, 14, Moscow and Leningrad, 1950.

Bernshtam, A. N., *Reports of the Semirechye Archeological Expedition: The Chu Valley*, MIA, 14, Moscow and Leningrad, 1950.

Bernshtam, A. N., *Po Sledam Drevnikh Kultur: Tyan-Shan and Pamirs Engravings*, 1954.

Bernshtam, A. N., *Saimaly-Tash: Fergana Rock Engravings*, Sovietskaya Etnografiya, 1952.

Bernshtam, A. N., *Scythian Art: Rock Engravings*, Materials of and Research into the Archeology of the USSR, 1952a.

Biscione, R., *Ceramica di Amlash*, Museo Nazionale d'Arte Orientale, Schede 6, Rome, 1974.

Bivar, B. D. H., *The Kanishka Dating from Surkh Kotal*, BSOAS, 15, 1963.

Blackwel, B., *Ikats: Woven Silk from Central Asia*, Oxford, 1988.

Blake, S. P., *Half the World*: Social Architecture of Safavids Isfahan 1590–1722.

Bode, W. von and E. Kuhnel, *Antique Rugs from the Near East*, fourth revised ed., trans. C. G. Ellis, Berlin, 1958.

Bonfante, L., *Etruscan Life and Afterlife*, Wayne State University Press, 1986.

Bosworth, C. E., *Legal and Political Sciences in the Eastern Iranian World and Central Asia in the Pre- Mongol Period*, History of Civilizations of Central Asia, Vol. IV, UNESCO Publishing, 2000.

Boulnois L., *Silk Road—Monks Warriors & Merchants on the Silk Road*, W. W. Norton & Company, New York, 2005.

Browder, M. H., Biruni Manichaean Sources, in P. Bryder, ed. Manichaean Studies, 1982.

Bruno, J., *Ceramics of Parthian Homeland: New data about the ceramic production of the early Arsacd period*, from the Italian excavation in Old Nisa, 2008.

Brzezinski, R. and M. Mielczarek, *The Sarmatians 600 BC—AD 450*, Bloomsbury USA; Osprey Publishing, 2002.
Bunker, Emma C., *Nomadic Art of the Eastern Eurasian Steppes*: the Eugene V. Thaw and other New York collections, New York: The Metropolitan Museum of Art, 2002.
Buriankov, I. U. F., *The watershed of the middle Jaxartes in ancient and early medieval times.* Tahskent, 1987.
Buswell, R. Jr, D. S. Lopez Jr, eds., "*Kucha,*" in Princeton Dictionary of Buddhism. Princeton University Press. 2013.
Calmard, J., *Cultural and Religious Cross-Fertilization between Central Asia and The Indo-Persian World*, in History of Civilizations of Central Asia, Vol. V, UNESCO Publishing, Turin, Italy, 2001.
Campbell, L.A., *Mithraic Iconography and Ideology*. E. J. Brill, Lieden, 1970.
Caubet, A., *Achaemenid Brick Decoration,* in P. O. Harper, J. Aruz, and F. Tallon, eds., The Royal City of Susa: Ancient Near Eastern Treasures in the Louvre, New York, 1992.
Cellerino, A., *La ceramica, In Nisa Partica, Ricerche nel compleso monumentale, Arsacide*, Monogra, 2008.
Chardin, J., *Travels in Persia* 1673–1677, Dover Publications, 2012.
Chernikov, S. S.,a *"Golden" kurgan in Chiliktin Valley: Origin of Scythian Art*, 1964.
Chernykh, E. N., *Ancient Metallurgy: The Early Metal Age*, Cambridge University Press, 1992.
Christensen, A. E., *L'empire des Sassanides*: Le people, l'etet, la cour, Levin and Munksgaard, Copenhagen, 1944.
Chuvin P. and G. Degeorge, *Samarkant, Bokhara and Khiva*, Flummarion, Paris, 1999.
Crawford, E. *Hasanlu,* Bulletin of the Metropolitan Museum of Art, Nov. 1961.
Cumont, F. and E. D. Francis, (ed., trans.) (1975), "The Dura Mithraeum," in Hinnells, John R. (ed.), Mithraic studies: Proceedings of the First International Congress of Mithraic Studies, Manchester University Press, 1975.
Curtis, J. E. and N. Tallis, *Forgotten Empire*: The World of Ancient Persia, Published in Association with The British Museum, 2005.
Curtis, J., *The Oxus Treasure*, British Museum Objects in Focus series, British Museum Press 2012.
Curtis, J., "The Oxus Treasure in the British Museum," *Ancient Civilizations from Scythia to Siberia*, Vol. 10, 2004.
D'iakonov, M. M., *Archeological work in the lower course of the Kafirnigana (Qobadian) River*, MIA, No. 37, 1953.
D'yakonov, M. M., *The murals of Panjikant and painting in Central Asia*, in Zhivopis' drevnego Pendzhikenta, Moscow, 1954.
Dabbs, J. A., *History of the Discovery and Exploration of Chinese Turkestan*, The Hague, 1963.
Dalley, S., "Foreign charioteer and cavalry in the armies of Tiglath-Pileser III and Sargon II," Iraq 47, 1985.
Dandamayev, M. A., *Media and Achaemenid Iran*, History of Civilizations of Central Asia, Vol. II, UNESCO Publishing, 1996.

Darmesteter, J., *The Zend Avesta*, Part II, Sacred Books of the East, Vol. 23, 1882.
Davidovich, E. A., *The monetary economy of Central Asia during the transitional period from ancient to feudal times*. In Blizhnii I Srednii Vostok, Moscow, 1980.
Davis, P. K., *One Hundred Decisive Battles from Ancient Times to the Present: The World Major Battles and How They Shaped History*, Oxford University Press, Oxford, 1999.
Deshayes, J., *Turang Tepe and the Plain of Gorgan in the Bronze Age*, Archaeologia, I(1), Paris.
Diakonoff, I.M., *Media*, The Cambridge History of Iran, 2, Cambridge University Press, 1985.
Duchesne-Guillemin, J., *Religions of Ancient Iran*. Tate Press, Bombay, 1973.
Dussaud, R., *The Bronzes of Luristan*, Survey, I, 1956.
Dyaduchenko, L. B., *Mystic Saimaluu-Tash*, Bishkek, 2008.
Dyson, R. H., *Glimpses of History at Ziwiye*, Expedition 4, 1963.
Dyson, Robert H., "Constructing the Chronology and Historical Implications of Hasanlu IV," Iran, Vol. 27, 22, 1989.
Enoki, K., G. A. Koshelenko, and Z. Haidary, *The Yuech-chih and their migrations in History*, History of Civilization of Central Asia,V, UNESCO Publishing, Vol. II, 1994, 171–90.
Erdmann, K., *Oriental Carpets*, second edition, trans. C. G. Ellis, London, 1960.
Ettinghausen, R., *Medieval Near Eastern Ceramics*, Freer Gallery of Art and Smithsonian Institute, Washington D. C., 1960.
Fairservice, W. A. Jr., *Archeology of Southern Gobi of Mongolia*, Durham, 1993.
Molodin V. I., Zh. Geneste, L. V. Zotkina, D. V. Cheremisin, C. Cretin, *The "Kalgutinsky" Style in the Rock Art of Central Asia*. Archaeology, Ethnology & Anthropology of Eurasia, 2019.
Falser, M. *The Bamiyan Buddhas*, performative iconoclasm and the "image" of heritage. In: Giometti, S.; Tomaszewski, A. (eds.): *The Image of Heritage. Changing Perception*, Permanent Responsibilities. Proceedings of the International Conference of the ICOMOS International Scientific Committee for the Theory and the Philosophy of Conservation and Restoration, 6–8 March 2009, Firenze, Florence, Italy, 2011.
Fergus M. and J. Jandosova, *Kazakhstan—Coming of Age*, Stacey International, London, 2003.
Fleming, S. J., V. C. Pigott, C. P. Swann, and S. K. Nash., *Bronze in Luristan: Preliminary analytical evidence from copper/bronze artifacts excavated by the Belgian mission in Iran*. Iranica Antiqua, 2005.
Foltz, R., *Religions of the Silk Road*. Palgrave Macmillan, New York, 2010.
Francis, E. D., "Mithraic graffiti from Dura-Europos," in Hinnells, John R. (ed.), Mithraic Studies: Proceedings of the First International Congress of Mithraic Studies, Manchester University Press, 1975.
Fraumkin, G., *Archaeology in Soviet Central Asia*, E. J. Brill, 1970.
Frye, R., *The Heritage of Central Asia - From Antiquity to the Turkish Expansion*, Markus Wiener Publishers, Princeton, 1996.

Frye, R., *The Samanids*, The Cambridge History of Iran, Vol. 4, Cambridge University Press, 1975.
Ganialin, A. F., *Altin Depe, The 1953 Excavations*, TIIAE AN TSSR, t. 5, 1953.
Ganialin, A. F., *The 1959 – 1961 Excavations at Altin-depe*, SA, No. 4, 1967.
Ghirshman, R., *Fouilles de Sialk pres de Kashan*, 1933, 1934, 1937, Vol. 1, P. Geuthner, 1938.
Ghirshman, R., *Fouilles de Sialk*, vol. 2, Paul Geuthner, 1939.
Ghirshman, R., *L'Iran et la migration des Indo-Iraniens*, Leiden, 1977.
Ghirshman, R., *Sept Mille Ans d'art en Iran* (Exposition: Petit Palais, Oct. 1961–Jan. 1962. Paris), 1961.
Ghirshman, R., *The Arts of Ancient Iran*, New York, 1967.
Ghirshman, R., *Iran: Parthian and Sassanian*, Thames & Hudson, London, 1962.
Ghose, R., *Kizil on the Silk Road: Crossroads of Commerce and Meeting of Minds*, Marg Publication, 2008.
Ghrishman, R., *The Scythians and the Royal Tomb of Ziwiyeh*, in Art of Ancient Iran, New York, 1964.
Godard, A. *Les Bronzes du Luristan*, Ars Asiatica XVII, 1931.
Godard, A., J. Godard, and J. Hackin, *Les antiquites bouddhiques de Bamiyan*, Mem. DAFA, 1968.
Godley, A. D. (ed.), *Herodotus' Histories*, with an English translation. Harvard University Press, Cambridge, 1920.
Goldman, B., *The Animal Style at Ziwiyeh, IPEK* 24, 1977.
Gorka, T. and J. W. E. Fassbinder, *Classifying and documenting kurgans*, Siberia, 2011.
Goryacheva, V. D., *The Early Medieval Monuments of Buddhism in Northern Kirgizia*, Buddhist for Peace, No. 4, Ulan Bator, 1980.
Gosudarstvennyj Ermitaz., *Trudy otdela istorii pervobytnoj kul'tury*, t. I, str. 237–71. Leningrad 1941.
Grach, A. D., *On Early Burials with Cremation: Balbals of Tuva*, Archeological Discoveries, 1968.
Grenet, F. E. and de la Vaissière, *The Last Days of Panjikent*, Silk Road Art and Archaeology 8, Kamakura 2002.
Grjaznov, M. P., *Drevnjaja bronza Minusinskich stepej. I. Bronzovye kelty.*
Grousset, R., *The Empire of the Steppe*, Rutgers University Press, 1991.
Grousset, R., *The Empire of the Steppes - A History of Central Asia*,
Gryaznov, M. P., *On the Question of the Formation of the Scytho-Siberian-type Cultures in Connection with the opening of the Arzhan Kurgan*, Moscow institute of Archeology, 1978, 9–12
Gryaznov, M. P., *Southern Sibiria*. Geneva: Archaeologia Mundi, 1969.
Gudkova, A. V. and V. A. Livshitz, *Inscriptions at Tok Kala*, Moscow, 1967.
Gudkova, A. V. and V. N. Yagodin, *Delta of Amu Darya: Tok Kala*, Moscow, 1968.
Guliamov, Y. A., G. Islamov, and A. Askarov, *Prehistoric Culture and the Rise of Irrigation Agriculture in the Lower Reaches of Zarafshan*, Tashkent, 1966.
Hammer, J., *Searching for Buddha in Afghanistan, Smithsonian Magazine*, Dec. 2010.
Hancar. F., *Luristan, Archéologie, Art et histoire*, Persée - Portail des revues scientifiques en SHS, Vol. 16, 1935.

Harmatta, J., *Scythians*, UNESCO Collection of History of Humanity: Volume III: From the Seventh Century BC to the Seventh Century AD, Routledge, 1996.

Harmatta, J., *The Emergence of the Indo-Iranians: The Indo-Iranian Languages*. In Dani, A. H. and V. M. Masson (eds.), History of Cicilizations of Central Asia: The Dawn of Civilization: Earliest Times to 700 BC, UNESCO, 1992.

Henning, W. B., *A Sogdian God*, Bulletin of the School of Oriental and African

Hermann, L., *Les Petroglyphes de Tcholpon-Ata*, Paris, 2010.

Herodotus, The History of Herodotus, *The Fourth Book: Melpomene*, translated by G. Rawlinson, Tudor Pub. Co., New York, 1956.

Herodotus, *The History, The Fourth Book: Melpomene*, translated by G. Tudor Pub. Co., New York, 1956.

Herzfeld, E., *The Persian Empire*, Franz Steiner Verlag GMBH, Wiesbaden, 1968.

Hiebert, F. T., *A Central Asian Village at the Dawn of Civilizations at Anau*, Turkmenistan, University of Pennsylvania, 2003.

Hiebert, F. T., *Pazyryk Chronology and Early Horse Nomads Reconsidered*, Bulletin of Asian Institute, New Series, Vol. 6, 1992.

Hinds, K., *Scythians and Sarmatians*, Marshall Cavendish, 2009.

Hookham, H., *Tamburlaine the Conqueror*, London, 1962.

Hopkins, C., *The discovery of Dura-Europos*. Yale University Press, New Haven, 1979.

Howard, A. F., *In Support of a New Chronology for the Kizil Mural Paintings*, Archives of Asian Art, XLIV, 1991.

Ibbotson, S., *Getting off the Silk Road: Uzbekistan's Hidden Archeological Sites*, Bradt Guides Ltd., 2020.

Isakov, A. I., *The citadel of ancient Panjikant*, Dushanbe, 1977.

Isakov, Kohl, Lamberg-Karlovsky, and Maddin, *Mettallurgical Analysis from Sarazm*, Tadjikistan SSR, Archeology 29, Feb. 1987.

Itina, M. A., *Excavations of a Cemetery of Tazabaiab Culture at Kokcha*, Materaly Khorezmskoi Eksepeditsii, Vol. 5, Moscow, 1961.

Itina, M. A., *The Farmers of Ancient Khorezm*, Moscow, 1968.

Itina, M. A., *The Steppe Tribes of the Central Asian Inter-River Area in the Second Half of the 2nd and the Early 1st Millennium BC*, 25th International Congress of orientalists, Moscow, 1960.

Itina, M. A., *The Farmers of Ancient Khorezm*, Moscow/Leningrad, 1968.

Izakov, A. I., "*Sarazm: An Agricultural Center of Ancient Sogdiana*," Bulletin of the Asia Institute, 8, 1994.

Izakov, A. I., *Excavations of the Bronze Age Settlement of Sarazm*. In: Soviet Anthropology and Archeology, 19, 1981.

Jackson, W. A. V., *From Constantinople to the Home of Omar Khayyam*, Ch. IV, Macmillan Co., 1911.

Jettmar, K., *Art of the Steppe*, New York, 1967.

Jettmar, K., *The Altai before the Turks*, Bulletin of the Museum of Far Eastern Antiquities, No. 23, Stockholm, 1951.

Jones, H. L., *The Geography of Strabo*, The Loeb Classical Library, Vol. 8.

Kadyrbayev, M. K., *Early Nomads: Central Asia Tasmola Kurgan Culture, Funeral rites, Early "Animal Style,"* 1966.

Kangxin, H., *The Study of Human Skeletons from Xinjiang*, Sino-Platonic Papers, China, 1994, 51.

Kennedy, A., *Central Asian Ikats*, Philadelphia, 1980.

Khlopin, I. N., *Dashlidji Depe and the Chalcolithic Farmers of Southern Turkmenistan*, TYuTAKE, t. X. Ashkhabad, 1960.

Khlopin, I. N., *Excavations at Namazga Depe*, Arkheologicheskiye otkrytiya goda, Moscow, 1968.

Khlopin, I. N., *The Geoksyur Group of Settlements in the Chalcolithic Period*, Moscow- Leningrad, 1964.

Khodzhaniyazov, G., *Fortified cities of Khorezma*, Soviet Archeology, 2, Moscow, 1981.

Kia, A., *Central Asian Cultures, Arts and Architecture*, Inner Eurasia from prehistory to the Medieval Golden Ages, (Second Edition), Lexington Books, An Imprint of Rowman and Littlefield, New York, 2018.

Kia, A., *Central Asian Cultures, Arts and Architecture*, Inner Eurasia from prehistory to the Medieval Golden Ages, (First Edition), Lexington Books, An Imprint of Rowman and Littlefield, New York, 2015.

Kia, A., *Central Asia: Rediscovering a Cultural Treasury*, Central & Southwest Asian Studies Program, Anthropology Department, the twelfth monograph in the contributions to Anthropology Series, (three articles), The University of Montana Press, 2010.

Kia, A., M. Kia, D. Bedunah, R. Graetz, A. Gunya, S. Hampson, M. S. Hendrix, A. Klaits, and W. S. Sears, *Discovering Central Asia*, The University of Montana Press, 2012.

Kia, A., *Central Asia: Ancient History*, From Pasargod to Cetisphon, In: Cultures of Central Asia, Vol. III, University of Montana Press, 2013.

Kia, A., *Gonbaz-i Manas*: An Analysis of Kyrgyzstan Cultural Heritage through Studying its Sacred Sites, In: Cultures of Central Asia, Vol. II, University of Montana Press, 2013.

Kia, A., *Prehistory and Early History*, In: Cultures of Central Asia, Vol. III, University of Montana Press, 2012.

King, L. W. and R. C. Thompson, *The Sculptures and Inscription of Darius the Great on the rock of Bisutun in Persia,* London, 1907.

Klimkei, H. J., *Gnosis on the Silk Road* (Gnostic Texts from Central Asia), Harper, San Francisco, 1993.

Klimkeit, H. J., *Christians, Buddhists, and Manichaeans in Medieval Central Asia,* Buddhist-Christian Studies, 1, 1981.

Klyosov, A. A., *The 3 R's in R1 Haplogroup*, Journal of Genetic Geneology, Vol. 5, No. 2, 2009.

Knobloch, E., *Monuments of Central Asia*, A Guide to the Archeology, Art and Architecture of Turkestan, I. B. Tauris Publishers, New York, 2001.

Kohl, P. L. and D. J. Dadson, (eds.), *The Culture and Social Institutions of Ancient Iran*, by Dandamaev, M. A. and G. Vladimir Lukonin, Cambridge University Press, 1989.

Komarova, M. N., *Detailed Survey of Andronovo Civilization: Analysis of Pottery in the Hermitage Museum*, 1962.

Komomaroff, L., *The Golden Disk of Heaven: Metal Work of Timurid Iran*, Cosa Mesa, California and New York, 1992.

Korobkova, G. F., *The Mesolithic and Neolithic Cultures of Central Asia, problems in the archeology of Western Central Asia*, Leningrad, 1968.

Korobkova, G. F., L. Krizhevskaya, A. Mandel'shtam, *The Neolithic of the East Coast of the Caspian Sea*, The History, Archeology and Ethnography of Central Asia, Moscow, 1968.

Korobkova, G. F., *The Production tools from the Settlements o Chopan-depe, Togolok-depe and Pessedjik-depe,* Karakumskiye drevnosti, I, Ashkhabad, 1968.

Korobkova, G. F., *The Determination of the Function of Stone and Bone Implements the Djeitun Site on the basis of Working Traces*, TYuTAKE, t. X. Ashkhabad, 1961.

Koshelenko G. A., *A survey of the literature on the archeology of Central Asia and Kazakhstan.* SA 1, 1973.

Koshelenko G. A., *Materials for an Archeological Map of Margiana*, Mesopotamia 26, 1991.

Koshelenko, G. A., and V. N. Pilipko, *Parthia*, History of Civilizations of Central Asia, Vol. II, UNESCO Publishing, 1994.

Kristensen, A. K. G., *Who were the Cimmerians, and where did they come from?, Sargon II, and the Cimmerians, and Rusa I.* Copenhagen Denmark: The Royal Danish Academy of Science and Letters, 1988.

Kuftin B. A., *Field Report on the work of Yu TAKE Team No. XIV on the Study of the Culture of the Settled Agricultural Population of the Copper and Bronze Age*, 1952.

Kuftin, B. A., *Research into the Anau Culture by the South Turkmenian Archeological Expedition in 1952*, IAN TSSR, I, 1954.

Kuz'mina, E. E., *Emba Region, West Kazakhstan: Neolithic and Bronze age Analysis*, 1961.

Kuz'mina, E. E., *The origin of the Indo-Iranians*, Brill, Leiden, Netherlands and Boston, 2007.

Kuzmina, E. E., *The Cemetary of Zaman-baba*, SE, No. 2, 1958.

Kyzlasov, L. R., *The Meaning of Babas*, Sovietskaya Arkheologiya, 1964.

Kyzlasov, L. R., *Archeological Explorations in Ak-Beshim Settlement*, Funze, 1953–1954.

Lawergren, B., B. E. Neubauer, and M. H. Kadyrov, *Music and Musiology, Theatre and Dance*, History of Civilizations of Central Asia, Vol. IV, UNESCO Publishing, 2000.

Le Coq, A. V., *Buried Treasures of Chinese Turkestan*, George Allen & Unwin Ltd. 1928. Paperback with introduction, Oxford University Press, 1985.

Le Coq, A., *Buried Treasures of Chinese Turkestan: An Account of the Activities and Adventures of the Second and Third German Turfan Expedition*, G. Allen & Unwin, London, 1928.

Lebedynsky, I., *Les Nomades, les peuples nomades de la steppe des origines aux invasions mongoles*, IXe siècle av. J.-C. - XIIIe siècle apr. J.-C., Errance, Paris, 2007.

Lee, S., *Recent Articles on Art and Archaeology of Kucha: A Review Article*, Archives of Asian Art, 68(2), 2018.
Lenz T. W. and D. L. Glenn, *Timur and Princely Vision*, Persian Art and Culture in the Fifteenth Century, Smithsonian Institution Press, 1989.
Litvinsky, B. A., *Parkhar Region: Adzhina-tepe*, Upper Zeravshan, 1967b.
Litvinsky, B. A., *Tadzhik Archeology*, Sovietskaya Arkheologiya, 1967a, 3.
Litvinsky, B. A., *Namazga -Tepe: 1949 – 1950 Excavations*, SE, No. 4, 1952.
Litvinsky, B. A., M. H. Shah, and R. S. Samghabadi, *The Rise of Sasanian Iran*, History of Civilizations of Central Asia, Vol. II, UNESCO Publishing, 1994.
Livshits, V. A., *Khwarazmian calendar and the eras of ancient Khwarazm*, Palestinskii sbornik 21, No. 84, 1970.
Livshits, V. A., *The Sogdians and the Turks*, Narody Azii I Afriki, 4, 1979.
Livshits, V. A., *A Sogdian document from ancient Samarkand*. In TSentral'naia Aziia. Moscow, 1975.
Lukonin, V. G., *Sassanian conquests in the East and the problem of Kushan absolute chronology*, VDI 2, 1969.
Ma, L., *The Original Xiongnu*, An Archaeological Exploration of the Xiongnu's History and Culture. Inner Mongolia University Press, Hohhot, 2005.
Maenchen-Helfen, O. J., *The Legend of the Origin of the Huns*, Byzantion, Vol. 17, 1944–1945.
Mair, V. H., *Mummies of Tarim Basin*, Archeology, 48, 2, 1995.
Maksimova, A. G., *Tamgaly Rock Engravings*, Viestnik Journal of Akademiya Nauk SSSR, 1958.
Mandel'shtam, A. M., *New Timber Graves in Southern Turkmenia*, KSIA, Vol. 112, Moscow, 1967.
Mandel'shtam, A. M., *Timber Graves in Southern Turkmenia*, KSIA, Vol. 108, Moscow, 1966.
Mandelshtam, A. M., *The Nomads on the Route to India*, Materials and investigations of the Archeology of U.S.S.R., Moscow, 1966.
Margulan, A. Kh., K. A. Akishev, *Analysis of nomad Tribes: Origin of Scythian Art*, 1966.
Markov, G. E., *Dam dam chashma cave no. 2 on the Eastern Shores of the Caspian*, SA, 1956.
Marshak, B. I., *The monumental paintings of Sogdiana and Tokharestan*, Moscow, 1983.
Marshak, B. I., *Report on the work on section XII in 1955 – 1960*, MIA, No. 124, 1964.
Marshak, B. I., *The Ceilings of the Varakhsha Palace*, In Parthica. Incontri di culture nel mondo antico. Issue 2. Pisa-Rome: Istituti editoriali e poligrafici internazionali, 2000.
Marshak, B. I. and V. I. Raspopova, *Buddha Icon from Panjikent*, Silk Road Art and Archaeology 5, Kamakura, 1997/1998.
Marshak, B. I. and V. I. Raspopova, *Wall Paintings from a House with a Granary: Panjikent, First Quarter of the Eight Century AD*, Silk Road Art and Archeology 1, Kamakura, 1990a.
Masson M. E., *Periodization of the ancient history of Samarkand*, VDI 4, 1950.

Masson V. M., *The monetary economy of Central Asia according to numismatics data*, VDI, 1955.
Masson V. M. and V. I. Sarianidi, *The Symbols on the Central Asian Bronze Age Figurines*, VDI, No. I, 1969.
Masson, V. M., *Kara Depe near Artyk*, TYuTAKE, t, X, Ashkhabad, 1960.
Masson, V. M., *Middle Chalcolithic Sites of South West Turkmenia*, Mocow, 1962.
Masson, V. M., *The Fourth Season of Excavation at Altin Depe*, Arkheologicheskiye otkrytiya goda, Moscow, 1969.
Masson, V. M., *The proto-urban civilization of southern Central Asia*, SA 3, 1967.
Masson, V. M., *The south Turkmenistan Center of Early Agriculturalists*, TYuTAKE, t.X, Ashkhabad, 1960.
Matthews, R., *Administrative Activity and technology at Godin Tepe in the Later Fourth Millennium BC*. In Proceedings of the International Symposium on Iranian Archaeology: Western Region, (Kermanshah, 1–3). Teheran: ICAR (Iranian Center for Archaeological Research), 2006.
Maximova, A. G., *Bronze Age of East Kazakhstan: A comprehensive survey of Chernikov's writings*, 1959.
Melikian-Chirvani, A. S., *Islamic Metalwork from Iranian World*, eighth to eighteen Centuries, London, 1982.
Michael, H. N., *Studies in Siberian Shamanism*, University of Toronto Press, 1963.
Kaykhusrow, M., Manuscript known as the "*miscellaneous codex*" or *MK* (after, the Indian Zoroastrian [Parsi] copyist who created it), dated to 1322.
Mongait, A. L., *Archeology*, On the Tracks of the Ancient Khorezmian Civilization of the U.S.S.R., Penguin Books, Baltimore, Maryland, 1955.
Mongiatti, A., *A gold four horse mode chariot from the Oxus Treasure: A fine Illustration of Achaemenid goldwork*, The British Museum Technical Research Bulletin. British Museum, 2010.
Moorey, P. R. S., *Ancient Bronzes from Luristan*, British Museum: London, 1974.
Moreau, K. *Tureng Depe*, Expedition records, University of Pennsylvania, Penn Museum Archives, 2010.
Moreau, K., *Tureng Tepe, Iran expedition records* (finding aid), University of Pennsylvania, Penn Museum Archives, 2010, Retrieved July 19, 2010
Morita, M., *The Kizil Paintings in the Metropolitan* in *The Metropolitan Museum Journal*, Vol. 50, pp. 115–36, 2015.
Muller, F. M., *The Sacred Books of the East*: Vol. 23, The Zend Avesta, Adamant Media Corporation, Oxford, 2000.
Muscarella, O. W, A. Caubet, and Tallon, F., *Susa in Achaemenid Period*, in The Royal City of Susa, The Metropolitan Museum of Art, Harry N. Abrams, New York, 1993.
Muscarella, O. W., *Achaemenid Art and Architecture at Susa*, in P. O. Harper, J. Aruz, and F. Tallon, eds., The Royal City of Susa, New York, 1992.
Muscarella, O. W., *Surkh Dum at The Metropolitan Museum of Art*, Journal of Field Archaeology, Vol. 8, No. 3, 1981, pp. 327–59.
Mushtaq, Q. and J. L. Berggren, *Mathematical Sciences*, History of Civilizations of Central Asia, Vol. IV, UNESCO Publishing, 2000, 177–94.

Negahban, E., *Excavations of Marlik*. Tehran: Cultural heritage Organization Iran, (ResearchCenter). Vol. 1, 1st ed, 1999.

Negahban, E., *Royal Gold of Marlik Tepe*, Hhorizon Magazine, V, Nov. 1962.

Negmatov, N. N., *States in north-western Central Asia*, History of Civilizations of Central Asia, Vol. II, UNESCO Publishing, 1994.

Nerazik, E. E., *Village Settlements of Khorezm*, Moscow, 1966.

Nerazik, E. E., *Detailed survey of post-Kushan Khorezmian pottery*, Moscow, 1959.

Nerazik, E. E., *Some questions about the history and culture of ancient Khwarazmian cities in the light of excavations at the Topraq qala site*, Moscow, 1981.

Nerazile, E. E., and P. G. Bulgakov, *History of Civilization of Central Asia*, Vol. III, Ch. 9, *Khwarazmia*, 2000.

Newman, A. J., *Safavid Iran: Rebirth of a Persian Empire*, St. Martin Press, New York, 2006.

Okladnikov, A. M., *Djebel cave, an early prehistoric site on the Caspian shores of Turkmenia*, TYu—TAKE, VII, 1956.

Okladnikov, A. M., *On Stone Age*, Ch. 1, 2, 3 in Sredniaya Aziya, Academy of Sciences of Kazakhstan, 1966.

Olson, K. G. and Christopher P. Thornton, "*Tureng Tepe, a Bronze Age Centre in Northeastern Iran Revisited.*" Journal of the British Institute of Persian Studies 59(1):, 2021.

Orazbayev, A. M., *Survey on Bronze Age and early Nomads in North Kazakhstan*, 1958.

Overlaet, B., *Luristan Metalwork in the Iron Age*, Persia's Ancient Splendour: Mining, Handicraft and Archaeology, Deutsches Bergbau-Museum, Bochum, 2004.

P'iankov, I. V., *A Central Asian city of Achaemenid period from the information of ancient authors*. In G. Kh. Sarkisian (ed.), Drevnii Vostok: Goroda I torgovlia III-I tys, Erevan, 1973.

P'iankov, I. V., *The Askatakas—Scythians and the eastern Kaspians*, Pamirovedenie 1, 1984.

Parlato, S., *The Saka and Xiongnu: A Comparative Reading of Literary Sources*. In B. Genito, The Archeology of the Steppes—Methods and Strategies, Naples, 1992, 9–12.

Parrot, A., Acquisitions et inédits du Musée du Louvre, 13. *Animaux et ceramiques d'Amlash*, Syria 40, 1963.

Passarelli, M., *Petroglyphs Along the Yaghnob River*, University of Bolobna, Yaghnob Valley Mission, 2007.

Pavlinkaya, L. R., *The Scythians and Sakians*, Eight to Third Centuries B.C., Nomads of Eurasia, Academy of Sciences of U.S.S.R., Natural History Museum of Los Angeles County, 1989.

Perevalov, S. M., *The Sarmatian Lance and the Sarmatian Horse-Riding Posture*. Anthropology & Archeology of Eurasia 40(4), 2002.

Plutarch, *Parallel Lives*, translated by Bernadotte Perrin, Loeb Classical Library, 1916.

Potemkina, T. M., *On the Question of Bronze Age Steppe Tribal Migration to the South*: Interaction between Nomadic Cultures and Ancient Civilization, Science, Alma-Ata, 1987.

Priestman, S. *Sassanian Ceramics from the Gogan Wall and other Sites on the Gorgan Plain*, 2013.
Pugachenkova, G. A., *Elements of Sogdian architecture in Central Asian terra cottas. In Materialy po arkheologii I etnografii Uzbekistana*, Vol. 2, Tashkent, 1950.
Pugachenkova, G. A., *A survey of the ancient monuments of Sogdiana*, ONU 4, 1965.
Pumpelly, R., *Expolartion in Turkestan, Expedition of 1904: Prehistoric Civilizations of Anau*, Vol. I–II, Washington, 1908
Pyankova, L. T., *The Bronze Age Cemetery of Tigrovaya Balka*, Soviet Archeology, 3, 1974.
Radner, K., "An Assyrian View on the Medes," in G. B. Lanfranchi et al. (eds.), *Continuity of Empire: Assyria, Media, Persia* (History of the Ancient Near East Monographs 5), Padova, Sargon, 2003.
Ranov, V. A., *Stone Age engravings in the Shakhta cave*, SE, No. 6, 1961.
Ranov, V. A., *Toward a New Outline of the Soviet Central Asian Paleolithic*. Can, Vol. 20, No. 2, 1979.
Rapoport, IU. A., *Chorasmia: Archeology and pre-Islamic History*. In EIr, Vol. 5, 1987.
Rapoport, IU. A., *Out of town palaces and temples of Topraq Qala*. VDI 4, 1993.
Rapoport, IU. A., *The Kurgans on the Chach Tepe heights*. TKhAEE, Vol. 9, Moscow, 1979.
Rawlinson, G., *The Sixth Oriental Monarchy*, Ch. XI, Longmans, Green and Co., London, 1873.
Reade, J. E., "*Iran in the Neo-Assyrian period*," in M. Liverani (ed.), Neo-Assyrian Geography (Quaderni di geografia storica 5), Università di Roma "La Sapienza," Rome, 1993.
Rempel, L. I., *Taraz, South Kazakhstan, Zoroastrian ossuaries*, Figurines, 1957.
Rice, T. T., *The Scythians*, 3rd edition, London, 1961.
Rice, T. T., *Ancient Arts of Central Asia*, F. A. Praeger Publishers, New York, 1965.
Rostovtzeff, M. I., *Dura-Europos and Its Art*, Oxford University Press, 1938.
Rowland, B., The Art of Central Asia, Crown Publishers, p. 103, 1974.
Rozwadowski, A., *Symbols Through Time, Interpreting the Rock Art of Central Asia*, Poznan, 2004.
Rtvelladze, E. V., *Religious and funerary structures of the Kushan ers at Kampir Tepe*, Moscow, 1989.
Rubinson, K. S., *A Study in the Transfer and Transformation of Artistic Motifs,* The Textiles from Pazyryk, Penn Museum, Vol. 32, Issue one, 1990.
Rudenko, S. I., *Frozen Tombs of Siberia*, the Pazyryk Burials of Iron Age Horsemen, University of California Press, 1970.
Rudenko, S. I., *The Pazirik burial of Altai*. American Journal of Archaeology XXXVII, 1933.
Santoro, A. *Miran: The Visvantara Jataka on Visual Narration Along the Silk Road,* Rivista degli studi orientali, Sapienza - Universita di Roma, 2006.
Sarianidi V. I., *The Bacterian center of goldsmithing*. SA 1, 1987.
Sarianidi, V. I., *Excavations at Khapuz Depe and Altin Depe*, Arkheologicheskiye otkrytiya goda, Moscow, 1967.

Sarianidi, V. I., *Further Investigations at Ulug-depe, Arkheologicheskiye otkrytiya* 1966 goda, Moscow, 1969.
Sarianidi, V. I., *Khapuz Depe, A Bronze Age Site*, KSIA, Vol. 98, 1964.
Sarianidi, V. I., *Pottery Manufacture in the settlements of Ancient Margiana*, TYu-TAKE, t. VIII, Ashkhabad, 1958.
Sarianidi, V. I., *The Treasure of Golden Hill*, American Journal of Archeology, V. No. 2, Apr. 1980.
Savory, R., *Iran under Safavids*, Cambridge University Press, 1980.
Schlumberger, D., *Surkh Kotal,* Antiquity, Vol. 33, No. 130, 1959.
Schmidt, E. F., *Persepolis* 3 v. University of Chicago Press, 1953–1970.
Schmidt, H., *Archeological Excavations in Anau and Old Merv*, Carnegie Institution of Washington, 1908.
Schmidt, E., N.Maurits, and H. H. Curvers, *Expedition to Luristan*, The Oriental Institute of the University of Chicago, 1989.
Senigova, T. N., *Novaya Kazanka, West Kazakhstan, Bronze Age: Sarmatian Period*, 1956.
Shchetenko, A. Y. A., *Taichanak Depe*, Karaumskiye drevnosti, Vol. 2, Ashkhabad, 1969.
Shishkin, V. A., *Varakhsha*. Moscow: Izdatel'stvo Akademii Nauk, 1963.
Sima Qian, *Shih chi,* Chapter 123, Vols. 46–48, B. Watson, New York, 1925.
Sinitzyn, I. V., *West Kazakhstan: Neolithic, Bronze Age, Scythians and Sarmatians*, 1956.
Sinor, D., *The Cambridge History of Early Inner Asia*, Cambridge University Press, 1994.
Sinor, D. (ed.), *The Cambridge History of Early Inner Asia*, Cambridge University Press, 1990.
Sircar, D. C., *The Kushanas*, in The History and Culture of the Indian People, Ch. 9, A. D. Puusalkar, Bombay, 1990.
Smith, P. and T. Cuyler Young T. C., *The Evolution of Early Agriculture and Culture in Greater Mesopotamia*. In Population Growth: Anthropological Implications, B. Spooner (ed.), MIT Press, Cambridge, 1–59, 1972.
Smith, P. E. L., *Ganj Dareh Tepe*, Paleorient, Vol. 2, No. 1., 1974.
Starr, S. F., *Lost Enlightenment*, Princeton University Press, 2015.
Staviskii, B. I,. *Historical data on the upper section of the Zarafshan valley*. IMKU, No. 1, 1959.
Staviskii, B. I., *The northern limits of Kushan Empire*. EVD, I, 1961.
Stein, A., *Ancient Khotan*, Oxford University Press, 1907.
Stierlin, H., *Splendors of the Persian Empire* (Timeless Treasures), White Star, 2006.
Stronach, D. *Archeology of Median and Achaemenid*, Routledge & Kegan Paul, 1982.
Stronach, D. *Depe Nush-I Jan: A Mound in Medaia*, The Metropolitan Museum, New Series, 27, 3, 1973.
Sykhova, N., *Traditional Jewellery from Soviet Central Asia and Kazakhstan*, Museum of Oriental Art, Moscow, 1984.
Tacon, P. S. C., H. Tang, and M. Aubert, *Naturalistic animals and hand stencils in the rock art of Xinjiang Uyghur Autonomous Region*, Rock Art Research 33 (1): 2016.
Taizi, Z. *Architecture et décor rupestre des grottes de Bamiyan*, Paris, 1977.

Tallgren, A. M., *Collection Tovostine des antiquites prehistoriques de Minoussinsk*. Helsing, 1930.
Tallgren, A. M., *Dolmens of North Caucasia*, Antiquity Journal, 1933.
Tallgren, A. M., *Eurasia Septentrionalis,* Antiqua III, Journal of East European and North Asiatic Archeology and Ethnography, ESA III, 1928.
Tallgren, A. M., *La Pontide prescythique apress l'introduction des metaux*, ESA II, 1926,
Taylor, A., *Diversity and Identity in Seventeenth Century Persia*, Getty Publications, 1995.
Tewinkle, K., *Miran,* Xinjiang Uyghur Autonomous Region, Central Asian Archeological Landscapes, 2020.
Tolstov, P., *Ancient Khorezm—Retracing Ancient Civilizations*, Moscow, 1948.
Tolstov, S. P., *On the Tracks of the Ancient Khorezmian Civilization*, Berlin, 1953.
Tolstov, S. P., M. A. Itina, and A. V. Vinogradov, *On New Exploratrion in Akcha Darya delta, Kokcha, Western Kizil Kum, Toprak Kala, and Syr Darya*, Moscow, 1967.
Tolstov, S. P., *At the Ancient Delta of the Oxus and Yaksarta: Documents found at Toprak Kala*, Moscow, 1962.
Tolstov, S. P., *Scythians of Aral and Khorezm*, XXVth Congress, Vol. III, 1960.
Tongerloo, A. van., *Notes on the Iranian Elements in the Uygur Manichaean Texts*, in P. Bryder, (ed.), Manichaean Studies, Lund, 1987.
Trever, K. V., *Terracottas from Afrasiab*, Leningrad, 1934.
Tucker, J., *The Silk Road: Art and History*, Art Media Resources, Chicago, 2003.
Vamberry, A., *History of Bokhara from earliest Period down to the Present*, Eliborn Classics, London, 2005, pp. 35–87.
Vermaseren, M. J., *Mithra, The Secret God*. Chatto and Windus, Uppsala, 1963.
Viatkin, V. L., *Afrasiab: Gorodishche bylogo Sarakanda*, Tashkent, 1927.
Vorobeva, M. G., *Reports of Khorezm Archeological and Ethnographical Expedition*, IV, 1959.
Waugh, D. C., *Kucha and the Kizil Caves*, Silk Road Seattle, University of Washington, 2014.
Widengren, G., *Mani and Manichaeism*, translated by Charles Kessler, Upsala, 1965.
Wilkinson, J. V. S., *Shahnameh of Ferdowsi*, The Book of the Persian Kings, London, 1937.
Wulsin, F. R., *Excavation at Tureng Tepe, near Asterabad*. Supplement to the Bull. American Inst. Persian Art and Archaeology, New York, 1932.
Yablonsky, L. T., *The Saka of the Southern Aral Sea Area: The Archeology and Anthropology of the Ceremonies*, Moscow, 1966.
Yamauchi, E., Review of *The Treasure of the Oxus with Other Examples of Early Oriental Metal-Work*, *Journal of the American Oriental Society*, Vol. 90, No. 2 JSTOR, Apr.–Jun., 1970.
Yamauchi, E., *Persia and The Bible*, Baker Book House, Grand Rapids, Michigan, 1990.
Yong, M. and S. Yutang, *The Western Regions under the Hsiung-nu and the Han*, History of Civilization of Central Asia, UNESCO Publishing, Vol. II, 1994.
Young T. C. Jr and Louis D. Levine L., *Excavations at Godin Tepe*. Second Progress Report, Royal Ontario Museum Occasional Paper 26, 1974.

Young, T. C., *Excavations of the Godin Project: First Progress Report*. Toronto Royal Ontario Museum 1969.
Young, T. C. Medes, *The Early History of the Medes and the Persians and the Achaemenid Empire*, in Cambridge Ancient History, 4, Cambridge University Press.
Young, T. C., *The Kangavar Survey*, Periods VI to IV. In Antonio Sargona (ed.), A view from the highlands: Archaeological Studies in Honour of Charles Burney, Peeters, Herent, Belgium, 2004.
Young, T. C., *Medes, The Early History of the Medes and the Persians and the Achaemenid Empire*, In Cambridge Ancient History, 4, Cambridge University Press, 1988.
Yu, Y., *The Hsiung-nu*, The Cambridge History of Early Inner Asia, Cambridge University Press, 1994.
Zeimal, E. V., *Periodization of the ancient history of Central Asia*, mid-first millennium B.C. to mid-first millennium A. D. Moscow, 1987.
Zeimal, E. V., *The Political History of Ancient Transoxania according to numismatic data*. In CHIr, Vol. 3.1, 1983.
Zhang, G., *The city-states of the Tarim Basin*,"Chapters 11, 12, in History of Civilizations of Central Asia. Vol. III. The crossroads of civilizations: A. D. 250 to 750, B. A. Litvinsky et al., eds. Paris: UNESCO, 1996.
Zhu, J., J. Ma, and F. Zhang, *The Baigetuobie cemetery: New discovery and human genetic features of Andronovo community's diffusion to the Eastern Tianshan Mountains (1800–1500 BC)*, Sage Journals, 2020.
Zin, M., *The Identification of the Kizil Paintings II* [3. Sudåya, 4. Brhaddyuti] in Indo-Asiatische Zeitschrift, Berlin, 11, 2007.
Zyablin, L. P., *Second Buddhist Temple of Ak-Beshim*, Settlement, Funze, 1961.

Index

Abbasi, Reza, 157, 176
Abetekov, Asan, 52
Achaemenid Empire, 61, 79, 81, 129, *182*;
Achaemenid palaces, 118, 175
animal-style art of, 43, 72–73;
    capital cities and megalithic architecture in, 84–85;
    Darius I as emperor of, 28, 54;
    decorative and utilitarian arts of, 87–88;
    Eurasian art, Achaemenid influence on, 58, 105, 115;
    first central Asian states in, 83–84;
    Khwarazmia as a satrapy of, 92, 94;
    Parthian Art, Achaemenid elements in, 106, 107, 109, 110;
    relief sculptures of, 86–87;
    Soghdia as a satrapy of, 139, 140;
    Susa as third capital of, 28, 88
Afrasiab, city of, 1, 29, 30, 148–49, 153, 155
Ahuramazda and Ahriman, 43, 72
Airymach-Tau site, 12
Ak Beshim, settlement of, 119
Ak Saray (White House), 150

Akch-Darya sites, 9
Akishev, Kimal Akishevich, 7, 51, 52, 56
Aktobe region, 12
Alaverdi Khan bridge, 176
Alay region, 8, 51
Aleksieyev, Valery Pavlovich, 50
Ali Qapu palace, 175–76
Alpysbayev, Kh. A., 7, 12
Altai Mountains, 8, 50, 116;
    Andronovo culture of, 49;
    "animal style" art found in, 56, 57;
    kurgans of, 53, 54;
    Pazyryk, 55, 155;
    rock painting in, 5–6;
    western region, mummified bodies of, 115
Altin Depe, 24, 26, 39
Amirabad, 93–94
Amlash pottery, 24, 70–71
Amu Darya river, 11, 31, 73, 92, 93, 94, 95, 139, 148
Anahita (deity), 130–31,149
Ananino culture, 58
Anau, 10;
    Anau pottery, 17, 18, 19, 21, 24
    Copper Age culture of, 35–36
Andronovo culture, 8, 51;

Andronovo metallurgy, 49–50;
    dwelling sites from Andronovo
        period, 55;
    Indo-Iranians and, 52–53;
    western Kazakhstan
        variant of, 26–27
animal style art;
    as art of the steppes, 2, 46, 61
    Scythian animal art, rise of, 58
    Scythian/Saka animal art
        style, 51, 53–54
Anthony, David W., 52
Apadana palace, 28–29, 85, 86,
    88, 140, 177
Aravan area, 13
Arsaces, King, 105
Arsalan, Sultan, 31, 147
Arzhan site, 52
Assur, 106, 107, 132
Ateas, King, 52
Attila the Hun, 117
Augustine, Saint, 135
Augustus, Emperor, 111
Avesta text, 27, 43, 72, 93, 139, 165–66
Avicenna, 30, 99, 146
Azar Borzin Mehr, 134
Azar Faranbagh, 134
Azar Goshnasb fire temple, 133–34

Babas/Balbals sculptures, 38–39
Babur, 148
Baghdad Museum, 109, 110
Bagram, city of, 25, 117
Baigetuobie cemetery, 49
Baimiaozishan, 6, 7
Baipakov, Karl Moldakhmetovich, 119
Bakharzi, Sayf al Din, 155
Bakhtaran (Bactra), 2, 73, 87, 117, 122,
    139, 140, 141
Baku, city of, 134
Balkh, city of, 30, 142, 145
Al-Balkhi, 146
Bamyan art center, 118, 122
Ban Chao, 120
Ban Gu, 116

Bazaklik monastic center, 124
Bazar-kala, 95
Beckwith, Christopher, 26, 67
Beg, Nar Buta, 101
Beg, Ulug, 148
Behzad, training by, 157, 173–74
Belenitsky, A. M., 143
Bernshtam, Aleksandr Natanovich,
    12–13, 51, 119
Beurme, 18, 36
Bibi Khanum, 32, 150
Binghua, Wang, 17, 127
Biruni, Abu Rayhan, 30, 96, 98–99, 146
Bishapur, 131–32
Bistun, 109, 130
Bokhara region:
    bookmaking in, 156–57, 176;
    Bukhara, city of, 2,
        30–31, 100, 155;
    as a cultural and artistic center,
        30, 98, 153;
    golden age of, 144–45;
    khanate rule in, 32, 148, 154;
    mausoleum wood carving in, 155;
    pottery schools of, 29, 32;
    as Samanid capital, 98,
        143, 146–47;
    Storehouse of Wisdom as
        library of, 31;
    as an urban center, 147, 150;
book making/book art, 96, 135,
    156–58, 176;
British Museum, 42, 71, 73, 111;
Bronze Age, 5, 14, 49, 177;
    Andronovo Bronze culture,
        50–51, 55;
    art of the Bronze Age, 117;
    early Bronze Age pottery, 23–27
    in Ferghana Valley, 13
    Khwarazmian cultures and
        arts, 92, 94
    kurgans as characteristic of, 53
    Late Bronze Age, 7, 19, 94
    Middle Bronze Age, 7, 25

Minusinsk, Bronze Age
    culture of, 60
  mummies of, 116
  Ordos as a Bronze Age culture, 45
  Pamir petroglyphs, 8
  Uzbekistan, petroglyphs from, 9
  Zaman Baba culture of, 22
bronze art and jewelry:
  bronze ornaments, 51, 144;
  bronze tools, 51;
  of Luristan, 42, 71–73;
  Nisa, bronze weapons of, 106;
  pre-Mongol period bronze
    pieces, 154;
  Sarmatian gold, silver, and bronze
    art, 44–45;
  Talysh culture, flourishing in, 41
Buddhism and Buddhist art, 108, 117,
  118–24, 125
Burli-kala, 95

calligraphical writing, 4, 161
caravanserais, 175, 177
carpets, 58, 61–62, 154, 155
Carrhae, Battle of, 111–12
carvings, 1, 12, 86;
  rock carvings, 6, 9;
  wood carvings, 60, 100, 144, 155
Caspian Sea Group, 11, 49
ceramic art/ceramic tile, 31–32, 100,
  149, 150, 153–54
Chaacha Sai, 18, 36
Chach (Tashkand), 29, 145, 153
Chagilli Depe, 18, 20
Chakin Chur Bilga, 143
Chalcolithic period, 37, 177;
  human figurines in early
    period, 36;
  Middle Chalcolithic, 19, 21;
  pottery of, 23, 24;
  in Southern Central Asia, 17;
  Turang Tepe complex,
    Chalcolithic layers of, 75
Chang Yen-yuan, 120
Chernikov, Sergei S., 7, 12, 51

Chertomlyk, 57, 58
Chifeng region, 6, 7
Chiliktin Valley, 51
Chirchik region, 9, 12
Cholpon Ata, 14
Chu Valley, 22, 51
Chulak Mountains, 12
Chust Culture, 14, 19
Cimmerians:
  animal shape as specialty
    of, 44, 73
  Cimmerian art, 41–42, 87
  Cimmerian mercenaries, 71
Cincinnati Art Museum, 43, 72
Copper Age, 17, 18, 35, 177. *See also*
  Chalcolithic period
crowns, 85, 110, 130–31, 132
Ctesiphon, city of, 106, 107, 109, 129,
  130, 135, 170

Dalverzin settlement, 13
Dam Dam Cheshma caves, 10, 11, 19
Dandamaev, Muhammad
  Abdulkadyrovich, 42
Daqiqi, Abu Mansur, 146
Dariush I, Emperor, 109;
  Apadana Palace of, 28–29, 85, 88;
  Behistun inscription, 84;
  Greater Media, forming, 80, 83;
  Naqsh-I Rustam inscription, 54;
  reliefs portraying, 87, 140;
  Tachara Palace of, 86;
Dashlidji-depe, 18, 36
Demidov, Alexis, 55
Deshayes, Jean, 74
Divashtich (Soghdian ruler), 142
Djebel caves, 11
Djeitun culture, 17, 18, 20–21, 35–36
Dnieper region, 41, 58
domes, 32, 100, 107, 108, 129, 130,
  147, 149, 150, 176
Dugat paintings, 5–6
Dura Europos, 106–107, 108–109
Dushak, 18, 36
Dzhanbas-Kala, 91, 95

Dzheytun, 10, 22

Ecbatana (Hamadan), 81, 84, 106
Ekin Depe, 18, 36
Elen-Depe, 19, 21
engravings, 12, 13, 14, 154
Esarhaddon, King, 53–54
etchings, 5, 10, 12

fabrics and fabric design, 117, 140, 155, 174;
    animal-patterned fabric, 60
    "Beauty of Loulan," fabric covering, 116
    Persian fabrics, 61
    silk fabric of Khotan, 119
    wool fabric of Hun warriors, 56
face/mask motifs, 6
Fars province, 84, 129, 131, 134, 142, 176
Ferdowsi, Abul-Qâsem, 146
Fergana Valley, 10, 11, 13, 27, 51, 141, 145
Ferghana region, 54, 93, 97, 170
figurines, 18, 19, 21, 26;
    of animals, 22, 35;
    figurine art style, 36–38;
    individualized styles of, 39;
    Khurvin metal work and, 69;
    of Marlik necropolis, 71;
    Parthian clay figurines, 110;
    stone figurines of Turang Tepe, 75;
    terracotta figurines of Koy Krylgan Kala, 95
Firdawsi, Abul-Qâsem, 30
fire temples, 133–34, 143
Firuzabad, 97, 130
frontalism, 106, 108, 109
Frumkin, Grégoire, 50

Gagarin, Matvey P., 55
Gandhara School, 120–21, 123
Geoksyur, figurines of, 36–37, 38
Ghaffurov, Bobodzhan Gafurovich, 143

Ghrishman, Roman, 18, 27, 68, 73, 74
glazed ware:
    Afrasiab glazed ceramics, 30
    glazed brick, 4, 28–29, 88, 178
    green glaze of Susa, 111
    lead glaze technique, 153
    Seljuk Turks, glazed ceramics of, 31, 147
gold, 81, 87, 99, 106, 117, 129, 135;
    animal-style golden articles, 54, 57, 58, 59;
    art of gold, pottery, and bronze tools, 50–51;
    gold coins, 110;
    gold embroidery, 155;
    gold funerary, 19;
    gold harnesses, 60;
    gold jewelry, 55, 69, 70, 74, 140, 144, 155;
    gold plaques, 41, 44, 55, 59, 73;
    gold trays, 130;
    gold vases, 69–70;
    Marlik gold beakers, 71;
    Sarazm settlement, gold objects found in, 139;
    Sassanian courts, gold discovered from, 132;
    Scythian motifs on gold objects, 28;
    Siberian burials, gold found in, 56;
    Soghdian trade in, 141
Gordian III, Emperor, 131
Goryacheva, V. D., 119
Govich Depe agricultural settlement, 17
Grach, Aleksandr Danilovich, 38
Great Wall of China, 140, 142
grey ware, 19, 21, 22, 23–24, 26
Griaznov, Mikhail, 59, 60, 61
Grunwedel, Albert, 123, 124
Gulyamov, Yahya G., 22
Gur-e Amir tomb, 149

Haba River county, 5
Hamedan, 81, 135

Han Kangxin, 116
Han Wudi, Emperor, 117, 141, 142–43
Harmatta, János, 42, 45
Hasanlu pottery center, 25, 28, 69–70, 74, 133
Hatra art, 106, 107–8, 109, 110
Hedin, Sven, 115
Hellenistic artifacts, 111–12
Hephtalites, 38, 92–93, 142
Herat, 29, 145, 153, 154, 156–57, 176
Hermitage Museum, 56, 57, 59, 61, 132, 144
Herodotus, 44, 52, 54, 79, 93, 116
Hissar community, 26, 57
Hodja Su I site, 11
Hori, Kenyu, 123
Hsuan-tsang, 120
Hunnic sub-culture, 53, 61
Huns (Hsiung-nu), 2, 38, 57, 116–17, 142

Ili River, 51, 56
Illi Valley, 7
Indo-Iranian Styles, 123–24
Indo-Iranians, 26, 27, 52–53, 67, 79
Inner Mongolia, 6–7, 45, 46
Iron Age, 19, 70, 178;
    early Iron Age, 7, 45, 69, 71, 93;
    Khwarazmian Iron Age, 93–94;
    Minusinsk as a triumph of, 60;
    rock art created in, 13;
    Scythian/Saka style during, 9;
    Turang Tepe, Iron Age layers of, 75
Irtysh area, 7, 12, 55
Isfahan, city of, 68, 156, 157, 175–76
Isfahani, Mohamad Mahmud, 149
Ishan Kala, 100
Issyk Kurgan, 55, 56, 57
Itina, Marianna Aleksandrovna, 51
iwan (porches), 100, 150, 178;
    Parthian *iwan*, 107–8, 132;
    Sassanian *iwan*, 129, 130, 131

Jackson, W. A. V., 134

Jalal-Abad province, 13
Janaid dynasty, 148
jewelry and jewelry making, 44, 55, 74, 87, 139;
    of Hasanlu, 69–70;
    Hun warriors, jewelry pieces of, 56;
    metal works and jewelry, 154–55;
    Nisa and Parthian art, use of jewels for, 106;
    Panjkent excavation, jewelry pieces found in, 144;
    Scythian/Saka jewelry, 51, 57–59, 179;
    Sialk II, copper and silver jewelry of, 68;
    Soghdian merchants as offering, 141

Kadyrbayev, M. K., 50–51
kala sites:
    Dishan Kala, 100;
    Koy Krylgan Kala, 95–96;
    Tok-Kala, 92, 95;
    Toprak-Kala site, 1, 91, 95

Kalar Dasht, 74, 133
Kalteminar culture, 91–92
Kamberi, Dolkon, 115
Kangavar temple, 107
Kangjiashimenzi petroglyph site, 6
Kara Depe, 18, 19, 21, 36, 38
Karaganda region, 7, 51
Karantki Tokai, 18, 36
Karatau Mountains, 7, 51
Kashgar, 29, 30, 120, 142, 153, 156
Katanda cultural center, 46, 59, 60–61
Kaufmann, Konstantine Petrovich von, 148
Kazakhstan, 3, 9, 55, 158;
    Central Kazakhstan, 50–51;
    eastern kurgans of, 56;
    petroglyphs and paintings, 7–8;
    rock art of, 12, 38;
    western Kazakhstan, 26–27, 92

Khaneghah-e Khoja Zaynadin, 148
Khapuz Depe, 24, 25, 39
Khiva city center, 97;
 book making in, 156–57, 176;
 as a cultural and artistic
  center, 98, 153;
 golden age of, 100–101, 145;
 khanate rule in, 2, 32, 154;
 pottery schools of, 29–30
Khoda, Saman, 145
Khorasan province, 97, 105, 134, 144, 145, 146, 170
Khorazmia, walled city of, 95, 106
Khorezm site, 19, 108
Khosrow (Khusro), 38–39, 142, 146
Khotan city center, 115, 125;
 art school of, 119–20;
 pottery school of, 29;
 trade and culture in, 30, 141–42, 153, 156
Khurasan, 30, 97, 170
Khurvin, 28, 69, 70, 74
Khuzestan province, 21, 28, 88, 109
Khvatai namak text, 146–47
Khwarazmi, Muhammad bin Musa, 97–98, 146, 170
Khwarazmia region, 2, 31, 50, 98, 140, 145, 156;
 Azar Faranbagh fire
  temple of, 134;
 calendars and book art of, 96–97;
 Gurganj as capital of empire, 147;
 in Iron Age, 87, 93–94;
 Khiva as located in, 100–101;
 Khotan School, influence on, 120;
 metal art of, 154, 155;
 music and dance of, 99–100;
 neolithic era, Kalteminar culture
  of, 91–92;
 walled cities of, 95, 96
Kizil Arvat, 18, 36
Kizil mural painting, 123–24
Kokand, city of, 2, 32, 100, 101, 154
Komarova M. N., 50, 51
Kopet Dag Mountains, 37

Koy Krylgan kala, 95–96
Kozhemyako, P. N., 119
Krasnovodsk, 10, 11
Kuban region, 41, 44, 45, 57–58, 59, 70
Kucha, 120, 122–23, 124, 125, 141, 153
Kuftin, Boris Alekseevich, 18, 36
Kuh-I-Kwadja site, 106, 107, 108
Kui Bulien site, 11
Kulya, Shams al Din, 155
Kunstkammer Museum, 55–56
kurgans (burial mounds), 22, 41, 45;
 art treasury of, 1, 54–56;
 Golden Kurgan, 51;
 in Northern Mongolia, 56–57;
 in Pazyryk, 60, 61, 84, 155;
 Scythian kurgans, 53, 58;
 war trophies in Hun kurgans, 117
Kushaev, G. A., 52;
 Kushan Empire, 79, 92, 116, 122;
 Gandhara area,
  dominance in, 121;
 Kushan-style vessels, 96;
 Surkh Kotal sanctuary,
  106, 117, 118;
 trade practices, 111, 141
Kuzmina, Elena Efimovna, 51
Kyrgyzstan, 3, 14, 22, 38, 119, 158;
 Andronovo traditions of, 27;
 animal figures found in, 51;
 rock art of, 8, 9, 12–13
Kyzlasov, Leonid Romanovich, 39, 119

Lab-e Hawz complex, 148
Lake Issykul, 14, 51
Langar village, 8
Latynin, B. A., 13
Le Coq, Albert von, 115, 135
Leizu, Queen, 140
Lev, D. N., 9
Litvinskiy, Boris Anatol'evich, 14
Lukonin, Vladimir Grigoor'evich, 42
Luristan province:
 Luristan tradition, 28, 74
 metallurgy of, 42–44, 71–73
Maikop belt, 44

male statuettes, 37
Mandelshtam, A. M., 14
Mani and Manichaeism, 2, 120, 124, 125, 134–35
manuscript illuminations, 157, 173–74
Al-Maqdasi, 146
Margiana region, 17, 93, 111
Margulan, Alkey Khakanovic, 50
Marikovsky, Pavel Iustinovich, 12
Marlik necropolis, 24, 25, 71
Marushchenko, A. A., 10
Masson, Vadim Mikhailovich, 18, 149
Mathura, city of, 117, 118
Maximova, A. G., 51
Mazandaran Province, 25, 74
Meana Sai, 18, 36
Median Empire, 105;
    eastern Media, Iranian tribes in, 27;
    Median revolt, 42, 71;
    Oxus Treasure as a Median collection, 73
Merv, city of, 29, 30, 112, 153, 155, 170
Mesolithic period, 178;
    Late Mesolithic, 11, 19;
    Mesolithic rock art of Inner Eurasia, 10;
    Mesolithic rock art of the South and Southwest, 11;
    micro-lithic techniques as perfected during, 12
Messerschmidt, Daniel, 55
metal art/metallurgy:
    Andronovo metallurgy, 49–50, 52;
    Khurvin, metal workers of, 69;
    of Luristan, 42–44, 71–73;
    metal works and jewelry, 154–55;
    of Minusinsk, 59–60;
    in Namazga and Djeitun cultures, 35–36;
    of Pazyryk, 60–61;
    potters as inspired by metal works, 28, 74;
    in Sassanid art, 129, 132–33;
    Sialk II, appearance of metallurgy in, 68;
    silver vessels as inspired by early works, 132–33
Metropolitan Museum of Art, 28, 42, 72, 132
micro-lithic techniques, 11, 12
Mikhailovka treasure, 41
miniature illumination, 157, 176
miniature painting, 124, 135, 150, 156–58
Minusinsk center:
    Andronovo culture in Siberian Minusinsk region, 50;
    kurgans as distinctive feature of, 55;
    as a metallurgy capital, 59–60
Miran art school, 120–22
Mithra (sun god), 108, 130, 133–34, 178
Mithradates I, Emperor, 105
Mithradates II, Emperor, 109, 110, 141, 142–43
Mithraism, 2, 5, 80, 108
Mongolian massacres, 2, 31, 148, 149, 153–54
Morgan, Jacques de, 28, 88
mosaics, 149, 174, 178;
    in Chehel Sutun palace, 175;
    mosaic art, 4, 129, 131–32
Mount Meru, 118–19
Müller, Gerhard Friedrich, 55–56
mummies, 61, 115–16
mural painting, 123–24
Museum of Asian Art, 123

Namaga II and III periods, 35
Namazga Depe, 18, 19;
    metal art of, 35–36;
    Namazga II assemblage, 21;
    Namazga IV period, 24;
    Namazgah V period, 25
Naqsh-I-Rustam, 54, 131
Narshakhi, Abu Bakr Muhammad ibn Jafar, 146
Negahban, Ezzat, 71

Neolithic period, 9, 22, 35, 37, 70, 74, 178;
  Bronze Age tombs, Neolithic flints in, 51;
  Central Asia, Neolithic culture of, 19;
  Copper Age as Neolithic in character, 17;
  Neolithic cultures, 91–96;
  Neolithic petroglyphs, 6–7;
  Neolithic pottery cultures, 20–21;
  Saimaly-Tash, rock art of, 13;
  in Sialk excavations analysis, 163;
  Turang Tepe, Neolithic layers of, 75;
  Zhejiang site, silk items found at, 140
Nestorian Christianity, 2, 124
Neyshabur, city of, 134
Nihavand Treasure, 111
Nisa, 1, 20, 29, 105, 109, 132;
  Parthian art and, 106–107;
  Parthian dome discovered in, 108
Nishapur, city of, 29, 30, 153
Novaya Kazanka (Dzhangaly), 51
Nuh II, Emir, 146

Ob River, 50, 55, 60
Okladnikov, Aleksei M., 7, 8, 9, 10
Orazbayev, A. M., 50–51
Ordos art, 45, 46, 59
Ovadan settlement, 18, 36
Oxus Treasure, 73, 85, 94, 129, 139, 142

Paleolithic period, 3, 7, 14, 161;
  Kayrak-Kumy, Paleolithic finds in, 8;
  as Old Stone Age, 178, 179;
  Turkmenistan, Paleolithic artifacts of, 10;
  upper Chirchik, Paleolithic cave sites of, 9;
  Xinjiang, Paleolithic art of region, 5–6

Palmyra art center, 106, 107, 109
Pamir Area, 8, 11–12, 14, 52
Panjkent:
  art school of, 140;
  Old City Panjkent, art treasury of, 142–44;
  Panjikent District, 9, 150;
  Sassanid royalty of, 142
Parthians, 112, 117, 135, 145;
  amphoras, craters, and bowls of, 29;
  Ashur, Parthian palace of, 107, 130;
  Eurasian art styles, Parthian return to, 105–106;
  Han empire, trade with, 141, 142–43;
  Mathura, Scytho-Parthian school of, 118;
  Mithra cult under Parthian rule, 133–34;
  Nisa and Parthian art, 106–107;
  Parthian dome, 108;
  Parthian pottery, 111;
  queen sculptures, 109–10;
  Sassanians ending domination of, 129, 142
Pazyryk:
  Altai group, as part of, 45;
  burial grounds of, 55, 57, 59;
  knotted rug, early example of, 155;
  as a metallurgy center, 46, 60–61
Persepolis, 25, 43, 72, 85, 86–87, 140
Peter the Great, 44, 55, 59
petroglyphs, 14, 161, 178;
  in inner Mongolia, 6–7;
  in Kazakhstan, 7–8;
  in Kyrgyzstan, 13;
  in Tajikistan, 8–9;
  in Uzbekistan, 9–10;
  in Xinjiang, 5–6
Philip the Arab, 131
pictographs, 5, 178
Piruz, Emperor, 142

pit graves, 53
Po-chih-na, 120
Pomazkina, Larisa Vasilevna, 13
pottery, 106, 144, 147, 149, 153, 155;
    defining, 178–79;
    Akch-Darya, round-bottomed vessels of, 9;
    of Anau I-A, 17;
    animal style pottery, 164;
    art of gold, pottery, and bronze tools, 50–51;
    art of pottery and origins of trade, 25;
    in burial mounds of Northern Mongolian Hun warriors, 56;
    Chust pottery, variety of forms in, 14;
    of Dam Dam Chashma I cave, 11;
    earthenware pottery, 177;
    Hasanlu pottery, 70;
    in Kalteminar culture, 91–92;
    Khurvin tombs, pottery pieces found in, 69;
    Khwarazmian pottery, 92, 93–94, 96;
    late Chalcolithic period, improved painting of, 37;
    neolithic pottery cultures, 20–21;
    Organic Style Pottery, 164;
    Parthian pottery, 111;
    pink pottery rhytons of Marlik, 71;
    polychromatic pottery, 19, 21, 22;
    potter's wheel, 18, 22, 23, 24, 25, 68, 94, 163;
    pottery kilns, 22–23, 24, 25, 26;
    pottery schools of Eurasia, 29–30;
    professionalization in pottery, 21;
    Sialk pottery, 27–32, 68, 163–64;
    of the Western Zone, 36;
    Ziwiyeh pottery, 28, 74
proto-Elamite seals, 43, 72
proto-urban settlements, 23, 26
Pumpelly, Raphael, 10, 17

Qadr, Yusef, 125
Qaghan Sinjibu, 39, 142
Qaznavi, Mahmud, 98, 99
Qoco (Kao-ch'ang), 124
Qongrat dynasty, 31, 100, 147
Quli Khan, Allah, 100, 148

Rabate Sefid dome, 108
Rahim Khan, Mohamad, II, 100
Ranov, Vadim Aleksandrovich, 8, 9, 14
Ratm fortress, 8
Rempel, Lazar' Izrailevich, 51
rhytons (drinking cups), 71, 74, 87, 106, 111
Rig Veda, 27
rock art, 5, 14, 179;
    Buddha, rock images of, 118, 122, 123;
    of Inner Mongolia, 6–7;
    in Kyrgyzstan, 8, 12–13;
    Sarmishay rock art, 9–10;
    Sassanian rock reliefs, 130, 131;
    in Tajikistan, 8, 11–12
Rostovtzeff, Michael, 107, 109
Rudaki, Abu Abdollah, 30
Rudaki Samarkandi, 146
Rudenko, Sergei, 59, 60, 61
rug making, 155–56

Safavi, Ismail, 32, 150, 157
Safavid Empire, 32, 150, 157, 175–76
Saka tribal confederations, 54
Samani, Ismail, 145, 147
Samanid dynasty, 2, 93;
    Bokhara as capital of, 31, 98, 143, 144;
    golden age of, 30–31, 145–46;
    model of patronage and support, 146–47
Samarkand:
    architectural structures built in, 32;
    as a cultural center, 30;
    golden age of Samarkand and Timurid Arts, 150;

as a Manichaean center, 135;
Old Samarkand, 148–49;
Saman grandson appointed governor of, 145;
Shirdar and Telakari Schools of, 148;
in Timurid reign, 2, 31
Al-Sami, Ibrahim bin, 97, 171
Saratov, 58
Sarazm, pottery of, 25, 139, 150
Sargon II, King, 42
Sarmatian art, 60, 105;
Sarmatian gold, silver, and bronze art, 44–45;
Scythians/Sakans as predecessors, 2, 46
Sarmishsay rock art, 9–10
Saromishastovskaya area, 41
Sassanid Empire, 38, 75, 98, 107, 108, 120, 122, 124, 125, 154, 170, 183;
amphoras, craters, and bowls of, 29;
architectural entities of, 129–30;
Azar Goshnasb as fire timple of, 134;
Ctesiphon as capital of, 135;
fall of, 133, 146;
Manichaeism in, 135;
metal art works from, 132;
Middle Persian as official language of, 169;
rock reliefs of Fars province, 131;
Sassanian ancestry, Samanid dynasty, 144, 145;
Sassanian royal palaces, 175;
Sassanid architectural entities, 129–36;
Zoroastrianism as official religion of, 43, 72, 129, 133, 142
Saymali Tash, 9, 13–14
Schmidt, Erich, 42, 71
School of Gandhara, 58, 115
School of Isfahan, 157, 176
Scythia/Saka, 2, 71, 74, 105, 115, 117, *181;*

animal style art, 51, 53–54, 57, 58–59, 60, 87, 106, 179;
culture of, 8, 9, 27, 52, 56;
Detached Scythians, 116;
funerary sites, 55, 59, 84, 94, 110;
Hasanlu, Scythian influences on, 70;
jewelry making, Scythian style of, 57–59;
Khwarazmia as dominated by, 92;
Medes and, 67, 79, 80;
at Nowruz festivities, 87;
Sakkis, Scythians migrating to, 73;
Scythian art, 45, 46, 58;
wool carpet from Scythian chieftan, 61;
Ziwiyeh as a Scythian settlement, 28
Seljuk Turks, 31, 100, 147
Selucids, 105
Semirechiye site, 51
Semirechye region, 52, 54, 56
Senigova, Taisiya Nikolayevna, 12, 51
Sermancha Depe, 18, 36
Seyrig, Henri, 107
Seyu Se Pol bridge, 176
Shah Zinda, 32, 150
Shakhta cave, 12
Shamanism, 2, 5, 42–43, 51, 56–57, 72, 119, 133, 179
Shanameh (Book of Kings), 146
Shapur I, King, 131
Shetkovo treasure, 41
Shi Huang Di, Emperor, 140–41
Shibe area, 45, 59
Shiraz, city of, 25, 31, 100, 130, 154, 156, 157, 176
Sialk, 74;
excavations analysis, 27, 163–64;
jewelry of Sialk sites, 70;
Sialk pottery, 25, 28, 69;
silver production in, 68
silk fabric, 4, 116, 119, 130, 133, 140, 141, 161

Silk Road, 2, 29, 95, 110, 149, *183;*
   Buddhism spreading east
      along, 121;
   Sassanian textile art
      traveling on, 129;
   trade along, 31, 111,
      140, 143, 147;
   Turfan on route of, 120, 135
silver, 4, 19, 41, 43, 44, 55, 56, 57,
   59, 68, 70–71, 72, 73, 81, 99, 106,
   110, 130, 132, 135, 139, 141, 144,
   154–55, 161, 163
Sima Qian, 116–17
Sinitzyn, I. V., 51
Sintasha culture site, 8, 52
Smith, Philip, 21
Social Realism, 157
Soghdia, 2, 57, 87, 93, 119, 120, 135;
   art school of Panjkent, 140–42;
   art treasury of Panjkent Old
      City, 142–44;
   artistic patronage, Samanid's
      model of, 146–47;
   Bokhara, golden age in, 145–46;
   metal works of, 154;
   Soghdiana and Timurid's golden
      age, 148–50;
   Tajikistan province of, 9, 84;
   urbanized centers of,
      136, 139–40;
solar images, 13, 14
Solokha, 57, 58
Sprishevsky, V. I., 13
Ssu-ma Ch'ien, 45
Stalin, Josef, 2, 157
stamped ware, 9, 11, 22, 29–30,
   91–92, 153, 157
Starr, S. Frederick, 144
Stein, Marc Aural, 115, 121
Stone Age, 179;
   Middle Stone Age, 3, 10;
   Old Stone Age, 3, 178;
   Stone Age excavations, 7, 8
Strabo, historiography of, 54
Stronach, David, 81

Sulayman (Sufi Lord), 31, 147
sun heads, 5, 7
sun-wheels, 27, 68
Surakhany fire temple, 134
Surkh Dum, 42–44, 71–72
Surkh Kotal, 106, 117, 118
Susa:
   Achaemenid Empire, as
      capital, 88;
   column capital in palaces
      of, 43, 72;
   glass industry in, 129;
   glazed brick walls of, 28–29;
   Parthian queen sculptures, 109;
   pottery found in, 21, 111
suzani (embroidery), 155–56
Syr Darya river, 51, 52, 54, 55, 93, 139

Tabriz, 156–57, 176
Taichanak Depe, 39
Tajikistan, 3, 13, 25, 38, 57, 111, 117,
   143, 144, 158;
   engravings, 14;
   Kushan Empire and, 117;
   petroglyphs and paintings, 8–9;
   rock art of, 11–12
talar (hall), 130, 175–76, 179
Talas region, 51
Tallgren, Aarne Michaël, 57–58
Talysh culture, 41
Tamgaly, 7–8, 9, 12
Tang dynasty, 120, 122, 123, 124
Taqe Kasra, 130
Taq-I Bustan, 131, 133
Tarim Basin, 49, 120, 135
Tash Kauli Palace, 100
Tashik Tash cave, 9
Tashkent, 10, 145
Tasmola burial site, 51
tepe (artificial mounds), 1;
   Tepe Ganje Dara, 21;
   Tepe Hissar, 24, 25;
   Tilla Tepe, 110;
   Turang Tepe, 25, 74–75
Terenozhkin, Alekseĭ Ivanovich, 52

Termez, 9, 30, 155
Tian Shan Mountain range, 6, 51
Tianshan Mountains, 49, 141
Tien-Shan territory, 10, 57
Tilkin Depe settlement, 18, 19, 21, 36
Timber Grave, 26–27, 49, 53
Timurid era, 2, 31–32, 100, 148, 149, 150, 154, *184*
Titus, Emperor, 111
Tokharians, 26, 49, 67, 87, 105, 116, 117, 123, 135
Tolstaya Mogila, 55, 57
Tolstov, Sergej, 9, 91, 92, 94
Toprak-Kala site, 1, 91, 95
Treasure of Karen Pahlavs, 111
Ts'ao Chung-ta, 120
Tuo Gan Bai, 6
Turfan, city of, 29, 115, 120, 124–25, 135, 153
Turgar of Samarkand, 143
Turkmen rugs, 156
Turkmenistan, 3, 10, 18, 25, 38, 100–101, 105, 111, 117, 158
Tuva region, 38, 52

Ulug-depe pottery, 24
unglazed ware, 29, 153
Ural River, 50, 52
Urartu mercenaries, 42, 71
Urganj city center, 29, 95, 153
Uyghurs, 3, 119–20, 124–25, 135
Uzbekistan, 3, 9–10, 13, 14, 25, 38, 106, 111, 135, 143, 149, 158;
  Bibi Khanum complex, completing, 32, 150;
  Bokhara as assigned to, 145;
  Kushan Empire and, 117;
  Uzbek Shaibanids, 2, 100, 148

Vagishton petroglyphs, 9
Vagoman, 143
Valerian, Emperor, 131
Varakhsha, city of, 1, 139–40, 150
Vinogradov, Nikolai B., 52
Vishnevskaya, O. A., 52

Volga area, 26, 41, 44, 58, 92
Voronets, E., 13
Vyatkin, V. L., 149

Wang Binghua, 5, 115
Watanabe, Tesshin, 123
Wei ch'ih I-seng, 120
wood working, 100, 155
Wulsin, Frederick, 74

Xia Paozi village, 6, 7
Xiang'nu:
  cup cauldrons of Xiang'nu period, 59;
  Xiang'nu art, 45–46;
  Xiang'nu Empire and Chinese historiography, 116–17
Xinjiang, 49, 92, 119–20, 125;
  mummies of, 115–16;
  paintings and petroglyphs, 5–6
Xiongnu tribe warriors, 141

Yalangach-depe, 37
Yassi Depe, 18, 36
Yenisei River, 50, 55, 59, 135
Young, Tuyler, Jr., 81
Yuezhi (Yueh-chih), 116–17
Yusuf (Sufi Lord), 31, 147
Yusupov, Hammid, 52

Zadneprovsky, Yuriy A., 12, 13
Zaman Baba culture, 19, 22, 26
Zarafshan River, 8, 14, 26, 27, 139, 143, 145
Zerafshan Valley, 22, 149
Zhang Qian, 141
Zima, B. M., 13
Ziwiyeh pottery, 28, 73–74
zoomorphic motifs, 7, 23, 36, 38
Zoroastrianism, 2, 80, 97, 120, 145, 149;
  Avesta as holy book of, 43, 139;
  Khwarazm as first region spread to, 93;
  Mithra cult, 133–34;

Sassanian Empire, as state
    religion of, 43, 72, 129, 142;
Talas River bank, Zoroastrian
    ossuaries of, 51;
Zoroaster as founding, 72, 133;

Zoroastrian burial rite, 96;
Zoroastrian temples, 118, 143
Zurvanism, 2, 43, 72, 80, 179
Zyablin, L. P., 119

About the Author

Ardi Kia is the award-winning co-founder and co-director of the Central and Southwest Asian Studies Program (CSWA Center) at The University of Montana. Professor Kia has developed a number of courses in Central and Southwest Asian studies which are now components of both minor and major degrees in this field. More than seventy of the courses he has taught since 1993 have concentrated exclusively on Central Asia, and are cross listed in anthropology and history, including: "Silk Road," "Central Asia: People and Environments," "Central Asia and Its Neighbors," "Cities and Landscapes of Central Asia," "Artistic Traditions of Central Asia," and "Central Asia: Seminar." Dr. Kia first received a Teaching Excellence and Scholarship Award during the sixth annual Central and Southwest Asian Studies Conference in April 2007. President Royce Engstrom and professor John Douglas, Chair of the Anthropology Department, presented the award in recognition of Dr. Kia's high-quality teaching of thousands of students since 1993. In Spring 2010, Dr. Kia was awarded an Honorary Doctoral Degree and Professorship from Nasser Khosrow State University in Tajikistan, Central Asia. He is one of the most popular professors at The University of Montana. Dr. Kia then received teaching excellence and scholarship awards during the annual Central and Southwest Asian Studies Conferences in 2012, 2013, and 2014. For the last twenty-five years he has written and lectured extensively on the history, archaeology, cultures, and artistic traditions of Central Asia with no sabbatical. Dr. Kia received a teaching excellence and scholarship award during the 15th Annual Central and Southwest Asian Studies Conferences in 2017 from Mr. Clay Christian, the Commissioner of Higher Education, and Provost Beverly Edmond, in recognition of Dr. Kia's high-quality teaching and scholarship. In Spring 2018, President Seth Bodnar presented a teaching and scholarship award to Dr. Kia during the 16th annual International Conference on Central and Southwest Asia.

www.ingramcontent.com/pod-product-compliance
Lightning Source LLC
Chambersburg PA
CBHW020118010526
44115CB00008B/874